THE MILLINGTON SITE

Modern view across the Presidio Bolson of La Junta. Photo by W. A. Cloud

THE MILLINGTON SITE

Archaeological and Human Osteological Investigations
Presidio County, Texas

William A. Cloud
Jennifer C. Piehl

Papers of the Trans-Pecos Archaeological Program
Number 4

Texas Antiquities Permit Nos. 4004 & 4691
Center for Big Bend Studies
Sul Ross State University
A Member of the Texas State University System

Alpine, Texas

2008

ISBN-13: 978-0-9707709-8-1

Printed in the United States of America
Center for Big Bend Studies
Papers of the Trans-Pecos Archaeological Program, No. 4

ABSTRACT

Between January 20 and February 17, 2006, the Center for Big Bend Studies (CBBS) of Sul Ross State University (SRSU) conducted an archaeological salvage and testing project at the Millington site in southern Presidio County, Texas. Undertaken after inadvertent damages from a city backhoe uncovered several human interments, the project was funded through the Texas Preservation Trust Fund, the City of Presidio, and the Trans-Pecos Archaeological Program of the CBBS. The site is an important village of the La Junta archaeological district that was occupied over a lengthy time span (Late Prehistoric through early Historic periods). The CBBS research team documented 14 features and 5 burials, and collected 314 artifacts on the surface through controlled means. The features consisted of five burials and burial pits, portions of three structures, two hearths, two pits of unknown function, a buried ring midden/earth oven, and a historic trench. Radiocarbon data indicates most of the features date to the La Junta phase (ca. A.D. 1200–1450). Artifacts collected from the surface include a wide range of prehistoric and historic ceramic sherds as well as cupreous metal items suspected to be of Spanish origin. Geophysical investigations conducted during the project identified a 7 x 7 m possible structure in the area of the site where a late seventeenth/early eighteenth century Spanish mission is thought to have been located. Materials recovered during the excavation are curated at the Museum of the Big Bend of SRSU.

TABLE OF CONTENTS

List of Figures

List of Tables

ACKNOWLEDGMENTS

The senior author would like to thank a number of individuals for the successful completion of the Millington site (41PS14) investigation. Special thanks are extended to staff of the Archeology Division of the Texas Historical Commission (THC) for providing support, guidance, and assistance during all phases of the work: State Archeologist Pat Mercado-Allinger and Staff Archeologists Brett Cruse, Tiffany Osborn, and Debra Beene. Also, many thanks to the funding organizations for their vision and support: the Texas Preservation Trust Fund administered by the THC, the City of Presidio, and the Trans-Pecos Archaeological Program (TAP) of the Center for Big Bend Studies (CBBS)/Sul Ross State University (SRSU).

A heartfelt thanks is extended to the field crew: Assistant Project Archaeologist Dr. Jennifer Piehl; Crew Chiefs Ann Ohl, Richard Walter, David Keller, and John Seebach; and Field Technicians Barbara Baskin, Bobby Gray, Roger Boren, Steve Kennedy, Jason Bush, Kendra Luedecke, Ashley Baker, and Candace Covington, who was also the talented camp cook. Dr. Piehl oversaw all of the burial recoveries, which often had her running to and fro to keep up with these simultaneous excavations. We also enjoyed the dedicated, cheerful assistance of many volunteers: Dawnella Petrey, Benny Roberts, Gena Roberts, Tom Crum, Ted Gephardt, Claude Hudspeth, and Tanya So. The crews often assisted with after-hours chores and continually performed necessary tasks before being asked. Thanks to five members of the field crew who, once back in the CBBS laboratory, assisted in several ways with materials and data recovered from the site: Dr. Jennifer Piehl, Ashley Baker, David Keller, John Seebach, and Dawnella Petrey.

A number of City of Presidio personnel are acknowledged for their assistance with the project. Former City Manager Tom Nance alerted the THC and the CBBS once he learned of the inadvertent exposure of human burials at the site. Current City Manager Cindi Clarke secured City of Presidio funding for the project and facilitated a wide range of logistical assistance during the fieldwork, and is sincerely thanked for her support throughout the project. Chief of Maintenance Carlos Mendoza had his crews available whenever the trench was covered or uncovered and also allowed the CBBS to store field equipment in the city maintenance yard during the fieldwork. City workers who assisted with backhoe work at the site are Moises Herrara, Miguel Gonzalez, Omar Guerrero, and Arturo Alvarez.

A number of consultants contributed to the findings presented in this report. Dr. David Hill provided the ceramic analysis and presented it as Appendix I. Dr. Hill's expertise on ceramics of the Southwest allowed him to recognize nuances within the collection and his efforts are greatly appreciated. The faunal analysis was completed by Steve Kennedy and Sarah Willet, who also served as junior authors to the report which is presented as Appendix II. Geophysical work at the site was completed in 2006 by Jaime Hincapié and Oscar Dena and in 2008 by Chester Walker, and reports on these investigations are presented as Appendices III and IV, respectively. Photographer Jim Bones is acknowledged for his excellent work photographs during the excavation, several of which appear in the report.

Former and present CBBS staff members assisted in various ways to bring this investigation to a finalized published report. As always, Robert J. Mallouf, Director of the CBBS, provided sage advice during all phases of the work, from his observations in the field and during the analysis to content editing, and the author extends the warmest thanks to him for these contributions and for his unflagging support throughout the project. Erin Caro Aguayo, Center Editor, is acknowledged for her technical editing and layout skills as well as her cheerful attitude during the process of bringing this project to a conclusion. Avram Dumitrescu, Scientific Illustrator for the Center, is acknowledged for his drafted figures, solving problems with some of the photographs, and his attention to myriad details. Bobby Gray took all of the set-up photography that appears in this report. Becky Hart, former Administrative Assistant for the Center, helped with administrative details preceding, during, and after fieldwork. Her replacement, Susan Chisholm handled these chores during later stages of the project and typed the tables that appear in the report, among other tasks. Ellen A. Kelley helped secure copies of obscure publications used in the background chapters and with other details in the office. Thanks are also extended to Ann Ohl, Richard Walter, and David Keller for helping the senior author with select analyses and editorial comments on the manuscript. Two student workers, Caleb Waters and Casey Riggs, assisted with various chores during the analysis and report preparation. These students did what needed to be done with smiles on their faces, and their efforts are much appreciated by the authors.

Finally, the late Dr. J. Charles Kelley is acknowledged for his pioneering contributions to La Junta archaeology. His initial work at the Millington site and subsequent field and archival research efforts at La Junta were ahead of their time, allowing the construction of a solid archaeological database for the area which facilitated our investigation.

INTRODUCTION

In the eastern Trans-Pecos region of Texas and adjacent portions of northeastern Chihuahua, the term La Junta or La Junta de los Ríos refers to the confluence of the Rio Grande and Río Conchos, two of only three rivers found within the vast Chihuahuan Desert. Along their paths the rivers breathe life into otherwise arid and inhospitable areas of the geologically diverse landscape. Floral and faunal communities in these narrow corridors are diverse in comparison to those found across the majority of the desert. Human populations have also clustered along the two river courses, with both historic and current concentrations just below their joining at the sister cities of Presidio, Texas and Ojinaga, Chihuahua. During the latter portions of prehistory, select parts of these environs were also a focus of cultural activities. Indian villages with sedentary or semi-sedentary lifeways and economies including agriculture sprang up at and near the confluence by around A.D. 1200 and generally persisted in these locations until the latter portion of the eighteenth century (Kelley et al. 1940; Kelley 1952a, 1952b, 1953).

A cultural construct known as the Bravo Valley aspect was developed over 65 years ago to encompass the long-lived occupation of the La Junta village sites (Kelley et al. 1940), and the area containing the villages is known as the La Junta archaeological district (Kelley et al. 1940; Kelley 1952b). The district, as defined by J. Charles Kelley (1952b:259), is contained within a roughly triangular area formed by Cuchillo Parado, Chihuahua, about 48 km up the Río Conchos, Ruidosa, Texas, approximately 56 km up the Rio Grande, and Redford, Texas, some 29 km down the Rio Grande (measurements are from the confluence).

In the 1930s–1940s, Kelley's pioneering efforts in villages of the La Junta district allowed him to formulate numerous hypotheses about cultural groups that lived in this hot, arid environment. His body of work in the district included extensive excavations at two important sites in the Presidio valley, the Millington site (41PS14/San Cristóbal) and Loma Alta (41PS15/San Juan Evangelista) (Kelley 1947, 1985, 1986), as well as investigations at the Polvo site (41PS21/Tapacolmes) in the Redford valley (Kelley 1949; Shackelford 1951, 1955), the Shiner site (Shafter 6:1) along Alamito Creek (Kelley et al. 1940), and Loma Seca in Chihuahua along the Río Conchos (Kelley 1951). In addition to his excavations, Kelley's research efforts within the district included cultural ecological hypotheses (Kelley 1952a) and ethnohistorical analogy (Kelley 1952b, 1953), the latter providing on-the-ground identifications for most of the Indian pueblos. Since there has been a bare minimum of work conducted at any of these or other La Junta village sites in the more than 50 intervening years—the Polvo site was tested in 1994 (Cloud et al. 1994)—most of Kelley's theories have gone unchallenged, although a few have been verified through modern analyses (Kelley 1990:38; Cloud 2004:143–145). Despite the body of data from these sites, generated almost exclusively by Kelley, there has been a pressing need to understand the La Junta cultures using up-to-date analytical techniques and methodologies. It was within this context that the Millington site investigation reported here was undertaken.

Located at the southeastern edge of Presidio, the heart of the Millington site became the property of the Texas Historical Commission (THC) in December 1986 as the neighborhood was targeted for a federally funded housing project which became known as the Millington Edition. This preservation effort spared most of the site from the bulldozer, but adjacent portions of this large village were subsequently impacted by city roads and the housing project. Shortly after the purchase, a fence was erected around the property and metal signs in both English and Spanish were positioned just inside the fence to explain ownership and state protection of the site. In recognition of its significance, the site was listed on the National Register of Historic Places (NRHP) as part of the La Junta archaeological district on February

14, 1978, and became a State Archeological Landmark (SAL) on July 10, 1987. The fenced area (ca. 1.6 hectares/4 acres) and SAL designation also include small tracts of land still under private ownership. The protective designations, in tandem with the fencing and signage, have served to protect the Millington site from human impacts over the last ca. 20 years.

However, on June 25, 2003, city workers using a backhoe accidentally uncovered several human interments in the roadway east of the site (Third Street) during an attempt to refurbish an old, out-of-use water line. To address these impacts, the THC and Center for Big Bend Studies (CBBS) of Sul Ross State University in Alpine, Texas were contacted by the city manager and through consultations between these three parties a plan was formulated. The CBBS agreed to send archaeologists to the site for an assessment and appraisal of the impacts and report their findings to the THC. A one-day field visit by William A. Cloud and Andrea J. Ohl of the CBBS occurred two days later with assistance from local volunteers Barbara J. Baskin and Jeff Moore. The crew documented at least three burials and several other probable cultural features within the lengthy backhoe trench (ca. 90 m long) at that time. They also made discrete collections of loose human bone in the trench and from adjacent backdirt piles. The crew used plastic to cover the burials and backdirt from which the human bone had been found, and filled the trench with sterile sediment.

Due to previous commitments and financial considerations, it was not until January, 2006 that the CBBS could return to the site to mitigate damages inflicted by the backhoe. Armed with $20,000.00 from a Preservation Texas Trust Fund grant and matching dollars from the City of Presidio ($10,000.00) and Trans-Pecos Archaeological Program (TAP) of the CBBS ($10,000.00), the CBBS conducted a 23-day investigation over the period of January 20–February 17. Because research of La Junta sites is one of the stated goals of this program, TAP ultimately contributed appreciably more than the $10,000.00 matching fund towards the successful completion of the project. The THC through Texas Antiquities Committee Permit No. 4004 authorized the investigation, and William A. Cloud served as Principal Investigator and Project Archaeologist.

While excavation and analysis of the human remains was of primary concern, additional work included profiling portions of the trench walls, excavating additional features along the trench, conducting geophysical investigations of the subsurface in select areas, and generating an instrument map of the site in tandem with a controlled surface collection. Seven excavation units were employed to salvage the burials and test some of the features exposed in the backhoe trench. An additional hand-excavated unit sampled deposits in the southeastern portion of the site. Supplemental stratigraphic data in peripheral portions of the site was recovered with four additional and relatively short backhoe trenches. Crews uncovered and documented a total of 14 features during the project: portions of three structures, five human burials and burial pits, a buried ring midden/earth oven, two small hearths, two pits of unknown function, and a historic trench.

Artifactual materials recovered during the investigation include Toyah, Fresno, and Perdiz arrow points (Suhm et al. 1954; Suhm and Jelks 1962; Turner and Hester 1985), a number of small, untyped arrow points with various morphologies, ground stone artifacts and other stone tools, and debitage. A wide variety of prehistoric and historic ceramic sherds, cupreous metal objects and fragments, other historic debris, and marine shell ornaments were also recovered.

An additional geophysical investigation was conducted in 2007 at Millington and at the Polvo site (41PS21), with work at the latter conducted through Texas Antiquities Permit No. 4691. William A. Cloud also served as Principal Investigator for this investigation and the complete report of findings appears as Appendix IV.

Due to the scope of the recent Millington site investigation, data was only recovered from a relatively small portion of the site. However, these findings include new architectural and mortuary data for both the site and district. The project spawned a broader analysis and synthesis of La Junta district mortuary customs and human osteological data pertinent to the health and diet of these peoples. As a result, the CBBS investigations have revitalized archaeological inquiry of the distinctive prehistoric and protohistoric cultures of the La Junta district and have paved the way for further investigations.

ENVIRONMENTAL SETTING

The Millington site is located in the southeastern portion of Presidio, Texas, in southern Presidio County (Figure 1). It is within the eastern Trans-Pecos region of Texas and in the northeastern portion of the vast Chihuahuan Desert. While the area actually encompassed by the Chihuahuan Desert varies depending on the defining criteria, estimates of its size range from 357,000 km² to 505,000 km² (Powell and Hilsenbeck 1995:4). At its greatest extent, it is approximately 1,900 km long and 1,300 km wide, stretching north-south from south central New Mexico to just north of Mexico City and east-west from the Pecos River in West Texas to the central portion of the Mexican state of Chihuahua.

Much of the desert environs in the region are rugged and stark when viewed from a perspective of geologic and climatic factors, although more hospitable settings are found along the Rio Grande (Río Bravo del Norte) and Río Conchos of northeastern Chihuahua. These ribbons of life meander through the parched area providing an important supply of water to the current inhabitants of the region. Given the lack of conveniences such as wells, pipelines, storage tanks, and water systems that sustain modern populations, the significance of these water sources was probably much greater during prehistoric times than they are today.

The confluence of the Rio Grande and Río Conchos occurs at an elevation of about 780 m above mean sea level (AMSL), and areas downstream along the Rio Grande have the lowest elevations in the region. The Rio Grande basin below the confluence of the two rivers is generally broad, with an average width of approximately 1.6–2.4 km. However, near the downstream end of the La Junta archaeological district, at the head of Canyon Colorado, the river becomes narrowly constricted by mountainous terrain associated with the Bofecillos Mountains in Texas and the Sierra Rica in Chihuahua.

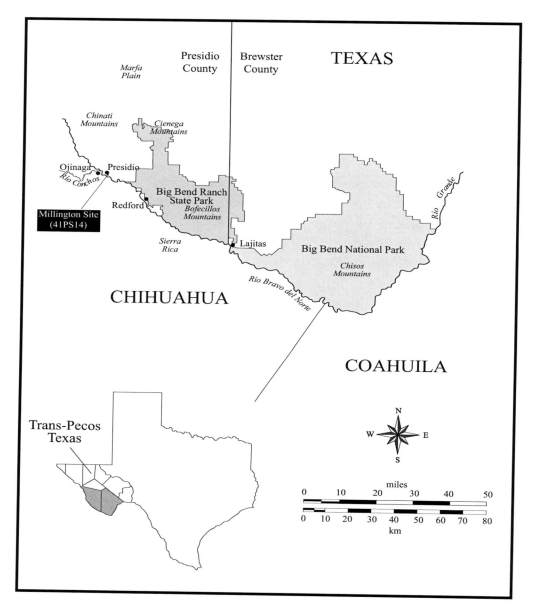

Figure 1. Location of Presidio County and the Millington site (41PS14) within the State of Texas.

These mountain ranges and others throughout the Chihuahuan Desert region are part of the Basin and Range province, a broad area in the western United States and northern Mexico typified by southeast/northwest-trending fault-block mountain ranges separated by extensive sediment-filled basins or bolsons (Fenneman 1931). More specifically, the ranges on either side of the Rio Grande in the Big Bend are within the Mexican Highlands section of the province, although this area does not fit the conventional picture of basin-range structure typified by fault block mountains (Fenneman 1931; Thornbury 1965; Groat 1972). Henry (1998) has indicated that normal faulting in the region, beginning in the late Miocene and terminating at the end of the Pliocene (ca. 23.7–1.6 million years ago), produced a complex system of horsts (uplifted blocks or ranges) and grabens (down-dropped blocks or basins) which resulted in the formation of two closed basins. Subsequently, thick detritus shed from the adjacent mountains filled these basins, forming the Presidio Bolson and downstream, the much smaller, but interconnected Redford Bolson. These closed basins were then breached when the ancestral Rio Grande formed about two million years ago and cut a path through their lower areas (Groat 1972; Henry 1998). Since that time, extensive erosion from both downcutting and lateral movement of the river, and the development of associated tributary drainages have helped shape the modern landscape.

Terraces formed along both the river and tributary drainages as a result of overbank flooding, and these settings shifted horizontally through time, especially along the Rio Grande in the Presidio and Redford bolsons. Today the river is situated ca. 1.6 km south-southwest of the Millington site, whereas in 1747 Spanish Captain Commander Joseph de Ydoiaga indicated the river bank was right up against the terrace edge at the site, then referred to as the Pueblo of San Cristóbal (Madrid 1992:60–61). These data demonstrate the dynamic nature of terrace formation along the river and its meandering tendencies across the bolson deposits.

Positioned along the edge of a low terrace immediately above the floodplain of the Rio Grande, the Millington site rests at an elevation of ca. 782 m AMSL on recent (Holocene) alluvium deposited during overbank flooding of the river. These deposits consist of silty sand and channel gravel, the latter composed of rounded pebbles, cobbles, and boulders up to three feet in diameter (Barnes 1979). While the surface of the Millington site is relatively flat and characterized by silty sand and pea gravels, an appreciable quantity of larger gravels were found buried in the northeast and northern portions of the site. These unsorted gravel lenses mark former channels of the river or perhaps tributary arroyos, channels that would have been active prior to establishment of the village now known as the Millington site. Soils at the site are classified within the Nickel-Canutio association and characterized as deep to shallow, undulating to rolling, calcareous gravelly soils on basins and valleys. At the Millington site it appears Canutio soils are present, with a pale brown, friable, calcareous cobbly loam ca. 15 cm thick overlying a very pale brown, loose, calcareous very cobbly loam with patchy lime coating on pebbles and cobbles ca. 45 cm thick. Immediately downslope on the floodplain of the Rio Grande soils are classified as belonging to the Glendale-Anthony-Toyah association. This association is characterized as deep, nearly level, calcareous soils on the floodplains (Soil Conservation Service 1992).

While the Rio Grande served the human populations in the area through time in a number of ways (i.e., drinking water, cooling/bathing water, irrigation water, source of sustenance, a travel route, a barrier, etc.), it also undoubtedly at times wreaked havoc on the occupants along its course. Historic Spanish, Mexican, and American accounts all testify to the power of the river during unpredictable flood episodes. In more recent times, dams in Chihuahua and New Mexico have served to contain its waters, but it still occasionally overflows its banks during periods of extreme rainfall. The prehistoric inhabitants that frequented the lush riverine environment must have been constantly aware of the river's potential for destruction. Most of their sites are situated on relatively high terrace systems, which were spared during all but the worst floods.

All of Trans-Pecos Texas, except the Guadalupe Mountains, falls within the Chihuahuan biotic province, and the "plants and animals of this province are mostly species that are widely distributed in the mountains and deserts of southwestern North America" (Blair 1950:116). From the Trans-Pecos region, the Chihuahuan province extends into northern Mexico, roughly mirroring the extent of the Chihuahuan Desert (Dice 1943). Both flora and fauna within the province are highly varied due to the complex geological settings and the attendant elevation ranges that occur. The plant and animal resources found along the Rio Grande and Río Conchos are unique and not duplicated to any extent in other areas of the province.

The river and adjacent areas would have provided a number of resources to the prehistoric inhabitants. Since the surface of many of the terraces, including the one at the Millington site, are relatively stone-free, pits for houses, storage, burials, etc. could be excavated fairly easily. Construction materials used for houses, *ramadas*, and other purposes could be secured from the riparian zone along the river, which contains cane (*Arundinaria gigantea*), cottonwood (*Populus arizonica*), desert willow (*Chilopsis linearis*), seep willow (*Baccharis glutinosa*), and other useful

species. Abundant stone materials useful in the manufacture of chipped and ground stone tools are present along gravel bars of the river and in outwash deposits found upslope (materials redeposited by tributary drainages of the Rio Grande and during bolson formation). Many of these stones were also regularly used in hearths or other burned rock features for heating and cooking purposes. Fish were apparently procured from the river at times, as the bones of several varieties of catfish and unidentified fish have been found within the deposits at the Polvo (Cloud et al. 1994:119) and Arroyo de la Presa sites (Cloud 2004:78; Kennedy 2004:237–239). Notched pebbles interpreted as net sinkers (Sayles 1935, 1936; Kelly et al. 1940:32) are relatively common at these sites and others along the river, including the Millington site, testifying to at least one possible method of fishing. While further evidence for fishing can be gleaned from historical documents during the later occupations at the site, both archaeological and stable isotopic dietary data from earlier occupations suggest fishing may not have been an important component of the diet. Other fauna, including turtles, frogs, snakes, ducks, beavers, mussels, as well as other birds, reptiles, and mammals could be caught at or near the shoreline. Turtles, frogs, and ducks have been documented within the deposits at the Polvo site (Cloud et al. 1994:119), and a turtle bone was recovered at the Arroyo de la Presa site (Kennedy 2004:237–239).

Areas adjacent to the river also contain a variety of useful plant and animal resources. Flora commonly found in these areas include ocotillo (*Fouquieria splendens*), yucca (*Yucca* sp.), creosotebush (*Larrea tridentata*), lechuguilla (*Agave lechuguilla*), sotol (*Dasylirion leiophyllum*), mesquite (*Prosopis glandulosa*), catclaw acacia (*Acacia greggii*), guayacan (*Porlieria angustifolia*), leatherstem (*Jatropha dioica*), allthorn (*Koeberlinia spinosa*), chino grama (*Bou-*

teloua ramosa), mormon tea (*Ephedra* sp.), and numerous cactus species (Butterwick and Strong 1976). Stalks from the ocotillo, yucca, lechuguilla, and sotol plants were probably used as poles in the construction of dwellings and windbreaks, while other parts of these plants were used for a wide range of additional purposes, such as sewing and the manufacture of baskets and cordage. Yucca, sotol, mesquite, and a number of other plants provided readily available foodstuffs. Wood for fuel could be secured from driftwood, trees growing along the river, or from woody trees and shrubs in the desert environment adjacent to the floodplain. Generally speaking, the flora found in the vicinity of the river supplied an array of resources that contributed to the prehistoric inhabitants' economy and way of life. Animals found within this zone today include jackrabbits, cottontail rabbits, mule deer, black bears, raccoons, foxes, coyotes, javelinas, skunks, porcupines, mountain lions, badgers, ringtail cats, muskrats, prairie dogs, gophers, rats and woodrats, snakes, lizards, squirrels, quails, doves, hawks, and eagles (Scuddy 1976).

Few studies have been carried out in the vicinity of the La Junta district which would illuminate past changes in the biotic communities within the study area. Using data from packrat (*Neotoma* sp.) midden, pollen, and faunal studies in the region, Mallouf (1981:139–140) has formulated a hypothesis that the eastern Big Bend was "a transitional biotic and cultural hub from which Archaic hunting-gathering adaptations spread into adjoining regions at a rate roughly concomitant to the upward displacement of xerophytic woodlands by desert shrub plant communities of the Chihuahuan Desert." Packrat midden studies within areas of the eastern Big Bend have allowed identification of desert shrub refugia within xerophytic woodlands at the end of the Pleistocene (Wells 1966, 1977). Gradually, drying conditions at the be-

ginning of the Holocene favored a retreat of the woodlands and the spreading of Chihuahuan Desert species throughout the region. This environmentally rich area would have contained plant and animal species endemic to both eco-niches, which would have been a highly favorable situation for human exploitation of these resources. Mallouf (1981) postulated that a localized cultural transition to an economy more reliant upon gathering developed as conditions became more xeric, and that these changes in climate, the resultant biotic communities, and adaptive human lifeways did not occur in areas north and west (including the La Junta district) of the eastern Big Bend until 1,500 to 2,000 years later. Packrat midden data from the Livingston Hills, south of Shafter, Texas, and from areas in the western Trans-Pecos seem to support this hypothesis (Van Devender 1977; Van Devender et al. 1978). However, additional work needs to be undertaken in portions of the western Big Bend to better understand the paleoenvironment and related human adaptations for this early period.

Subsequently, from about 5000–2500 B.C., a dry period known as the "Long Drought," or Altithermal, occurred throughout the American West with certain effects spread across the entire continent (Antevs 1955). This prolonged hot, dry climatic interval may have removed much of the stabilizing vegetation in the region, resulting in appreciable erosion of the landscape. Unfortunately, little is known or understood about the Altithermal in the Big Bend or eastern Trans-Pecos. Additional, more recent droughts of shorter duration have also been documented. There was a severe, several hundred years long drought across the mid-continent of North America centered at about 2200 B.C. (Booth et al. 2005). Droughts documented in the American Southwest include one around 500 B.C. and another around A.D. 330, labeled by Antevs (1955:330) as the "Fairbank Drought" and "Whitewater Drought," respectively. More pertinent to this project are two droughts dated by tree rings that occurred during occupations of the Bravo Valley aspect: one long distinguished as the "Great Drought" which occurred from A.D. 1276–1299 (Douglass 1935:42; Antevs 1955:330), and an unnamed drought that lasted from A.D. 1573–1593 (Antevs 1955:330). Of the latter four droughts, the Great Drought was thought to have been the most severe. This event occurred during the earliest portion of the Bravo Valley aspect and may have greatly affected the inhabitants at La Junta.

Based on limited paleoenvironmental data (including that which was derived from archaeological excavations) and early historical Spanish accounts (e.g., Madrid 1992), the modern biotic community may well have been in place within the La Junta district by around 2000 B.C. (Mallouf 1994:8). However, certain aspects of the environment undoubtedly have been altered by man's actions and historic and recent uses of the available resources. The plant communities along the river now include several species introduced during historic times. These include salt cedar or French tamarisk (*Tamarix gallica*), tree tobacco (*Nicotiana glauca*), carrizo or giant reed (*Arundo donax*), and bermuda grass (*Cynodon dactylon*) (Butterwick and Strong 1976; Mallouf 1994). Changes in water resources are attributable to historic wells in use throughout the region which have steadily dropped groundwater tables and greatly decreased the number and flow rates of springs. Similarly, ranching endeavors, which intro-

duced cattle, sheep, and goats to the area over the last 120 years, have depleted much of the grass cover that was once present. As noted above, flow patterns of the Rio Grande have been altered as a result of modern uses (i.e., recreation, irrigation, drinking water, etc.) upstream which has appreciably changed its character and predictability.

This area of the Chihuahuan Desert can be uncomfortably hot during the summer months, when high temperatures often soar well beyond the 100 degree Fahrenheit (F) mark. In contrast, winter months are typically mild, with few extended periods of temperatures below freezing. Data collected from 1951–1980 indicate the project area has an average annual temperature of over 69 degrees F, with an average annual low of over 53 degrees F and an average annual high of over 86 degrees F (Larkin and Bomar 1983:48–50). The warmest months are most often May and June, with January being the coldest. The region receives most of its rainfall during the summer monsoons that usually bring relief to the parched area from June or July through September. Rainfall in the project area during these months averages between 2.5–5 cm per month; however, these rains can be greatly abbreviated during periods of drought. The average annual precipitation hovers below 25.4 cm, with appreciable portions of this rain falling in short periods during intense thunderstorms. This rainfall pattern results in much of the water flowing off the landscape as runoff which constantly reshapes the gullies and arroyos and contributes to the destructive power of the Rio Grande.

ARCHAEOLOGICAL AND HISTORICAL BACKGROUND

History of Investigations

Previous archaeological investigations within the Presidio and Redford Bolsons have consisted of survey and reconnaissance projects, testing projects, and large scale excavations, which, for the most part, have produced data on the Transitional Late Archaic and Early Late Prehistoric (ca. A.D. 700–1000), the Late Prehistoric (ca. A.D. 1000–1535), and the Protohistoric (ca. A.D. 1535–1700) periods. Since the following discussion is focused on findings from the La Junta archaeological district and other pertinent projects, the reader is referred to Kelley et al. (1940), Campbell (1970), Mallouf (1985), and Cloud (2004) for background data from peripheral areas and the greater eastern Trans-Pecos region.

The first glimpse of the rich archaeological record in this portion of Texas occurred in 1895 when local residents unearthed over 1,500 arrow points beneath a cairn on top of Mount Livermore, the highest peak in the Davis Mountains. Together with the arrow points were an unidentified dart point, and a few flat stone beads, all clustered together in a small pit beneath the cairn (Janes 1930:8). The find became known as the Livermore Cache, and the small, distinctively shaped arrow points within it were later given the type name "Livermore." Discovery of the Livermore Cache put the Big Bend on the map archaeologically and paved the way for the scientific investigations that followed.

In response to this find, although almost 15 years later, in April 1909, the first investigation in the region by a professional archaeologist occurred when Charles Peabody of Harvard University conducted a 17-day reconnaissance through the western Big Bend. Peabody (1909) was also the first archaeologist to visit what would later be referred to as the La Junta district. Although his time in the district was brief, he investigated areas on both sides of the Rio Grande at Presidio, Texas and Ojinaga, Chihuahua. He indicated archaeological specimens were extremely rare on both sides of the river beyond the flood limits and was puzzled by this absence. By these statements, one can assume he did not visit any of the prehistoric villages of the district.

The first conceptualization of the cultural history of West Texas was offered by E. B. Sayles of the Gila Pueblo in Arizona, who visited the Big Bend region of Texas during a broad-based archaeological reconnaissance of the state in the early 1930s. Taking the known archaeological record of the region, he devised nomenclature and definitions for a series of cultural units—from oldest to most recent—which he termed the Pecos River Cave Dweller group, the Big Bend Cave Dweller group, the Edwards Plateau culture, the Jumano phase, and the Lipan phase (Sayles 1935). The latter two were for a late agricultural group and late food-gathering group, respectively. Although little was known about La Junta archaeology at that time, Sayles included the confluence of the Rio Grande and Río Conchos along with a swath of land paralleling the river from Big Bend to El Paso in his Jumano phase. He indicated, however, only one house site had been found, that occurring in the Fort Hancock area well upstream of La Junta. Characteristics of the Jumano phase included large campsites with big hearths along sandy ridges at the mouths of small arroyos, beveled knives, Red-on-Brown wares, notched "sinkers," and shaft abraders, the latter two artifact types noted as confined to the phase. While Sayles' work failed to recognize the distinctive villages at La Junta, he did create a framework that helped pave the way for subsequent researchers.

Further data applicable to La Junta were supplied through Sayles' (1936) archaeological survey of Chihuahua, Mexico. It was during this effort that he cursorily defined the protohistoric Conchos phase. Only a list of

traits, accompanying artifact photographs, and a map with hypothesized boundaries is supplied for the phase, the mention of missions and Spanish and Mexican pottery in the list of traits and the map showing boundaries of "Late Archaeological Phases" the only indications of its chronological placement. He made no clear distinction between the Conchos and Jumano phases in relation to content or chronology.

Shortly after Sayles published his proposed culture histories, J. Charles Kelley, an archaeologist working at Sul Ross State Teachers College in Alpine, Texas and a fellow of the School of American Research, began to pursue a program of research in the Presidio area. Through these efforts, which began in the Spring of 1936, he became interested in the findings of "amateur archaeologist" V. J. Shiner of Presidio, Texas. Shiner had excavated a 1.5-m diameter pit into the deposits of a site at the southeast edge of Presidio, which later was named the Millington site. Upon inspecting the pit in June 1937, Kelley noted a buried lens of ash, charred materials, and burnt clay that was found, through subsequent excavation, to be the remains of a superstructure and roof of a circular pithouse. A flexed adult burial was discovered within a pit covered by a stone cairn that extended above the level of the floor (Kelley 1939). This work marked the beginnings of focused archaeological research at La Junta.

Beginning in 1938, the Peabody Museum of Archaeology and Ethnology of Harvard University and Sul Ross State Teachers College in Alpine jointly sponsored an important interdisciplinary project in the Big Bend. It was organized to "investigate the occurrence of human skeletal remains and archaeological materials in association with geological deposits" (Kelley et al. 1940:11). This project, completed well before the advent of radiocarbon dating, attempted to correlate archaeological finds with the Quaternary deposits in which they were found for a better understanding of their respective ages. The project geologists, Kirk Bryan and Claude C. Albritton, identified three broad depositional formations within the deposits, from oldest to youngest being the Neville, the Calamity, and the Kokernot (Albritton and Bryan 1939; Kelley et al. 1940:49–51). Meanwhile, the archaeological team, headed by J. Charles Kelley and T. N. Campbell, conducted both reconnaissance and substantive and test excavations in open sites throughout the Big Bend—in the vicinity of Alpine, Texas, and south-southeast, southwest, and west-northwest of Alpine.

Kelley and Campbell's work spanned the period of January 1–September 1, 1938, and, in combination with the stratigraphic sequence developed by the project geologists, led to a revised synthesis of Trans-Pecos Texas cultural history. Using the McKern classification system, Kelley et al. (1940) proposed several encompassing cultural constructs—the Big Bend Cave aspect (Archaic to Late Prehistoric foragers) and the Bravo Valley aspect (Late Prehistoric to Historic agriculturalists). The former was subdivided into two units, the Pecos River (Middle to Late Archaic foragers) and Chisos (Late Archaic foragers) foci, while the latter was divided into five units, the La Junta (Late Prehistoric agriculturalists), Concepcion (Late Prehistoric to Historic agriculturalists), Conchos (Historic agriculturalists), Alamito (Mexican-period occupants), and Presidio (Anglo-American and Mexican-American occupants) foci (Kelley et al. 1940:23–38). In addition, a construct was offered for a distinctive group of foragers centered in the Davis Mountains area from ca. A.D. 800/900–1200. It was named the Livermore focus and characterized by Livermore arrow points, but was not subsumed by either of the proposed aspects. All of the foci presented in this construct remain in use today, although the term

"foci" has been replaced by the term "phase" (Kelley 1990; Mallouf 1990). However, efforts still continue today to re-evaluate, revise, and restructure these constructs.

Shortly after completion of the Peabody/Harvard-Sul Ross expedition, Kelley and his associate, Donald J. Lehmer, conducted extensive excavations at two La Junta sites. The project was carried out under the auspices of Sul Ross State Teacher's College (now Sul Ross State University), with principle funding through the Work Progress Administration. Additional financing was provided by the School of American Research and E. B. Sayles of the Gila Pueblo (Kelley 1985). Kelley planned and supervised excavations at the Millington and Loma Alta sites, which occurred from October 1938 through July 1939. Lehmer was the field director for most of the excavations at Millington until May 1939. Kelley took over this role for final excavations at Millington and all of the work at Loma Alta which was upstream several kilometers, almost directly north of the confluence of the Rio Grande and Río Conchos.

Work at the Millington site was extensive, and 21 additional houses were excavated—another nine were documented in trench walls. Excavations were concentrated in the heart of the site, but were supplemented with testing in other areas. The efforts at Loma Alta were also extensive, as Kelley excavated wholly or in part 13 house structures and identified several likely plazas (Kelley 1947, 1986). Through these efforts, a variety of construction techniques were documented for the La Junta, Concepcion, and Conchos phase pithouses. Rectangular and circular house traditions were associated with all three phases, while a single near surficial, adobe-walled structure with five contiguous rooms at Millington was linked to the La Junta phase. The latter structure was thought to be similar to early Jornada Mogollon houses around and north of El Paso and perhaps be the earliest structure at the site. Although it is beyond the scope of the project reported here, a synthesis of the Millington and Loma Alta excavations is sorely needed. While some efforts in this regard were made for the current project, especially in relation to burial findings, a more comprehensive attempt is being planned for the near future.

Kelley's efforts in the La Junta district that are detailed above formed the basis of his dissertation (Kelley 1947) from Harvard University entitled "Jumano and Patarabueye: Relations at La Junta de los Ríos," which was later published by the University of Michigan (Kelley 1986). This archaeological and archival synthesis implied the La Junta phase groups were ethnically and socially linked to sedentary peoples of the Jornada Branch of the Mogollon to the northwest.

After completion of his dissertation, J. Charles Kelley continued his La Junta research in the late 1940s and early 1950s (e.g., 1949, 1951, 1952a, 1952b, 1953, 1957, 1985, 1990, n.d.a, n.d.b; see Shackelford 1951, 1955). These efforts were focused on Bravo Valley aspect occupations on both sides of the river, although most of the work was done in Texas. This body of work has continually guided further research in the area and stands as the definitive field and archival research relative to La Junta sites.

Kelley's body of work brought him to conclude that a symbiotic relationship existed during the Late Prehistoric and into the Protohistoric periods between the villagers and nomadic to semi-nomadic foragers of the area. He further theorized that the La Junta groups were Jornada Mogollon colonists from the El Paso area of West Texas (Kelley 1985). A theory expounded later by Kelley (1990) offered that the La Junta villages provided foodstuffs and other products to Casas Grandes, a major redistribution center in north-central Chihuahua during the Late Prehistoric period. An alternative model for

the La Junta area has been offered by Mallouf (1990, 1999), who suggests the La Junta villagers might have been non-puebloan peoples linked to Puebloan cultures through a symbiotic trade relationship. Furthermore, Mallouf suggests the La Junta peoples may never have fully made the transition to a sedentary lifestyle. La Junta variations of Puebloan architecture and an associated hunting and gathering material culture found at La Junta were used in this argument.

Following a ca. 25 year absence of work in or near the La Junta district, an international flood control and channel relocation project occurred in 1973–1974. Archaeologists Vance Holliday and James Ivey, affiliated with the Texas Archeological Survey of the University of Texas at Austin, discovered several exposed burials at Loma Alta during the project and subsequently conducted salvage excavations (Holliday and Ivey 1974).

A few years later, in 1979 and 1980, the Office of the State Archeologist (OSA) of the THC conducted a reconnaissance and testing project in the Rosillos Mountains (Mallouf and Wulfkuhle 1989), now within Big Bend National Park (BBNP), which led to identification of a previously unknown Late Prehistoric to Protohistoric social group. Research continued on this group of hunter-gatherers in the mid- to late-1980s and 1990s under the direction of State Archeologist Robert J. Mallouf (1985, 1986, 1990, 1993, 1995, 1999), who called this manifestation the Cielo complex. These efforts included excavations at select sites, two of which are within the La Junta district near Redford—Cielo Bravo and Arroyo de las Burras (Mallouf 1990, 1995, 1999). Both of these type sites, positioned on high pediments overlooking the river, yielded abundant surface and subsurface data which allowed a temporal estimate of A.D. 1250–1680 for the complex (Mallouf 1999:65).

Information on two possible Cielo complex cairn burials came to light in the

1980s and early 1990s through involvement of the OSA. The first of these was a cairn burial outside the small community of Las Haciendas, Chihuahua, about 20 km south of BBNP's Santa Elena Canyon that had been destroyed by relic collectors. Mallouf (1987) was able to reassemble and analyze the grave goods—195 arrow points, one small pendant, and one small discoidal bead—and complete a detailed report of the artifacts, most of which were Perdiz arrow points. This study provided invaluable metric and other data associated with the Perdiz projectile point type. The other burial was discovered in the western portion of BBNP in 1987 during an in-house survey and was scientifically excavated in 1988 and 1990 through a cooperative effort between BBNP and OSA/THC personnel. Known as the Rough Run Burial, this secondary interment lay beneath a semi-subterranean cairn which contained 73 arrow point and arrow point fragments, all but one adhering to the Perdiz type. Two radiocarbon dates secured from it indicate the burial was executed sometime between A.D. 1400–1640 (Cloud 2002). While both of these could be Cielo complex interments, the slightly elevated Las Haciendas setting, compared to that at Rough Run, offers greater support for such an affiliation.

There were several other noteworthy testing projects that occurred in the 1990s within or adjacent to the La Junta district, or which provided significant data relative to occupations of the Bravo Valley aspect. These consist of work at the Sam Nail site in BBNP (Alex et al. 1992; Corrick 1992, 2000:8), at the Polvo site (Cloud et al. 1994), at Cuevas Amarillas in Big Bend Ranch State Park (BBRSP) (Beene 1994), and at the Arroyo de las Burras site (Mallouf 1995).

In 1992, testing at the Sam Nail site (41BS188) yielded 33 Toyah arrow points, including several from a hearth which was excavated. Charcoal from this feature yielded

a corrected and calibrated radiocarbon date of A.D. 1233–1377 (Alex et al. 1992; Corrick 1992, 2000:8), thus providing the first date in the region for Toyah points, which are a type commonly found in Bravo Valley aspect sites (Kelley et al. 1940; Kelley 1957). However, as Kelley (1957) has pointed out, Toyah points in hunter-gatherer contexts are quite different from those typically found in La Junta villages. This issue needs to be revisited in the near future for a better understanding of cultural complexities at work in the region.

The OSA/THC conducted testing at the Polvo site in 1994 in response to inadvertent damages inflicted during an emergency repair of the Presidio-Redford earthen retaining levee (Cloud et al. 1994). Several areas of the site were investigated and two probable pithouse remnants were documented and profiled in a cutbank. Radiocarbon samples from one of the houses provided an average date of A.D. 1330, or roughly in the middle of the La Junta phase (Cloud et al. 1994:122). A large refuse pit containing a Toyah arrow point yielded a date of A.D. 1190–1280, confirming the chronological data secured earlier at the Sam Nail site for this point type.

In 1991 and 1992, test excavations were carried out at Cuevas Amarillas under the direction of Debra L. Beene, a University of Texas at Austin graduate student. Beene, noting the presence of unusual items such as turquoise, *Olivella* sp. shells, obsidian, ceramics, and glass beads within the recovered specimens, offered that there was a direct connection between Cuevas Amarillas peoples and those living in the villages along the main stem river in Late Prehistoric and Historic times (Beene 1994:179).

Additional information was forthcoming on La Junta with publication of historical data on the Ydoiaga *entrada* of 1747–1748 (Madrid 1992), and through research on cultural interactions in the district (Kenmotsu

1994a, 2001). The Ydoiaga *entrada* visited many of the villages of the district, taking censuses and describing different aspects of the respective Indian lifeways. During this endeavor, the Spaniards visited the Millington site over a three-day period (December 2–4, 1747) and described it as the Pueblo of San Cristóbal. Important information about the village and the people's lifeways was obtained and is provided in the Culture History section below.

A recent, and what amounted to be a very substantive archaeological investigation, occurred in the district in the early 2000s prior to renovation and rejuvenation of a section of FM 170 between Presidio and Redford. Texas Department of Transportation archaeologists identified six sites and recommended further work at several of these, including the Arroyo de la Presa site (41PS800), an open campsite on an upper terrace of the Rio Grande (Kenmotsu and Hickman 2000). William A. Cloud of the CBBS directed test excavations at this site in 2000 (Cloud 2001) and then a large-scale excavation in 2001 (Cloud 2004).

Confined to the highway right-of-way, work at the Arroyo de la Presa site consisted of both hand-excavated units and backhoe trenches, and was aided by results from 38 radiocarbon and 33 flotation/macro-botanical samples. The mitigation program was focused on a buried cultural zone thought to date from ca. A.D. 700–1250 and on a zone above terminating between A.D. 1600–1800. Within these zones were a number of plant food processing features, suggesting the upper terrace was used through time for food preparation. Projectile points within the deposits indicated the site had been used by Livermore phase peoples and other hunter-gatherers of the area, while two pieces of burned daub recovered from a trash pit dated from A.D. 1040–1260 suggests La Junta phase peoples also had a presence there. Analyses of Millington and Arroyo de la Presa pot-

tery sherds indicated the Arroyo de la Presa sherds were likely made in northern Chihuahua and that El Paso Polychrome sherds from Millington were made in the El Paso, Texas area. Furthermore, these analyses indicated Concepcion and Conchos phase wares could have been made at La Junta, lending support to a theory that had been expounded much earlier (Kelley et al. 1940).

Taken as a whole, these investigations provide an extensive amount of information about the cultural manifestations within and surrounding the La Junta district. Most of the more substantive data is from the latter portions of prehistory and protohistoric times and was recovered from village sites along either the Rio Grande or Río Conchos. While these data shed appreciable light on these early farming cultures, most of it was recovered when the discipline of archaeology was in its infancy. As a result, there is a need to evaluate sites in the district using modern field techniques and analytical means. It was within this context that the current project was undertaken.

Culture History

The above review of archaeological accomplishments in the La Junta district and surrounding areas allows for a general understanding of the culture history in the La Junta district during the Transitional Late Archaic-Early Late Prehistoric (ca. A.D. 700–1000), Late Prehistoric (ca. A.D. 1000–1535), Protohistoric (ca. A.D. 1535–1700), and Historic (ca. A.D. 1700–1950) periods. Since no evidence of earlier occupations has been documented at the Millington site, the brief review or synthesis presented below only covers what is known from these periods.

As mentioned previously, Kelley et al. (1940:23–41) developed a scheme to subdivide the regional cultural manifestations from the Archaic to the present using the terms *as-*

pect and *focus*, with the former encompassing the latter. A more recent construct for a unique hunter-gatherer archaeological manifestation in the region—the Cielo complex—has been offered by Mallouf (1985, 1990, 1993, 1995, 1999). This culture was roughly coeval with the Bravo Valley aspect, although it began a little later and terminated earlier. The following discussion is organized chronologically by these constructs: Livermore phase, Bravo Valley aspect (La Junta, Concepcion, and Conchos phases), Cielo complex, Alamito phase, and Presidio phase.

Livermore Phase (A.D. 800/900–1200)

The Livermore phase construct offered in Kelley et al. (1940:30–31) was based largely on work conducted in the region by Kelley and Victor J. Smith. Characterized by the consistent presence of three arrow point types (Livermore Barbed, Toyah Triple Notched, and Fresno Triangular) and a hunting-gathering tool kit, including double beveled "Plains" knives, small snub-nosed scrapers, and distinctive gravers (Kelley et al. 1940:30–31; Kelley 1957), the Livermore phase is concentrated in the Davis Mountains and Lobo Valley within the central and western portions of the region. Mallouf (1990:9 and Figure 5, 1999:62 and Figure 5) has suggested a distribution for the phase which essentially encompasses the entire eastern Trans-Pecos and extends beyond those boundaries relatively short distances: a western boundary along the Sierra Vieja, Van Horn, and Sierra Diablo mountain ranges, a northern boundary in southeastern New Mexico, an eastern boundary east of the Pecos River, and a southern boundary roughly mirroring the distribution of Late Archaic Paisano dart points in northern Coahuila and northeastern Chihuahua—ca. 30–50 km south of the Rio Grande.

Kelley et al. (1940:39–41) indicated the Livermore phase had been found in consistent association with the Chisos phase, suggesting a degree of contemporaneity with the Late Archaic foragers of that construct. Furthermore, Kelley has stated that the phase was "associated quite clearly with the erosional disconformity separating the Calamity and Kokernot Formations" (Kelley 1957:49), and accordingly predated the Bravo Valley aspect that is within the upper strata of the subsequent Kokernot deposition. Livermore points have been reportedly found associated with El Paso Polychrome ceramics in southeastern New Mexico, but this occurrence was thought to be relatively late and isolated for the phase (Kelley et al. 1940:30–31, 40). Based on stratigraphic relations and a tree ring date from southern New Mexico, Kelley et al. (1940:163) thought the Livermore phase began around A.D. 800 and ended by ca. A.D. 1200. Kelley (1957:51) later revised the suggested dates for the phase to A.D. 900–1200, noting that it may have appeared somewhat earlier and persisted a little later. It should be noted that recent chronometric dating of El Paso Polychrome associations indicates the type was developed some time after A.D. 1200 and persisted until ca. A.D. 1450 (Miller 1996).

Kelley et al. (1940:162–163) originally hypothesized that the Livermore phase represented an influx of new peoples in the region, and Kelley (1952a:359, 1986:143) later suggested this group may have originally been Plains Indians. Mallouf (1990:10, 1999:62) has cautioned that the group could also have been indigenous to the Trans-Pecos region, noting that neither hypothesis has been seriously investigated. Regardless of its origins, Kelley et al. (1940:40) indicated the phase "is the typological ancestor of the Bravo Valley aspect, and modified Livermore focus [phase] types of projectile points occasionally occur in La Junta focus [phase] sites." Later, Kelley (1957:50) softened this conclusion, stating "there is some evidence that the

Livermore Focus [phase] may have been one of the cultural elements that entered into the development of the La Junta Focus [phase] of the Bravo Valley Aspect."

It is clear much work remains to be done for a sound understanding of this enigmatic hunting and gathering group. Recent Livermore phase findings at Tall Rockshelter (Mallouf 2001) and Wolf Den Cave in the Davis Mountains (Mallouf 2002, 2007) and at the Arroyo de la Presa site in the La Junta district (Cloud 2001, 2004) have shed additional light on this culture and a comprehensive summary of the phase is currently being prepared by Mallouf (in prep.).

Bravo Valley Aspect
(A.D. *1200–1760*)

As stated above, the cultural continuum in the La Junta district referred to as the Bravo Valley aspect forms the cornerstone of the cultural classificatory scheme developed by Kelley et al. (1940:39). This aspect was subdivided into the La Junta, Concepcion, and Conchos phases. The La Junta phase (ca. A.D. 1200–1450) is confined to the Late Prehistoric period and the Concepcion phase (ca. A.D. 1450–1684) cross-cuts what is now the Late Prehistoric/Protohistoric temporal boundary. The Conchos phase (ca. A.D. 1684–1760) or "Mission period" (Kelley 1990:39) straddles the Protohistoric and Early Historic periods, and has been characterized as "the period of Spanish acculturation of the Indian villages" (Kelley et al. 1940:39). Important aspects of the theoretical continuum, all quite distinctive when compared to hunter-gatherers of the region, were the use of pithouses within village settings, consistent attempts at agriculture, and the use of various pottery types (Kelley et al. 1940:31–33). More recently Kelley (1990:39) revised his thoughts on the hypothesized continuum, suggesting La Junta could

have been almost completely abandoned by pottery-making agriculturalists between A.D. 1400/1450–1550, "leaving the area occupied only by semi-sedentary hunters and gatherers living in simple structures."

La Junta Phase (A.D. *1200–1450*)

The La Junta phase represents the first cultural manifestation in the La Junta district representative of sedentary or semi-sedentary occupations. The inhabitants of the La Junta phase lived in *jacal* structures placed in pits on terraces along the Rio Grande and lower Río Conchos, used non-local pottery, and according to Kelley et al. (1940:31–34), derived their sustenance from agriculture, hunting, fishing, and from the gathering of plant foodstuffs. It should be noted that stable isotopic dietary data, predominantly from the La Junta phase and presented later in this report, questions how much of a role agriculture and fishing contributed to the diet. Most of the recovered data from the Bravo Valley aspect, especially architectural and mortuary remains, are attributable to this phase. Whether this is due to sampling bias, or perhaps evidence of a greater population, remains in question at this time. While the impetus responsible for the relatively sudden appearance of the La Junta phase is also still open to conjecture, Kelley et al. (1940), Kelley (1957, 1990), and Mallouf (1990, 1999) have offered possible explanations.

As indicated in the discussion above, it was originally proposed that the Livermore phase was ancestral to the La Junta phase (Kelley et al. 1940:40). Kelley later (1957:50) altered this suggestion, saying it may have played a role in development of that phase. However, taking into account published data from the Jornada Mogollon (Lehmer 1948) and more recent findings within the La Junta district (Mallouf 1985, 1990) and at Casas Grandes (Paquime) (Di Peso 1974a; Ravesloot 1988)—a major redistribution center of the Gran Chichimeca in northeastern Chihuahua from which ornamental shell and other artifacts were most likely traded to the La Junta district (Di Peso 1974a, 1974b; Di Peso and Fenner 1974; Kelley et al. 1940)—Kelley offered a revised concept. Here he postulated the La Junta phase "essentially represents an isolated colony of the El Paso phase of the Jornada Branch of the Mogollon," and that the related sites "were procurement stations producing surplus local plant foods (especially mescal and mesquite beans); bison skin and dried bison meat obtained from Plains groups trading at La Junta; and were extractive areas for minerals and stones; all supplying the needs of the great redistribution center of Casas Grandes" (Kelley 1990:38).

Mallouf (1990:19, 1999:82–83) has offered an alternative hypothesis suggesting that the La Junta phase could have origins in a hunting and gathering society either indigenous to the region or intrusive from the Southern Plains, rather than from a direct linkage with sedentary peoples of the Jornada Branch of the Mogollon. He has argued that differences in both architecture and material culture between the Jornada Mogollon and La Junta phase support such a conclusion. He has further suggested that there are strong parallels in the cultural interactions that transpired at this time between the La Junta culture area and the Antelope Creek phase of the Texas Panhandle, with both involving the symbiotic exchange of goods with Puebloan cultures to the west (Mallouf 1990, 1999).

The Millington site is the type site for the La Junta phase (Kelley et al. 1940:33; Kelley 1986:72). Houses of the phase had various shapes and forms, entrance ways, and roof supports, with most all of these having *jacal* wattle and daub superstructures. During this phase three types of houses have been identified: 1) rectangular structures; 2) circular structures; and 3) a single example

of a multi-roomed structure constructed in a shallow pit.

Dominant houses during the La Junta phase were rectangular, built within or over pits, and encompassed from 10–21 square meters. All but one of these small, isolated houses had *jacal* superstructures placed within the pits, the exception being from Polvo, where adobe bricks formed the walls beginning at ground surface (Shackelford 1951, 1955). Floors were of puddled adobe or tramped gravel, occasionally with low adobe curbs around their periphery. The *jacal* superstructures were anchored by both large and smaller interior posts. Walls were of a pole framework, and often plastered with mud/daub. Circular to oval structures used at this time were relatively small, with diameters of less than three meters. They had tramped gravel floors and framework posts arranged around the periphery of the floor. It appears they were built over the pit, with pole walls starting at ground level.

The multi-roomed structure had adobe floors and a tier of five rooms arranged in an east-west direction that resulted from accretion—all traits seen in El Paso phase houses. The structure was placed within a ca. 45 cm-deep pit and small wall supports were embedded within the adobe. Furthermore, Kelley's notes (1985, 1986, 1990) suggested the walls were comprised of an adobe substructure with a *jacal* superstructure, architectural elements that seem to be more in line with Mallouf's (1990) model—a native copy of an El Paso phase structure. At this point, the origins of this structure remain very much open to debate.

La Junta phase artifacts present a conundrum of sorts, as they are represented by items manufactured both locally and remotely. Ceramics from the phase are predominantly Southwestern trade wares, with El Paso (Jornada Branch) and Chihuahua (Casas Grandes) polychromes consistently present

(Kelley et al. 1940:34). In sheer numbers, El Paso Polychrome sherds are dominant, and both Shackelford (1955) and Hilton (1986) have suggested some of the El Paso variant sherds at La Junta may have been locally produced—other possible threads of evidence for the colony theory. While recent petrographic and instrumental neutron activation analyses of select El Paso Polychrome sherds from the Millington site indicate manufacture in the El Paso area (Robinson 2004; Rodríguez-Alegría et al. 2004; Kenmotsu 2005), data from a larger sample would be needed to refute or support this hypothesis. Chihuahua polychromes identified include the Ramos, Babicora, and Villa Ahumada types, and other established types represented include Tusayan Polychrome, Playas Red, and Chupadero Black-on-White (Kelley et al. 1940:34). On the other hand, La Junta phase arrow points suggest affiliation or some type of relationship with local hunter-gatherers. The primary points found with the phase include Piedras Triple Notched, Perdiz Stemmed, and Fresno Triangular (Shackelford 1951)—now called Toyah, Perdiz, and Fresno (Turner and Hester 1985)—all types uncommon or nonexistent in the El Paso phase assemblages but regularly seen in hunter-gatherer settings across the Big Bend.

Kelley (1990) has pointed out that the end of the La Junta phase coincides with the collapse of both the El Paso phase of the Jornada Mogollon and the Casas Grandes interaction sphere. As a result of these coeval occurrences, he further suggested that the La Junta area "may have been almost entirely abandoned by pottery making agriculturalists, leaving the area occupied only by semi-sedentary hunters and gatherers living in simple structures" (Kelley 1990:39). Alternatively, Mallouf (1990:21, 1999:84) has offered that La Junta phase peoples were practicing a semi-sedentary rather than sedentary existence to begin with, and that upon

collapse of the phase reverted fully to a hunting-gathering lifeway.

Concepcion Phase (A.D. 1450–1684)

Kelley et al. (1940:35–36) used the Concepcion phase to distinguish changes in architecture and material culture within the La Junta district from those of the La Junta phase. He originally indicated an ending date for the phase of ca. A.D. 1700 (Kelley 1947, 1986). While he never formally revised the dates for the period, in several instances he referred to the subsequent Conchos phase as the Mission period (Kelley 1986:84–85, 1990:39; Kelley and Kelley 1990:10). Accordingly, since historical data indicates that the first missions at La Junta were established in ca. A.D. 1684, that date is used here to divide the Concepcion and Conchos phases.

During the Concepcion phase, houses were larger but very similar to those of the La Junta phase, with both rectangular and circular to oval varieties represented. Rectangular houses were dominant, either isolated or in east-west tiers, and about twice the size of those of the preceding phase—averaging 8.5 x 9.1 m. These houses also differed from those of the preceding phase by their lack of adobe. Tramped gravel or packed refuse served as floors within the pits, and adobe was not used at all. Circular houses had diameters of about 3.7–5.5 m and numerous supporting posts compared to those of the La Junta phase (Kelley 1985, 1986).

The Concepcion phase is further separated from the La Junta phase by the associated ceramic assemblage, although virtually all stone, bone, and shell artifacts are quite similar (Kelley 1986:82). The intrusive Southwestern types are no longer present within the assemblage, which is comprised almost completely of new wares—Chinati Plainware, Capote Red-on-Brown, and Paloma Red-on-Gray—thought to have been locally produced (Kelley et al. 1940:35–36). However, some trade wares were apparently being brought into the area at this time as indicated by the presence of two sherds of Patton Engraved, an East Texas Caddoan type, which were found in the deposits at Loma Alta (Kelley 1986:83, 90). This may be a small clue linking the La Junta villagers with the ubiquitous Jumano Indians, who are reported to have ranged as far east as the Caddo settlements in eastern Texas (Kelley 1947, 1986; Hickerson 1994:24).

The arrival of the first Europeans occurred during the Concepcion phase when Alvar Núñez Cabeza de Vaca and his three companions apparently traveled through La Junta in A.D. 1535. Shipwrecked off of Galveston Island in A.D. 1528, these men lived with various native groups, acting as shaman and traders during their long walk back to civilization. Their interactions with Indians along the way are described in a journal written by Núñez after returning to New Spain (Bandelier 1905). Although their exact route has long been debated (Chipman 1987), evidence for their passing through La Junta was suggested by chronicles of a A.D. 1582–1583 expedition led by Antonio de Espejo:

> They made us understand, through interpreters, that three Christians and one Negro had passed through there [La Junta], and by means of signs that they gave, it seemed that these had been Alvaro Núñez Cabeza de Vaca, and Dorantes, and Castillo Maldonado, and a negro (Espejo 1871:107 [in Kenmotsu 1994b:17]).

Núñez's apparent description of La Junta includes brief references about the environment, the people that lived there, their economy, and dress. The settlements there were spread out along a river that ran between several mountains. The people grew crops of beans, squash, and corn and wore buffalo robes (Bandelier 1905:151).

Spanish slave raiding parties are reported to have visited La Junta as early as A.D. 1563 to obtain slaves for the silver mines in north central Nueva Vizcaya. Thereafter, the slave raiders returned to the area frequently, the raids peaking in intensity between A.D. 1575–1585 (Applegate and Hanselka 1974:51; Hammond and Rey 1929:60; Scholes and Mera 1940:271). As might be expected, these raids made the natives hostile toward all Spanish intruders and would continue until the mid-eighteenth century.

The next historical record of life at La Junta comes from the Rodríguez-Chamuscado *entrada* of A.D. 1581–1582. Several after-the-fact accounts of the expedition were produced, with the Gallegos *Relación* apparently supplying the best information on La Junta (Kelley 1952b). This account described individual pueblos, and also gave a detailed description of some of the houses and how they were constructed, which is in line with the archaeological evidence from the district. Groups of Indians referred to as "Conchos," "Patarabueyes," and "Amotomancos" were described as living at La Junta, but no references as to the number of pueblos nor the size of the population were given (Kelley 1952b:264–265). A later historian, Obregón, indicated the expedition had observed more than 2,000 Indians in the Rio Grande valley, which was named "Valle de Nuestra Señora de la Concepción" (Kelley 1952b:265).

That expedition was quickly followed by the *entrada* of Antonio de Espejo in A.D. 1582–1583, which was documented in the journal of Diego Pérez de Luxán (Hammond and Rey 1929) as they traveled down the Río Conchos, explored the La Junta area, then went up the Rio Grande to present-day New Mexico. The return trip was by way of the Pecos River to the vicinity of Toyah Creek, where they were guided back to La Junta (Hammond and Rey 1929:124–126; Kelley 1952b:265, 1986:14). They returned to the northern frontier of New Spain by traveling up the Río Conchos. More information was produced on the villages and inhabitants of La Junta, with "Omotomoacos" and "Abriaches" Indians identified and collectively referred to as "Patarabueyes," who apparently had different languages than their neighbors to the south (Hammond and Rey 1929:57–64; Kenmotsu 1994b:17).

The account did relay that "Jumanos" Indians had brought the group to La Junta from the Toyah Creek area (Hammond and Rey 1929:124–126; Kelley 1986:14). In the records for the region this is the first mention of Jumano Indians, which some researchers associated or linked with the Patarabueyes (Bandelier 1890; Hodge 1911; Sauer 1934; Hickerson 1994). However, the preponderance of archaeological and historical evidence suggests they were a separate group of nomadic hunters and traders (Scholes and Mera 1940; Kelley 1947, 1986; Kenmotsu 1994a, 2001; Mallouf 1990, 1999). Archival data recently gathered apparently provides conflicting evidence on the presence of this group at La Junta. Kenmotsu (1994a, 2001), noting the Jumano were not mentioned in the Spanish records of La Junta at the Archivo del Hildalgo del Parral for a 100-year period (A.D. 1583–1682), suggests they were only sporadically present at this time. However, some records from the late seventeenth century indicate they spent the winter months at La Junta and much of the remainder of their time in Central, East, and West Texas on hunting and trading forays (Kelley 1986:30–31, 112). The Jumano remain one of the least understood groups of the region during Protohistoric times.

After the Spaniards found a more direct route to the pueblos of present-day New Mexico in A.D. 1599, they abandoned the dif-

ficult passage through La Junta de los Ríos. During the middle to later portion of the seventeenth century, Indian unrest in New Mexico, culminating with the Pueblo Revolt of A.D. 1680, made the Spanish focus their attentions on holding that territory. Thus, a presidio was established at El Paso in A.D. 1681 to protect the four missions in that area (Ing et al. 1996:28), while a 20-year war ensued between the Spanish and practically all major Indian groups in northern Nueva Vizcaya (Spanish province that included most of the modern state of Chihuahua) and New Mexico (Jones 1988:99–110).

Also during this period, the "Apache" Indian tribes had made their way into the region from the Southern Plains, constituting a new and more dangerous threat to the northeastern Spanish provinces (Jones 1988:115). It was during this social upheaval, in A.D. 1683, that several delegations of Indians from La Junta traveled to the El Paso missions to request that missionaries be sent to the valley and to a vast area of Central Texas. One of these delegations was apparently led by Juan Sabeata, a Jumano Indian, who supposedly desired baptism for the Jumanos and other tribes (Castañeda 1976:II:312; Kelley 1986:24). It has been suggested that Sabeata's motives were perhaps partly driven by a desire to have the Spanish push the intruding Apache out of Jumano territory (Kelley 1986:26; Ing et al. 1996:29). In response to the request, the Mendoza-López expedition (A.D. 1683–1684) left a padre in La Junta in late December A.D. 1683 before moving eastward into Central Texas (Kelley 1952b:266).

It was reported that "Julimes" Indian *rancherías,* with crosses of some type and maize and wheat crops, were positioned on both sides of the Rio Grande at La Junta (Kelley 1952b:266–267). The Spanish documents indicate that between six and nine grass and/or wood missions were eventually established, and over 500 Indians from nine separate nations were baptized (Kelley 1952b:267). These missions were apparently closed in the summer of A.D. 1684, shortly after being established during a general native revolt in northern Nueva Vizcaya that began with the Manso Indians of the El Paso area. The revolt quickly spread down the Rio Grande to the Julimes and Conchos Indians that were part of the collective Patarabueyes of La Junta. Although Christian Indians remained faithful to the Spanish, the missionaries and their sacraments were taken to Parral (Kelley 1986:57–58).

Conchos Phase (A.D. 1684–1760)

The establishment of missions at La Junta in ca. A.D. 1684 marked the formal end of the Concepcion phase and the beginning of the Conchos phase, which lasted until A.D. 1760 (Kelley 1986:84) or a little later (Kelley et al. 1940:163). This phase "represents the period of Spanish acculturation of the Indian villages" (Kelley et al. 1940:39), during which time large rectangular pithouses were still being constructed and lithic assemblages went virtually unchanged from the previous period (Kelley et al. 1940:36). The phase is distinguished archaeologically by the presence of artifacts of European or Mexican origin, including Spanish or Mexican majolica wares, associated Spanish utility wares, and metal items (Kelley et al. 1940:37). Indigenous pottery styles found associated with the phase include Conchos Red-on-Brown and Pulicos Red-on-Brown (Kelley et al. 1940:37), with some Capote Red-on-Brown, and Chinati Plain, Striated-Neck, and Neck-Banded (Kelley 1986:85).

Although missions were established at La Junta in A.D. 1684, a series of events left them only sporadically in use for the first ca. 30 years of the Conchos phase. The aforementioned native revolt caused the first lapse, from the summer of A.D. 1684 until

A.D. 1687. Then, after only a couple of years of operation they were again shut down in A.D. 1689 to protest renewed slave raids for the silver mines to the southwest. After that, there were apparently no official Spanish visits to La Junta until A.D. 1715, when missions were reestablished in the district.

With subjugation of most of the native tribes of the region, the Spanish were able to focus their attention on the Apache Indians, who had increased their presence in the region. By approximately A.D. 1720, the Jumano may have been assimilated by this aggressive group of horsemen, as the group is henceforth referred to in the historical record as 'los Apaches Jumanes' or 'Apaches Jumanos' (Newcomb 1961:233; Hickerson 1994:202; Kenmotsu 1994a:324; Kenmotsu and Wade 2002:50). The Jumano name no longer appears in these records by the latter portion of the eighteenth century. The Apache raided both Indian groups and Spanish alike—they also traded with both groups (Kelley 1952a; Jones 1991). At La Junta there is more evidence of trade relations than raids at this time. Deer and buffalo hides and some dried meat were exchanged for, among other things, corn and beans (Kelley 1952a:380). During the Conchos phase, the Apache role as the dominant tribe of the Southern Plains was taken over by the "Comanche" tribes, who had steadily moved southward from the Great Plains (Wallace and Hoebel 1986).

Several Spanish *entradas* focused on La Junta during the first half of the eighteenth century: the Trasviña Retis *entrada* in A.D. 1715, the Rábago y Therán *entrada* in A.D. 1747, the Ydoiaga *entrada* in A.D. 1747–1748, the Vidaurre *entrada* in A.D. 1747–1748, and the Rubín de Celis *entrada* in A.D. 1750–1751 (Kelley 1952b).

The Trasviña Retis *entrada* brought two priests to La Junta to help reestablish missions there, although "churches appear to have been standing in most if not all the villages, but in disrepair, European traits were already conspicuously present, including dress, use of the Spanish language, agricultural products, tools, and perhaps irrigation methods, and some architectural features, to mention only the more obvious" (Kelley 1952b:270). Six more priests were dispatched to La Junta in A.D. 1716, but the missions were temporarily abandoned for a short time in A.D. 1718, again over the issue of slave raids. They were reestablished later that year, but were once again abandoned between A.D. 1725 and A.D. 1732/1733 due to Apache and Comanche raids (Kelley 1952b:270). During each of the abandonments, the missionaries petitioned the Spanish authorities for establishment of a presidio at La Junta. There was little action on these requests, but eventually, as Apache and Comanche raids were extended deep into Nuevo Vizcaya through the Big Bend country and began impacting Spanish settlements and ranches, the need for a Spanish military force in the area was realized. To address this problem, three separate, but interconnected *entradas* visited and explored the region in A.D. 1747, primarily to research the feasibility of placing a presidio at La Junta to stop the incursions (Kelley 1992:xiii–xiv).

The first and most significant of these *entradas*, led by Captain Joseph de Ydoiaga, was launched down the traditional route to La Junta along the Río Conchos (Kelley 1952b; Madrid 1992). Ydoiaga found several of the previously reported outlying pueblo locations abandoned, with the former residents relocated to nearby pueblos more centrally positioned as a means of defense against the raiding Apache and Comanche. Ydoiaga spent three days at the Millington site (Pueblo of San Cristóbal), where the inhabitants indicated their farming efforts were successful only infrequently due to a reliance upon flood waters of the river. They said in good years there was enough corn to last the full year and to allow some trade with the Apache.

However, in poor years wheat was planted as an additional crop, and was supplemented by fish, game animals, prickly pear tunas, and a gruel-type beverage made from various ground seeds. The census indicated there were 158 residents at San Cristóbal, including 78 children. Ydoiaga tried to make the case that the Indians should move across the river to be better served by the priest from the Pueblo of Guadalupe, but was told there was no suitable location there for their pueblo or fields (Madrid 1992:59–63).

Both of the other *entradas* were launched from Coahuila, but neither of these spent appreciable time at La Junta nor added much to the point of discussion. On the other hand, Ydoiaga spent almost three months at La Junta during the expedition. He ultimately recommended that a presidio not be established at La Junta, citing that necessary lands for livestock and produce, as well as farmers, were lacking—elements needed to support a garrison (Kelley 1992:xv).

Ultimately, Ydoiaga's recommendation was disregarded and the Real Presidio de Nuestra Señora de Bethlen y Santiago de las Amarillas de la Junta de los Ríos Conchos y del Norte (later shortened to Presidio de Belén, Presidio de la Junta de los Ríos or Presidio del Norte) was constructed in A.D. 1759–1760 (Jones 1991:49; Kelley 1992:xv), bringing an end to the mission period and the Conchos phase (Kelley and Kelley 1990). Captain Manuel Muñoz established the presidio near the pueblo of Nuestra Señora de Guadalupe, probably within the present-day town of Ojinaga, Chihuahua (Kelley 1953, 1992:xv; Jones 1991:50).

Cielo Complex (A.D. 1250–1680)

Based upon extensive archaeological work in the region, Mallouf (1985, 1990, 1993, 1995, 1999) identified a unique cultural phenomenon that he has termed "the Cielo complex." It is described as "a Late Prehistoric to Contact period (ca. A.D. 1250–1680) aceramic manifestation that is found across most of the Texas Big Bend and for an undetermined distance southward into northeastern Chihuahua and northwestern Coahuila" (Mallouf 1999:65). In the La Junta district, Cielo complex sites, such as Cielo Bravo and Arroyo de las Burras, are present on "elevated pediments that overlook the river basin terraces that were used for farming and habitation by coeval La Junta phase agriculturalists" (Mallouf 1999:67). Mallouf feels the complex consists of a range of individual site types across the landscape, including base camps, short-term campsites, specialized resource procurement sites, and ritual locales (Mallouf 1999:65). Base camps and short-term campsites of the complex are characterized by above ground, circular-to-oval stacked stone wickiup foundations with narrow entranceway gaps, and a variety of constructions related to various special functions (Mallouf 1990, 1999).

Material culture associated with earlier occupations of the complex at Cielo Bravo includes Perdiz arrow points and preforms, flake drills, end and side scrapers, a few beveled knifes, a variety of expediency tools and ground stone, end-notched sinker stones, and a few Olivella shell beads (Mallouf 1999:69). Artifactual materials from the final occupation at that site were very similar to the earlier assemblages, with some notable differences: the addition of Garza/Soto-like arrow points, a lower incidence of ground stone, the lack of end-notched sinker stones, a higher incidence of triangular end scrapers and beveled-knife fragments, and the addition of small trianguloid shell (freshwater) pendants (Mallouf 1990:14, 1999:71).

Mallouf (1990, 1999) has theorized that both the La Junta phase and the Cielo complex are ancestral manifestations of the sixteenth century group identified in Spanish documents as "Jumano Indians." He further

suggests that these related groups had shared identities dating back as far as A.D. 1250 and that both had non-Athapaskan ethnic origins among hunter-gatherers indigenous to the Southern Plains or northeastern Chihuahuan Desert region. His model suggests that the La Junta phase and Cielo complex peoples were interacting somewhat like genetically-linked "cousins," with the La Junta folks practicing a semi-sedentary, agricultural-based (supplemented by hunting and gathering) lifestyle and Cielo complex groups relying on a hunting and gathering lifeway. The two groups interacted through seasonal trading where unknown goods were exchanged. After collapse of the Casas Grandes interaction sphere, Mallouf (1990, 1999) has offered that the La Junta phase peoples joined their cousins in the hunting and gathering lifeway, archaeologically manifested as the Cielo complex. Furthermore, using data from the final occupation at Cielo Bravo, he has suggested a linkage in the area between early Apachean groups and Cielo complex peoples (Jumano-Apache) by approximately A.D. 1650, or perhaps a little earlier (Mallouf 1990:21, 1999:85).

Alamito Phase (A.D. 1760–1850)

The Alamito phase, like the Livermore phase, lacked association with a defined aspect. This phase represents changes to the Indian settlements after the presidio had been established in A.D. 1760 at what is now Ojinaga. These changes were the result of both ethnic admixture and acculturation, which ultimately resulted in the formation of Mexican towns (Kelley et al. 1940:37). While Kelley never formally proposed an ending date for this phase, his description of the subsequent Presidio phase can be used to argue for a ca. A.D. 1850 closing date.

Kelley et al. (1940:37) indicated that many of the traits or characteristics of the Alamito phase derived from a Bravo Valley aspect or Conchos ancestry. During the evolution of this phase, agriculture, fishing, and the gathering of wild foodstuffs were the primary economic pursuits, while house styles and pottery types were modified only slightly from those of the Conchos phase. The phase is distinguished primarily by European artifacts such as modern chinaware, glass beads, metal cartridge cases, buttons, and other materials (Kelley et al. 1940:37–38).

At the beginning of the phase the La Junta presidio was immediately plagued with problems. It was attacked by Apaches at sunrise on the day it was to be dedicated, and a year later half of the natives of La Junta had fled the area due to the oppressive policies of the Spanish political and military officials. Many of the Indians moved up the Río Conchos and worked on Spanish farms. Yet the presidio remained at this location until A.D. 1767, when it was moved up the Río Conchos about 30 miles to the Pueblo of Julimes (Kelley 1953:35, 1986:65; Jones 1991:52). Six years later, at the command of the King of Spain, Presidio del Norte was reestablished at La Junta by Colonel Hugo O'Connor. During the same year (A.D. 1773), two presidios were established down the Rio Grande on the south side of the river, San Carlos and San Vicente, although the actual forts were not completely constructed until ca. A.D. 1775 (Ivey 1990:1). This created a line of forts to deter the Apache and Comanche raids in the extremely rough, expansive, and virtually unknown area along the Rio Grande between La Junta and San Juan Bautista de Coahuila called the *Despoblado*. This line of forts provided a degree of protection for Spanish settlers who slowly moved farther north and northeast on the Nueva Vizcaya frontier, yet the Indian raids continued. Regardless of their effectiveness in deterring the raids, the forts at San Carlos and San Vicente were both abandoned by A.D. 1784 when it was decided

that these locales were not appropriate for settlement (Ivey 1990:2–3).

The Spanish spent time courting peaceful relations with both the Apaches and Comanches through the ensuing years. The Apaches at La Junta served as auxiliaries on a number of occasions, and at times were coaxed into peaceful settlements through the issuance of rations (John 1991). However, these efforts were only sporadically fruitful, as the Apaches remained the biggest problem for the Spanish through their remaining years in the region. The Spanish also sought peace with the Comanche, and in A.D. 1785, Nueva Vizcaya Governor Domingo Cabello negotiated an agreement with the headmen of three of their bands that operated on the north side of the Rio Grande. The agreement, which called for the Comanches to wage war on their mortal enemies, the Apaches, in exchange for annual gifts and the cessation of hostilities by Spanish forces, essentially stayed in effect until Mexican Independence (Chipman 1992:199). Despite all of these efforts, Indian raids continued to plague the region and be the greatest impediment to settlement.

The struggle between Mexico and colonists in Texas in the mid-1830s impacted the La Junta area very little. Texas achieved independence from Mexico on March 2, 1836, but even after the Texans achieved victory at San Jacinto in April of that year, lands west of the Nueces River remained under Mexican control (Ing et al. 1996:41).

Trade became an important industry for the La Junta region in the next few decades despite dangers posed by the Indians, as several attempts were made to establish a route of commerce with Mexico through Presidio del Norte. As a result, an old trail between Indianola, Texas (through San Antonio), and Chihuahua City (by way of Presidio del Norte) began to see increased traffic at this time and became known as the Chihuahua Trail. In what later became Presidio County, this primitive road cut through Paisano Pass, then traveled down Alamito Creek, with several forks eventually crossing the Rio Grande at Presidio del Norte. Freighters using the road typically relied on ox-drawn carts and were heavily armed to dissuade Indian attacks (Swift and Corning 1988). Another road, this one going from El Paso to San Antonio, crossed through the northern reaches of the region as trade became increasingly important in the nineteenth century.

Presidio Phase (A.D. 1850–)

As stated above, the Presidio phase lacks association with a defined aspect and its beginning date has been somewhat arbitrarily placed at A.D. 1850. This is the period of Anglo-American and Spanish-American (or Mexican-American) cultural expressions in the region manifested archaeologically by adobe ruins, ranch houses, and the attendant material culture (Kelley et al. 1940:38).

In the late 1870s and early 1880s, railroads entered the region and settlement was encouraged by passage of the "fifty cent" law in A.D. 1879, which allowed sale of unappropriated lands at 50 cents/acre throughout much of West Texas (Ing et al. 1996:51–52). By the early 1880s, ranches and farms sprang up throughout the area, encouraging more Anglo-Americans, as well as additional Mexicans and Mexican-Americans to settle in the region.

The 1890s brought several changes to the area. A severe drought during the first portion of this decade greatly affected the ranchers of the area, a reminder to the early settlers that the region is within the Chihuahuan Desert and subject to annual (or longer) fluctuations in rainfall. At this time, mining had become an important industry in the region, with the Shafter district of the Chinati Mountains and, a few years later, the Terlingua district to the east, providing the largest

contributions. A large number of Mexican workers were employed in each of these districts, which ultimately helped shape the ethnic mixture now seen in the region. Also at this time, federal troops stationed in the area were reassigned as part of the army's efforts to consolidate its frontier garrisons. The fort at Fort Davis was abandoned in A.D. 1891, and, during this same year, the Seminole Negro scouts at Camp Neville Springs (now located in Big Bend National Park) received orders to relocate to Polvo, along the banks of the Rio Grande (Ing et al. 1996:56). The presence of these scouts at Polvo may be seen today in a small village known as El Mulato located on the Chihuahua side of the river immediately downstream from Polvo.

The drought was broken in A.D. 1895, and ranchers again stocked the range with cattle, sheep, and goats—the next prolonged drought would not come until the 1930s. During the early years of the twentieth century, social issues in Mexico reached a point that resulted in the Mexican Revolution (ca. A.D. 1910–1920). The unrest that enveloped that country spilled across the river at times during this struggle for reform. It was during this period that Camp Polvo, immediately east of the old town of Polvo, and Camp Fulton in Presidio were established (Earl H. Elam, personal communication 2000). Operations and associated travel between these and other camps along the river provided a strong military presence on the United States side of the river at this time.

Severe droughts in the 1930s and 1950s again devastated ranchers in the area, driving some out of the business, while others moved in to take advantage of lower land values. During this time, the government purchased a number of ranches in Brewster County and formed Big Bend National Park, which began operations in the 1940s. In A.D. 1988, the State of Texas purchased Big Bend Ranch, a vast tract in Brewster and Presidio counties located downstream of Presidio. This property ultimately became Big Bend Ranch State Park, the largest holding in the state park system.

The Presidio phase represents a time of change at La Junta. Early years were marked by Indian attacks and commerce associated with the Chihuahua Trail. Then, beginning in the 1880s, after Indians had been removed from the area, mining, ranching, and farming became the primary economic pursuits. Important events and activities associated with the Mexican Revolution (ca. A.D. 1910–1920) occurred at La Junta, resulting in an influx of new residents from Mexico. La Junta has always been a cross-roads of sorts and, accordingly, the resident population slowly, but steadily grew and evolved into a blended culture. Comprised of Indian, Spanish, Mexican, Mexican American, African American, and Anglo American blood-lines, this culture is certainly unique, with distinctive languages, food, art, customs, and lifestyles.

DESCRIPTION OF INVESTIGATION

Field Techniques

Archaeological fieldwork for the Millington site (41PS14) investigation generally conformed to the scope of work submitted to and approved by the THC in January 2006. The CBBS work plan consisted of mapping the site (areas both within and outside the fenced area owned by the THC) with a Total Data Station (TDS), conducting a provenienced surface collection, re-excavating and profiling portions of the backhoe trench (BHT #1) walls, excavating the burials and some of the other features exposed along the length of the trench, testing one or two other areas, and using several geophysical investigative efforts in select 10 x 10 m areas to locate subsurface anomalies. The only aspect of the investigation not explicitly included in the work plan was excavation of several backhoe trenches in the city-owned portion of the site.

The site was mapped with a Sokia SET 4110 TDS using three datums and two sub-datums (Figure 2). Since J. Charles Kelley's original site datum could not be found, the primary datum was placed in the eastern portion of the site just west of BHT #1 and designated MIL-A. This datum, a wooden stake driven deeply into the ground, was given arbitrary horizontal (North 1000.000 m-East 1000.000 m) and vertical (100.000 m) coordinates. Accordingly, all mapped points have coordinates in relation to it. Datums MIL-B (N984.443 m-E981.485 m—100.76 m) and MIL-C (N1026.689 m-E916.258 m—101.67

m), marked with rebar and protected on either side by wooden stakes, were placed within the THC-owned or fenced portion of the site. Both sub-datums, Sub-1 (N938.087 m-E1006.477 m—99.567 m) and Sub-2 (N1035.134 m-E1003.471 m—100.358 m), were positioned in the southeastern portion of the site and also served as southwestern corners of two of the 10 x 10 m areas (Areas A and C, respectively) investigated through geophysical means. This grid was established using "Fine Average" shots, that is, taking 20 unique readings (five shots at four readings per shot) with a 7 mm tolerance error

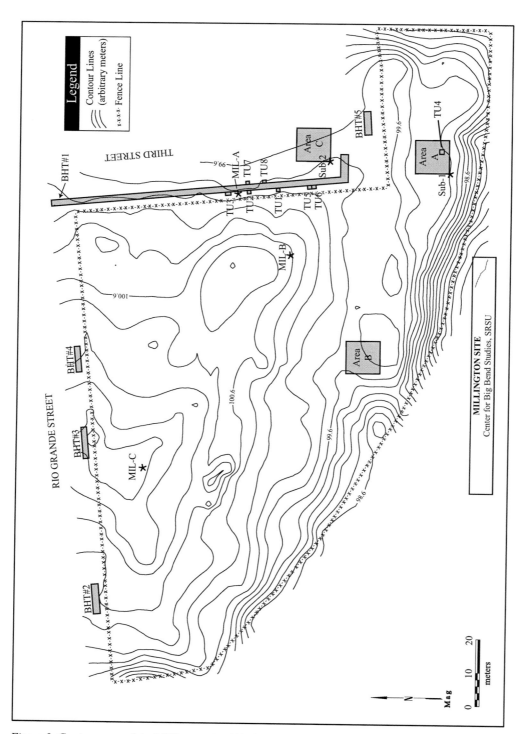

Figure 2. Contour map of the Millington site (41PS14) showing the fenced State Archeological Landmark portion, a historic ruin, backhoe trenches, and excavation units.

Figure 3. (left) View of the 2003 water line backhoe trench that generated the 2006 investigation.

Figure 4. (right) Re-excavation of BHT #1 in 2006. Shovels were utilized in burial locations and the backhoe in remaining portions.

for placement of each of the datums and sub-datums. All environmental (e.g., the terrace edge and gullies) and man-made features (e.g., house foundation, well, fence lines, roadways, backhoe trenches, and excavation units), as well as collected artifacts, were mapped in from one or more of these locations.

The collection of surface artifacts in the THC-owned portion of the site was accomplished in a systematic manner with a crew that varied in numbers from four to seven. This crew moved slowly across the site over a four-day period, often on their hands and knees for an up-close inspection of the surface. As was specified in the scope of work, these collections were selective. All ornamental objects and artifacts suspected to be of Spanish origin, and most formal stone tools and ceramic sherds were collected. Only representative samples of ground stone, notched pebbles, expediency tools, and certain types of ceramic sherds well represented in the surface assemblage were targeted for collection. Pin flags labeled with unique artifact numbers were used to mark all collected items and these locations were later provenienced with the TDS. A total of 314 artifacts were collected from the surface during this effort.

To begin ground breaking, the original backhoe trench excavated by the city (BHT #1), and located near the western edge of Third Street (Figure 3), was re-exposed. For this purpose, the city backhoe was utilized in non-burial locations (Figure 4) and the field

Figure 5. View of BHT #1 after re-excavation, with profile for Burial 1 prepared in right foreground.

crew used hand tools in the burial locations. Once this was completed, profiles of trench walls were drawn in locations where human bone was exposed prior to commencement of hand excavations (Figure 5). Additional profiles were drawn in locations along the trench where other cultural features were exposed. Due to myriad disturbances through the years, pit dug into pit, etc., it was impossible to correlate cultural and natural zones from one profile to the next, even when they were relatively close to one another.

A total of four test units (Test Units 1, 2, 3, and 7) were used to excavate the human interments identified in June 2003 along BHT #1 (Figure 6). Three other units (Test Units 5, 6, and 8) were used to explore other features along the length of the backhoe trench, one of these (Test Unit 8) containing the fifth burial excavated during the investigation. Since the upper deposits at the site were quite loose, each of these units were set back from the trench a short distance to protect corner

Figure 6. Crew beginning excavation of Test Unit 1, with survey crew in the background working on surface collection within the state-owned portion of the site.

Figure 7. (above) Crew working in Test Unit 5 (right) and Test Unit 6 (left). The latter unit was larger than usual to encompass several features exposed in the backhoe trench.

Figure 8. (right) Excavation of Burial 2 in Test Unit 3 showing removal and packaging of human remains.

stakes along it, the small additional areas excavated as part of the respective units. Thus, most unit sizes had east-west dimensions that varied from 1.3–1.4 m. Also, in order to completely encapsulate Burial 2 (Feature 2) and several other features (Features 4, 5, and 6), two of the test units had north-south dimensions of 1.5 m—Test Unit 2 and Test Unit 6 (Figure 7), respectively.

A single 1 x 1 m test unit (Test Unit 4) was used to explore deposits at the site away from BHT #1. This unit was placed in the southeast portion of the site within the fenced area (privately owned, but a portion of the SAL designated area of the site), and was positioned over a subsurface anomaly identified in the first of two geophysical investigations conducted at the site (see below).

Human remains were carefully excavated with wooden tools and brushes, and each element was identified in the field when possible, wrapped with padding and aluminum foil (Figure 8), and labeled accordingly. Levels were not employed during the burial pit excavations since all materials uncovered were point-plotted and from a single event in time. Data from the burials were recorded on individual CBBS burial forms. All other

Figure 9. Photographic technique in the bright sun of La Junta.

excavation was accomplished in 10 cm levels. Excavation level forms containing descriptive and mapped data were completed for each of these levels. Fill from both the burial pits and other excavations was passed through 1/8 in hardware cloth. Trowels, paint brushes of various sizes, dental picks, and wooden implements were used in the excavation. The triangulation method was employed to map in fire-cracked rock (FCR) and other stones, artifacts found in situ, charcoal and special samples, and soil anomalies. For this purpose, drawing compasses and plumb bobs were essential tools. Photographic documentation of the investigation was achieved with both digital and 35 mm color slide formats (Figure 9). All materials recovered in the field were assigned a field bag number which served as a temporary lot number. Charcoal samples (n=54) were plotted, given unique numbers, collected with trowels, and placed in aluminum foil pouches, and a total of 10 sediment samples were selectively collected.

Additionally, select portions of the June 2003 backdirt piles—those adjacent to the disturbed burials—were investigated with the goal of recovering displaced human remains. These deposits were usually screened until portions with concentrated remains were discovered. At that point, hand tools (wooden tools and brushes) were used until those efforts were exhausted, then screening was resumed. Recovery from backdirt piles adjacent to certain interments were labeled accordingly, i.e., BHT #1, Feature 3 (F-3?).

In addition to BHT #1, four backhoe trenches (BHT #2, BHT #3, BHT #4, and BHT #5) were excavated in city-owned portions of the site during the investigation. The backhoe bucket measured 61 cm in width, but due to looseness of the deposits the trenches varied from ca. 65–100 cm in width. Trench lengths ranged from ca. 9–10.5 m, and depths from ca.1.2–1.8 m. Backhoe trenches #2, #3, and #4 were placed on the north side of the site and on the south side of Rio Grande Street, a few meters from the fence line. BHT #5 was placed at the south end of Third Street, east-southeast of the south end of BHT #1 (Figure 10).

Of the three trenches on the north side of the site, BHT #2 was the westernmost. It measured 9 m long and 1 m wide and was excavated to a maximum depth of 1.7 m. Cultural residue in the form of FCR, charcoal, and ashy sheet midden deposit was visible in the upper 45 cm and overlay sterile sediments consisted primarily of dense, poorly sorted gravels. BHT #3, 10.5 m long, ca. 1 m wide, and 1.6 m deep, contained a similar profile. The midden-like deposit in this trench was much darker than the one in BHT #2 and extended to a maximum depth of 55 cm below the surface. However, across most of this trench the cultural zone was much thinner, perhaps averaging 20–30 cm. The cultural zones in both of these exposures were thickest on the south side of the trenches, thinning appreciably on the northern sides. BHT #4 was the easternmost trench positioned within Rio Grande Street. It had a length of 9 m, a width of 65 cm, and a depth of 1.8 m. It lacked a definable cultural zone, but contained a fine sandy silt in its upper 1.3 m. Poorly sorted gravels occurred below the sandy silt. BHT #5 was 7.8 m long, ca. 70 cm wide, and excavated to a depth of ca. 1.3 m. It revealed a sheet midden deposit in the upper ca. 20 cm that overlaid a more diffuse cultural zone ca. 45–80 cm thick. Cut into the bottom of the latter was an undefined pit that was designated F-10. Beneath this was a poorly sorted gravel deposit that likely corresponded to similar sediments observed in BHT #2–4.

Two separate geophysical investigations were conducted as part of the Millington project. The initial geophysical investigation was conducted by Jaime Hincapié during the field investigation in 2006 in three areas of the site that were targeted, to some extent, by a lack of vegetative cover. Chester Walker

Figure 10. View of BHT #5 at the southern end of Third Street with profile set up over an undefined pit (F-10) low in the trench.

performed the subsequent investigation in October, 2007.

The Hincapié investigation focused on three 10 x 10 m areas, designated Areas A, B, and C and oriented to cardinal directions using magnetic north. Areas A and B were positioned in the fenced/SAL area of the site and Area C adjacent to BHT #1 in the city-owned portion (Figure 11). Area A was placed in the southeast portion of the site, Area B in the south-central portion where the A.D. 1684 and/or A.D. 1715 mission is thought to have been located, and Area C within Third Street east of BHT #1. Two geophysical techniques were used in this investigation: conductivity and ground penetrating radar. Eight anomalies were identified in Area A, six in Area B, and 23 in Area C. The anomalies in Area A varied in depth from 0.9–1.9 m, the ones in Area B from 0.7–1.5 m, and those in Area C from 0.5–1.4 m. See Appendix III for the full report from this investigation.

After getting the results from Hincapié's geophysical investigation, a decision was made to field test one of the anomalies, so Test Unit 4 was placed over the shallowest anomaly in Area A. While the targeted anomaly was at a depth of 0.9 m, this unit reached sterile soil at a depth of 36 cm below the surface. A 40 x 40 cm corner test exca-

Figure 11. View of 2006 geophysical (conductivity) investigation in Area C near the southern end of Third Street.

vated an additional 20 cm into the deposits verified that these sediments were indeed culturally sterile. At this point work in the test unit ceased. Thus, it appears that this particular anomaly is likely a naturally occurring boulder or something similar.

Over a year and a half later, the opportunity presented itself for further geophysical investigations at Millington in tandem with an effort targeting the suspected mission location at the Polvo site (41PS21). Walker conducted the investigations at both sites using four techniques: magnetometer, conductivity, magnetic susceptibility, and ground penetrating radar (Figure 12). At Millington, the work simply targeted Area B from the previous investigation, the suspected location of the mission. Through the data retrieved from this investigation, Walker identified a possible ca. 7 x 7 m square structure positioned in the upper 12 cm of the deposit and pinching out around 36 cm below the surface. Appendix IV contains the report from this investigation.

Laboratory Procedures

Once all of the materials recovered from the site (i.e., human remains, field bags, charcoal samples, sediment samples, and special samples) were back in the CBBS laboratory, sediment and charcoal samples were opened and air-dried to avoid buildup of mold or other contaminants. All materials were then inventoried, compared to the list of field bag numbers, assigned lot numbers, then washed and labeled. Ceramic sherds were carefully washed to avoid impacting interior or exterior surfaces. Artifacts recovered from the surface were given "0-" lot numbers followed by sequential numbers in accordance with field designations. The remaining lot numbers (1–142) were assigned to various subsurface recoveries. To distinguish between items recovered from the screen and point-plotted specimens, the latter were given unique numbers with sequential numbers following the general lot number assigned to the level (e.g., "-1").

All artifacts were labeled with a Rapidoliner® drafting pen and then coated with polyvinyl acetate varnish. Artifact labels consisted of the state trinomial number (41PS14) placed above the individual lot number. Specimens too small to be labeled (e.g., micro-debitage) were placed in a plastic vial with an appropriately labeled acid-free tag. Tools recovered from the surface and subsurface were individually measured, weighed, and described during analysis. In addition, projectile points were scrutinized for their adherence to established types. Select specimens were photographed.

Charcoal samples chosen for radiocarbon analysis were hand-picked of foreign matter (i.e., plant and insect parts, rocks, carbonates, etc.), then re-bagged in foil and plastic bags and shipped to Beta Analytic Inc., a radiocarbon laboratory in Miami, Florida. Human skeletal remains were carefully cleaned, analyzed, wrapped with padding, and boxed with all elements that could be determined to be from individual interments. After analysis, select cortical bones from Burials 2, 4, and 5 were submitted to Geochron Laboratories in Billerica, Massachusetts. Results from both of these radiocarbon analyses are provided in Table 1.

Geochron Laboratories also conducted a stable isotope analysis of bone apatite and collagen on the Burial 2, 4, and 5 samples as well as on remains from three individuals recovered from Millington during the 1938–1939 investigation (Burials 3, 7, and 8—burial numbers are separate from those assigned during the 2006 investigation). These analyses, which yielded signatures of carbon and nitrogen isotopes which are reflective of diet over the last years of an individual's life, are provided in Chapter 6 (Analysis of Mortuary Contexts and Human Remains) of this report.

Figure 12. View of 2007 geophysical (magnetometer) investigation in Area B in the suspected location of the late seventeenth/early eighteenth century Spanish mission. Ground penetrating radar and conductivity units in foreground.

Table 1: Results of Radiocarbon Data from the Millington Site (41PS14)

Lab # *	Field Sample #	Context	Horizontal Provenience	Material Dated	13C/12C Ratio	Measured Radiocarbon Age	Conventional Radiocarbon Age	Calibrated Date A.D. (2–Sigma)** — Probability Distribution (.95)
Beta–221009	CS–14	Burial 3/ Lower Sheet Midden	Test Unit 1	Charcoal	(−24.3 ‰)	620±40 B.P.	630±40 B.P.	Cal. A.D. 1290–1410
Beta–221010	CS–15	Burial 1 (F–1)	Test Unit 2	Charcoal	(−27.1 ‰)	100±40 B.P.	70±40 B.P.	Cal. A.D. 1680–1740 Cal. A.D. 1810–1930 Cal. A.D. 1950–1960
Beta–221011	CS–23	Hearth (F–9)	Test Unit 8	Charcoal	(−23.7 ‰)	250±40 B.P.	270±40 B.P.	Cal. A.D. 1510–1600 Cal. A.D. 1620–1670 Cal. A.D. 1780–1800
Beta–221012	CS–27	Upper Sheet Midden	Test Unit 1	Charcoal	(−26.0 ‰)	240±40 B.P.	220±40 B.P.	Cal. A.D. 1640–1680 Cal. A.D. 1730–1810 Cal. A.D. 1930–1950
Beta–221013	CS–42	Rock Structure (F–12)	Test Unit 7	Charcoal	(−25.2 ‰)	230±40 B.P.	220±40 B.P.	Cal. A.D. 1640–1680 Cal. A.D. 1730–1810 Cal. A.D. 1930–1950
Beta–221014	CS–43	Ring Midden (F–6)	Test Unit 6	Charcoal	(−26.7 ‰)	620±40 B.P.	590±40 B.P.	Cal. A.D. 1300–1420
Beta–221015	CS–46	Undefined Pit (F–8)	Test Unit 8	Charcoal	(−25.7 ‰)	80±40 B.P.	70±40 B.P.	Cal. A.D. 1680–1740 Cal. A.D. 1810–1930 Cal. A.D. 1950–1960
Beta–221016	CS–48	Unknown Structure (F–5)	Test Unit 6	Charcoal	(−27.6 ‰)	670±40 B.P.	630±40 B.P.	Cal. A.D. 1290–1410
GX–32609–AMS	B–2	Burial 2 (F–2)	Test Unit 3	Human Bone	—	—	460±50 B.P.	Cal. A.D. 1330–1340 Cal. A.D. 1390–1520 Cal. A.D. 1570–1580 Cal. A.D. 1590–1620
GX–32610–AMS	B–4	Burial 4 (F–7)	Test Unit 7	Human Bone	—	—	630±50 B.P.	Cal. A.D. 1280–1410
GX–32611–AMS	B–5	Burial 5 (F–14)	Test Unit 8	Human Bone	—	—	780±50 B.P.	Cal. A.D. 1160–1290

* Beta Analytic, Inc., Miami, Florida (Beta) and Geochron Laboratories, Billerica, Massachusetts (GX)

** Beta calibrations based on Talma and Vogel (1993) and Stuiver et al. (1998); GX calibrations based on Reimer et al. (2004)

The analysis of human remains recovered during the project was conducted by Dr. Jennifer Piehl. The current project generated an investigation of remains previously recovered from the region (Piehl in press), including those from the Millington site during the 1938–1939 investigation. As a result, Chapter 6 provides data on the remains of 13 individuals, five from the project herein reported and eight from the Millington investigation in the 1930s.

All prehistoric and historic ceramics recovered from the surface and subsurface during the 2006 project were analyzed by Dr. David Hill. Individual specimens adhering to established types were classified according-ly, others were assigned to more descriptive groupings, such as Plain Brownware or Red-on-Brown. Although a formal petrographic analysis, or thin-sectioning, of sherds was not attempted, Hill's report (Appendix I) provides some basic information on temper attained with a hand lens.

An analysis of the faunal material recovered from the subsurface was completed by Steve Kennedy and Sarah Willet. Despite the fact that much of the faunal material recovered consists of small bone scraps and few specimens were burned, the analysis provides a list of probable animals targeted for food during site occupations. Data from this analysis is presented in Appendix II.

FEATURE DESCRIPTIONS

During the 2006 Millington site investigation, a total of 14 archaeological features were documented. These numbers are independent from feature numbers that may have been assigned during excavations at the site in the 1930s, as most of that data has not been published. All but one of the 14 features were uncovered during excavations along BHT #1—the lone exception was a pit documented in BHT #5. The features consist of five burial pits (F-1, F-2, F-3, F-7, and F-14), three structures (F-5, F-12, and F-13), a ring midden/earth oven (F-6), two hearths (F-9 and F-11), two undefined pits (F-8 and F-10), and a historic trench (F-4). For F-1, F-2, F-3, F-7, and F-14 only the burial pits are described here, see Chapter 6 (Analysis of Mortuary Contexts and Human Remains) for descriptions and findings from these discrete burials. The features are individually described below.

Feature 1

Feature 1 was the designation given for the burial pit containing Burial 1. Originally identified in the west wall of BHT #1 in 2003, this feature consists of an intrusive burial pit, which contained the interment of a subadult. The 2003 backhoe excavation and previous trenching associated with an early water line in this area apparently destroyed much of the pit and severely damaged the interment.

Based on exposures of the pit and human remains in the 2003 trench, a 1 x 1.3 m excavation unit (Test Unit 2) was centered over this feature. After excavation of ca. 15 cm in this unit, at an approximate elevation of 99.55 m, a sliver of the burial pit along the backhoe trench wall was clearly visible as a darker deposit in plan view. This matrix is a light brown (7.5YR6/3) sandy silt interspersed with rounded to subangular gravels. At 99.50 m the remaining portion of the pit had gotten a little larger, measuring ca. 8–10 cm (east-west) x 40 cm (north-south). As excavation proceeded, it became apparent that a large cavity in the deposit with a ca. 30 cm diameter had truncated the northern portion of the burial. In addition, along the western edge was a loose cluster of eight upright stones, with 6–14 cm maximum dimensions and basal elevations of 99.38–.37 m (Figure 13). Their clustered locations and common basal elevations next to the burial suggest they were pit defining markers. The burial pit was found to have its greatest dimensions at ca. 99.29 m, measuring ca. 30 x 30 cm with a somewhat irregular pit edge that had been damaged by rodent disturbances. The base of the preserved portion of the pit was documented at 99.14 m. Human remains were recovered from elevations of ca. 99.39–.14 m within the pit.

A single small charcoal sample (CS-15) was recovered from the burial pit. It was found well within the pit next to an in situ vertebra at an elevation of 99.28 m. Chosen for chronometric analysis using the Accelerator Mass Spectometry (AMS) method, it provided corrected and calibrated dates of A.D. 1680–1740, A.D. 1810–1930, and A.D. 1950–1960 (Beta-221010), with the second of these the most statistically viable at 71 percent (Reimer et al. 2004). Based on this data, it appears that Burial 1 dates to the Alamito or Presidio phase, although it could have been executed during the Conchos phase. It is also possible that the analyzed piece of charcoal entered the burial pit via a bioturbation and is completely unrelated to the interment.

Feature 2

Feature 2 was the designation given for the burial pit containing Burial 2, an interment of an adult male. Like F-1, it was originally identified in the west wall of BHT #1 in 2003 and had been severely impacted by the water line trenching. It represents the northernmost burial uncovered during the investigation.

The 2003 exposure of the remains and burial pit facilitated placement of a ca. 1.3 x 1.5 m excavation unit (Test Unit 3) during the 2006 investigation. In 2003, human remains were visible between ca. 99.20–.10 m in the trench wall (Figure 14); a 2006 profile

Figure 13. View of the upper portion of F-1 (burial pit) showing pit-defining stones on its western edge. Note the large cavity in the profile on the north side of the interment (Burial 1).

prior to excavation revealed remains from ca. 99.32–.13 m within a light gray matrix (10YR7/2). In plan view, a possible burial pit lining became visible at an elevation of 99.52 m. The clay or fine silt lining was observed as a 0.5–1 cm thick layer that corresponded to the western boundary of the pit, beginning around 99.52 m (Figure 15) and terminating at ca. 99.39 m, well above the base of the pit. Although it is here assumed to have a cultural origin, it is possible that it represents a post-depositional precipitate that entered a small crack at the edge of the burial pit. Without the eastern side of the pit, it is impossible to confirm or deny either of these possibilities. Similar to those seen associated with Burial 1 (F-1), four upright to angled pit-defining

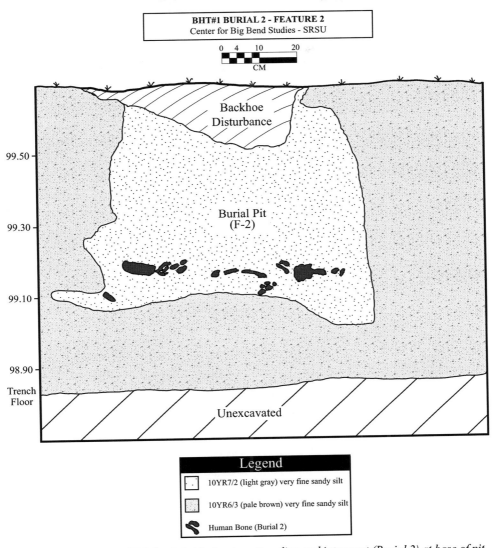

BHT#1 BURIAL 2 - FEATURE 2
Center for Big Bend Studies - SRSU

Legend

10YR7/2 (light gray) very fine sandy silt

10YR6/3 (pale brown) very fine sandy silt

Human Bone (Burial 2)

Figure 14. 2003 profile of F-2 (burial pit) showing pit outline and interment (Burial 2) at base of pit.

Figure 15. Close-up view of possible clay pit lining along western edge of F-2.

stones were found along the upper western edge of the burial pit. With 8–10 cm maximum dimensions, these stones had basal elevations within several centimeters of 99.40 m. Intact edges of the pit were found to be slightly bell-shaped. At its maximum extent (at an elevation of ca. 99.28 m) the intact portion of the pit measured ca. 19 cm (east-west) x 65 cm (north-south). Human remains were recovered between elevations of 99.36–.11 m, and elevation of the base of the pit varied between 99.10–.03 m.

Two notable pieces of chert debitage were recovered from the burial pit. Found overlying the head of the right femur was a relatively large corticate flake fragment. It is roughly square in plan view measuring ca. 37 x 45 mm, is unmodified, and has a maximum thickness of 9.9 mm. The other specimen was recovered from near the base of the pit at an elevation of 99.16 m. It is a small corticate flake fragment with a trimmed and utilized edge (Lot 18-8). Although not used extensively, it has the size and shape of a thumbnail scraper. Given the absence of grave goods in La Junta interments, these pieces of debitage likely entered the pit fortuitously, as is probable with a number of unburned faunal scraps.

Two small pieces of charcoal (CS-8 and CS-9) were found in the upper part of the burial pit at elevations of 99.49 m and 99.48 m, respectively, but neither of these was chosen for chronometric analysis. Instead, cortical bone from the interment was dated through the AMS method and provided corrected and calibrated dates of A.D. 1330–1340, A.D. 1390–1520, A.D. 1570–1580, and A.D. 1590–1620 (GX-32609-AMS), with the second of these the most statistically viable at 91 percent (Reimer et al. 2004). Therefore, this interment appears to date to the end of the La Junta phase or beginning of the Concepcion phase.

Feature 3

As with Burials 1 and 2, Burial 3 was originally identified through inspection of the west wall of BHT #1 in 2003. However, this interment was within a midden deposit and a definable pit could not be discerned at that time. The bone observed was badly disintegrated and occurred at an elevation that ranged from 99.46–99.27 m. This burial was subsequently uncovered in 2006 with a 1 x 1.3 m excavation unit (Test Unit 1). Since a burial pit could not be discerned in either the trench wall or the floor of the unit (and a formal pit may never have been present), the F-3 and Burial 3 designations both refer to this loosely defined interment.

Mostly represented by portions of long bone shafts, the poorly preserved skeletal elements were disarticulated, but somewhat clustered, within the very dark grayish brown (10YR3/2) midden deposit. During the excavation, the remains were found between elevations of 99.46–.32 m. Apparently, the chemistry of the midden soils had severely impacted the bones.

Two charcoal samples were collected from the general area and elevation of this burial: CS-4 (99.44 m) and CS-14 (99.32 m). The lower of these was in close proximity to several of the skeletal elements and was chosen for chronometric analysis through the AMS method. It provided a corrected and calibrated date of A.D. 1290–1410 (Beta-221009), suggesting interment during the La Junta phase. Since this date is from a sheet midden deposit where rodent disturbances are well documented, it should be used with caution. However, a charcoal sample (CS-27) from an overlying sheet midden provided corrected and calibrated dates of A.D. 1640–1680, A.D. 1730–1810, and A.D. 1930–1950 (Beta-221012), with the second of these the most statistically viable at 47 percent (Reimer et al. 2004). Thus, the midden depostis appear to be at least somewhat stratified, which lends support to the date for the burial.

Feature 4

A historic trench exposed on both the east and west sides of BHT #1 near its southern end was designated F-4. This feature was not identified in 2003 when the trench was initially inspected, but became well-delineated in both the eastern and western walls once they were troweled and profiled in 2006. Trench orientation was at a southeast-north-west angle. In the wall profiles, trench width measured from 1.3–1.45 m. Its base was at an elevation of ca. 99.22 m, roughly 55 cm below the surface. Trench walls varied from bell-shaped to slightly inwardly angled, and were obscured in places by very complex stratigraphy.

Feature 4, F-5 (unknown structure) and F-6 (ring midden/earth oven) were all located in close proximity and exposed in both walls of BHT #1 (Figure 16), so two excavation units (Test Units 5 and 6) were placed side-by-side on the west side of the trench to uncover these features. Test Unit 5 was positioned over most of F-4, but a portion of this feature lay beneath the northern portion of Test Unit 6. Test Unit 5 measured 1 x 1.3 m and Test Unit 6 measured 1.3 x 1.5 m. Excavation of the feature revealed the presence of both prehistoric and historic debris in its upper portion. These materials include two arrow points (Toyah-like and Sabinal-like), edge-modified and unmodified debitage, 27 prehistoric and historic ceramic sherds (15 Plain Brownware, two Polished Plain Brownware, one Polished El Paso Brownware, one El Paso Brownware, three El Paso Polychrome, one Red-on-Brown, one White Slipped Earthenware, two Majolica, and one Guanajuato Green Glaze), and assorted metal (including a complete rim-fired .44 caliber bullet) and glass debris. In addition, a number of small unburned fragments of faunal material were recovered from F-4, including rabbit, rodent, and unidentified mammals of all sizes. Additional troweling on the east wall of the trench revealed a metal can at the base of F-4 (Figure 17), making it clear the trench had been excavated during historic times. Accordingly, no charcoal samples were secured from this feature and, due to time constraints, complete excavation of Test Unit 5 was aborted.

Feature 5

When F-4 was first identified in 2006, it became apparent that a pit of some type lay immediately below the historic trench (see Figure 16). Vertical lines separating disturbed from undisturbed sediments lay directly beneath both the east and west exposures of F-4. Disturbed sediments were on the south side of this line beginning at an elevation of ca. 99.22 m, thus marking the northern edge of the F-5 pit.

As indicated above, Test Units 5 and 6 were placed in this area of BHT #1 to investigate F-4, F-5, and F-6. However, since Test Unit 5 was abandoned prior to reaching the northern wall of F-5, almost all efforts to delineate F-5 occurred in Test Unit 6. During excavation of this unit, it became apparent that F-5 represented a deep pit structure of unknown type and that it had been truncated by both F-4 and F-6 (ring midden/earth oven), the latter impacting the structure to a much lower elevation. Additionally, the lower 60 cm or so of the F-5 deposit (ca. 99.30–98.70 m) proved to be extremely confusing, as a complex of jumbled materials representing the walls and roof of the structure were uncovered amidst variously compacted sediments. Compounding the confusion were extensive rodent disturbances throughout the cultural detritus. Several burned posts, burned daub and mud dauber nests, and burned roof

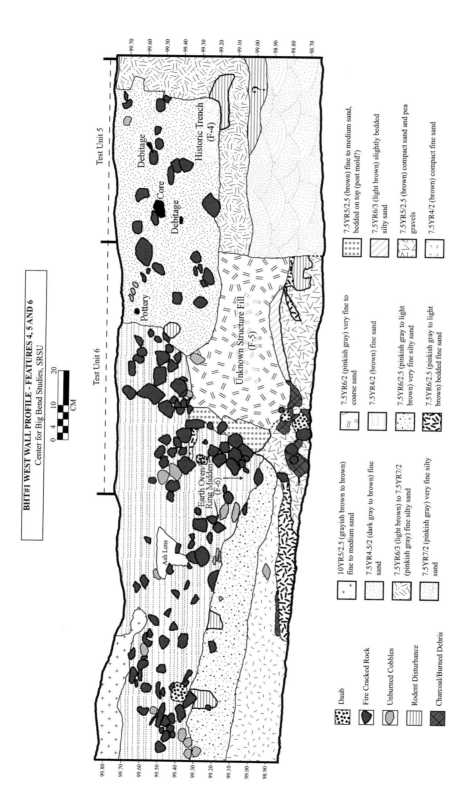

Figure 16. BHT #1 west wall profile showing F-4 (historic trench), F-5 (unknown structure), and F-6 (ring midden/earth oven).

Figure 17. View of F-4 (historic trench) in the east wall of BHT #1. Note the metal can exposed near the base of the pit.

and/or wall fall were uncovered during the excavation, but a firm indication of a floor of any type was not found.

The largest burned post had a diameter of 18–20 cm and was found in the northwest quadrant of the test unit, primarily within two elevation ranges: 99.36–99.20 m and 99.05–98.92 m. Only a small remnant of it was found between 99.20 m and 99.05 m. The post in the upper elevation range was burned completely and a large sample of it was collected as CS-37. In the lower elevation range only an outer 1–2 cm thick ring of charcoal remained as the interior of the lower portion of the post apparently never burned. This was likely due to collapse of the structure and an absence of oxygen at the lower elevation. A cross section of the lower portion indicated it was indeed a post and not the stump of a naturally burned tree. Since burned debris apparently associated with this structure was found at least 20 cm lower than the bottom of the post, this support may have been set into a pedestal above the layer of the floor. A smaller post with a maximum diam-

eter of 12 cm was uncovered in the northeast quadrant of the unit between ca. 99.06–98.76 m. As with the larger post, the upper portion was completely burned and the lower portion occurred as a ring of charcoal. A cross section of the lower portion revealed this anomaly was not a burned tap root of a small tree, as it had a blunted end. A charcoal sample (CS-47) was collected from the upper portion of this small post.

Further evidence of this structure was supplied by 31 pieces of burned and unburned daub and nine burned mud dauber nests. Fifteen of the pieces of daub were recovered from F-6 and one from F-4, although all of these likely emanated from F-5. The 15 pieces of daub recovered from F-5 contexts were found at elevations as high as 99.18 m and increased in frequency down toward the base of the excavation with the densest concentration occurring between ca. 99.00–98.70 m. Two relatively large pieces of burned daub, measuring ca. 12 x 14 x 19 cm and ca. 10 x 15 x 30 cm, were uncovered with basal elevations of ca. 98.86 m and 98.70 m, respective-

Figure 18. Burned daub with impression of cane from F-6 (ring midden/earth oven).

ly. These pieces, because of their size, could have been from one or more corners of the structure. Another piece of daub (from F-6) contains a clear impression of a piece of cane (Figure 18), likely a piece of wattle or the wall of the structure. All of the burned mud dauber nests were recovered from F-5 or the backhoe trench floor adjacent to F-5. Similar nests supplied one of the earliest clues for the first structure documented at the Millington site by J. Charles Kelley (1939:225–226).

The protected inner confines of the jacal structures apparently served as ideal locations for the nests of these wasps.

The first evidence of roof or wall fall, other than the burned daub and mud dauber nests, occurred between 99.05–.03 m as the tops of a large burned "log" and a thin layer of burned fibrous material were exposed in the central to northern part of the unit, respectively. There were both upper (ca. 99.03–.02 m) and lower (ca. 98.99–.91 m) layers of the fibrous material in this area, and these tended to angle downward to both the east and north. Each of these layers were about a centimeter thick, but the lower one was larger in plan view, extending over a ca. 20 x 100 cm area that was cut only by a rodent disturbance (Figure 19). Smaller scattered exposures of this material were documented in this area of the unit at an elevation of ca. 98.80 m. Possibly the remains of an unidentified variety of grass, these layers were likely a portion of the roof covering. Lower in elevation were other probable remains of the roof, including burned pieces of cane, several occurrences of criss-crossed materials (with basal elevations of 98.77–.76 m), and nine pieces of burned and unburned wood laying parallel to one another across a 50-cm area (Figure 20). The latter had basal elevations varying from 98.76–.71

Figure 19. Broad exposure of fibrous material, probably burned grass, in F-5 (unknown structure) fill. This material probably represents part of the structure's roof.

Figure 20. Burned roof or wall fall near the suspected floor of F-5 (unknown structure). Note the parallel-lying debris in the left midground.

m. In the first pithouse documented at the site in the 1930s Kelley (1939:226) indicated the roof had been constructed with poles (about 2 cm thick) "laid rather loosely across the framework of the house, then covered by two layers of reeds running in opposite directions across the poles, and then by a layer of grass, corn husks, etc. There was some evidence that a light layer of sandy clay, and possibly occasional thin stone slabs, had covered the roof thus formed." The F-5 findings seem to match this description fairly closely, with mottled sediments and occasional unburned cobbles or pieces of FCR possibly representing the sandy clay and stone slabs in Kelley's reconstruction. Other than the aforementioned daub and mud dauber nests, samples of residue collected from F-5 consist of 43 burned and partially burned wood samples, three samples of the fibrous material, and a burned river cane fragment.

It is estimated that the floor of this structure occurred around 98.70 m, but this was only based on negative information, as once the cultural detritus mentioned above was re-

moved from the unit, there was a general lack of further materials. There was varying compaction of the sediments from ca. 99.75–.70 m, but nothing widespread enough to indicate the presence of a floor, either prepared or unprepared. No diagnostic artifacts were recovered from this suspected elevation, although several specimens were found about 10 cm above it: a Fresno arrow point at an elevation of 98.79 m and a drill/perforator from 98.80 m (see Chapter 7 on Material Culture). Also found near the probable level of the floor (98.80–.70 m) were a number of unburned faunal materials, including an Artiodactyla long bone fragment containing possible cut marks and evidence of use in the form of polish. Other animals represented in this assemblage are rodents, an amphibian, a fish, and small and medium sized mammals. A variety of pottery sherds (six El Paso Polychrome, two El Paso Brownware, and one Red-on-Brown) and bone scraps from rabbit, rodent, deer or antelope, bird, and variously sized unidentified mammals were recovered from the F-5 fill, but none of these were within 15 cm of the apparent floor level. The ceramic specimens closest to the floor were a El Paso Polychrome sherd at 98.87 m and two sherds found in the screen from Level 10 (98.90–.80 m) identified as El Paso Polychrome and El Paso Brownware. Besides the charcoal samples from the suspected posts mentioned above, three radiocarbon samples were secured from the lower 35 cm of the F-5 fill: CS-48, CS-50, and CS-51. The first of these, dated through the radiometric technique, provided a corrected and calibrated date of A.D. 1290–1410 (Beta-221016). Thus, this unknown structure appears to date to the middle portion of the La Junta phase, which is supported to a degree by the ceramic specimens found in the lower fill.

A right proximal foot phalanx and an un-sided intermediate hand phalanx were recovered from the northwest quadrant of the unit, near the western wall, at elevations of 99.23 m and 98.98 m, respectively. The tops of two large, side-by-side cobbles were found ca. 20 cm below the lower bone, and could possibly be burial coverings like those at the top of F-14 (see below). These cobbles were left in place to facilitate further excavation of this structure in the future.

Due to the complexities encountered during the excavation, an expanded excavation will be needed to better understand the morphology and construction of this structure. At this point we know very little about it, despite the use of a large test unit and excavation of over a meter of the deposit. Given the focus of the current investigation on the burials impacted by the backhoe trench, further efforts to uncover and delineate F-5 were deemed inappropriate at this time. Furthermore, detailed analyses of the botanical and wood samples from F-5 will be attempted when more is known about the structure. An examination of Kelley's original file notes curated at the CBBS indicate several ramada-like structures attached to pithouses were

uncovered during the excavations at the site in the 1930s, and it is possible F-5 could be something similar.

Feature 6

Feature 6 was the designation given to a ring midden/earth oven originally identified in BHT #1 in the area of F-4 (historic trench) and F-5 (unknown structure). Like F-4 and F-5, this feature was not identified in 2003 when the trench was initially inspected, but became visible in 2006 in both its eastern and western walls once they were troweled and profiled (see Figure 16). This feature truncated F-5, and in turn, its northern edge was cut by F-4 (see Figure 17). It can be characterized as a pit containing a mass of stones and occasional pieces of burned daub. The stones consist of FCR, unburned and lightly burned cobbles, and ground stone fragments. Matrix within the pit is a brown (7.5YR4/2) fine silty sand interspersed with pea gravels. In the eastern wall of BHT #1 F-6 extends north-south a distance of ca. 2.2 m; its north-south extent in the western trench wall is ca. 2.4 m. In these exposures, the greatest concentration of stones were found on or near the bottom of the pit.

As with F-5, this feature was explored almost exclusively through excavation of Test Unit 6. Using the south wall of this unit as a guide (Figure 21), along with the backhoe trench exposures, the east-west extent of F-6 exceeds 2.2 m. It is unknown how much farther east of the trench the feature extends, but based on the information at hand it would seem the pit had an oval shape in plan view with the long axis in an east-west direction. The uppermost stones in this feature are buried about 5–10 cm below the current surface at an elevation that varies from 99.76–.73 m. The base of the feature occurs between ca. 99.00–98.95 m. The bottom of the pit angles up sharply to the north, at a more moderate

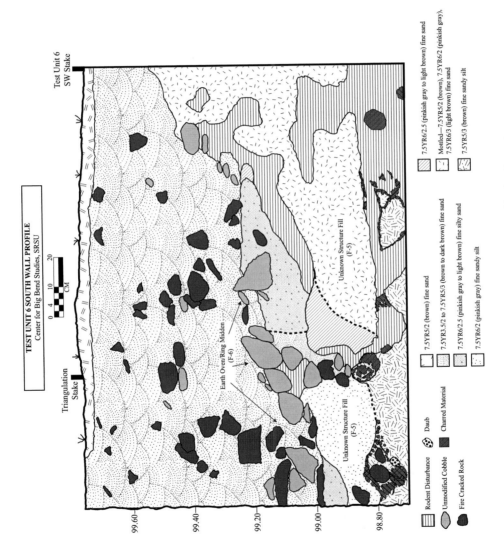

Figure 21. Profile of south wall of Test Unit 6 (ring midden/earth oven).

angle to the west, and at a relatively gentle angle to the south.

During excavation of Test Unit 6, the uppermost F-6 stones were found to be scattered with basal elevations varying between 99.72–.68 m. In Level 2 (99.70–.60 m), the northwestern edge became well-defined by an alignment of clustered stones that represented the bottom of the feature. As the excavation proceeded downward, this alignment shifted steadily to the southeast toward the base of the feature, providing further evidence that most feature stones were in close proximity to the bottom of the pit. Scattered flecks and chunks of charcoal were found amongst the feature stones, as were a variety of artifacts, mostly unmodified debitage. More meaningful artifacts from F-6 consist of a fragmentary Fresno arrow point, four pieces of edge-modified debitage, and three prehistoric pottery sherds (two El Paso Brownware, and one Plain Brownware). A few fragmentary pieces of possible ground stone were also uncovered within the feature, and were likely recycled materials used as heating elements like the rest of the stones. Due to their fragmentary nature, these items were not collected, just noted in the field. Faunal materials were also found scattered throughout the feature and included rabbit, reptile, amphibian, and variously sized unidentified mammal bones. Almost all of these were small and unburned and could have entered the feature as trash or perhaps through natural means.

Two matrix samples (SS-5 and SS-6) were collected from the heart of the feature in the eastern wall of the backhoe trench. Four charcoal samples (CS-20, CS-25, CS-31, and CS-43) were secured from various contexts within F-6. All of these were from locations within the feature that did not appear to have been compromised by bioturbations. One of these, CS-43, was chosen for chronometric analysis using the AMS method. It provided a corrected and calibrated date of A.D. 1300–

1420 (Beta-221014), indicating this feature was in use during the latter portion of the La Junta phase. Since F-6 truncates F-5, this date corresponds well with the slightly earlier date secured for that feature.

Ring middens/earth ovens are plant food baking features that have been documented across the Big Bend region, including at sites in the La Junta district. They were constructed in natural depressions or hand-dug pits which were lined with stones. Wood was then burned in these pits, creating a bed of hot coals that was covered with additional stones. Plant foods, probably lechuguilla bulbs or sotol hearts, were then added to the pits and covered with damp vegetation, more stones, and dirt. The ovens were then left to bake for two to three days. Uncovering the mass and retrieving the cooked food would leave these features in disorganized states rather than neatly layered. Repeated heating and cooling of the stones through multiple uses of the ovens would lead to fracturing of the stones. The overall appearance of F-6 conforms to this cooking technique, yet the high incidence of un-cracked stones in it suggests this feature was either used a single time or that it had been restocked with stone before its last use.

Feature 7

Burial 4 was uncovered in Test Unit 7, and the pit it rested in was designated F-7. Remains from this interment were originally identified in the east wall of BHT #1 in 2003, east of and almost directly across the trench from Burial 1. Despite the fact that the remains were exposed at a lower elevation, it was thought at that time to be an extension of Burial 1. However, during the 2006 investigation it became apparent after excavation of Burial 1 that the remains exposed on the opposite side of the trench were from a different interment. As was found with Burials 1 through 3, trenching associated with an early water line in this area had impacted both the pit and interment.

Based on exposures in the trench, a 1 x 1.4 m excavation unit (Test Unit 7) was centered over this feature. The burial pit became clearly visible in plan view at an elevation of 99.20 m within a light brown (10YR6/3) sandy silt matrix containing small angular and sub-rounded gravels (Figure 22). Although truncated on its western edge by the backhoe trench, the pit appears to have been circular to slightly oval in plan view when intact. Maximum east-west dimensions were ca. 57 cm at 99.00 m and a maximum north-south dimension of ca. 67 cm occurred at an elevation of 99.20 m. Human bone was uncovered in the pit between elevations of 99.20–99.84 m (Figure 23), the bottom of the pit corresponding to the latter of these (Figure 24). Evidence of rodent burrowing was

Figure 22. (above right) View of floor of Test Unit 7 with F-7 (burial pit) visible.

Figure 23. (below right) Burial 4 articulated within F-7 (burial pit).

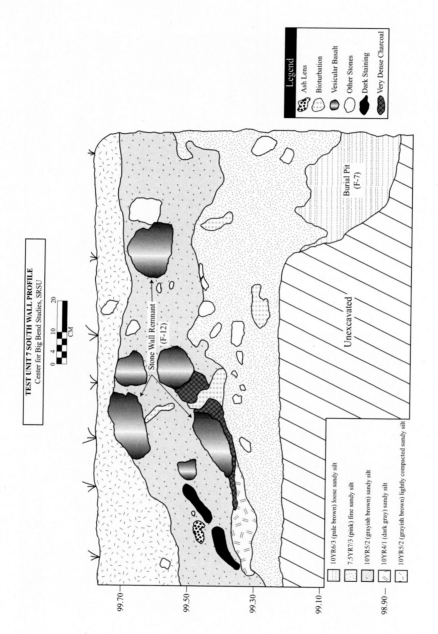

Figure 24. Profile of south wall of Test Unit 7 showing F-7 (burial pit) on right and F-12 (stone wall remnant).

documented throughout F-7, and a single Plain Brownware pottery sherd was recovered from within it at an elevation of 99.13 m. Small faunal materials representative of a snake, an even-toed ungulate, and medium to large unidentified mammals were widely scattered through the burial fill. Only three of these were burned, and all likely entered the pit fortuitously within the fill deposits.

A single small charcoal sample (CS-52) was recovered from the burial pit beneath the pelvis. However, cortical bone from the interment was chosen for radiometric analysis and dated through the AMS method. This analysis provided a corrected and calibrated date of A.D. 1280–1410 (GX-32610-AMS), indicating the interment dates to the La Junta phase.

Feature 8

Feature 8 is an undefined pit originally identified in the east wall of BHT #1 in 2006. A human fibula fragment was found about 25 cm south and a few centimeters lower than the base of this feature (Figure 25), suggesting the two could be related. Thus, a 1 x 1.4 m excavation unit (Test Unit 8) was positioned on the east side of the trench over the anomaly to investigate this occurrence.

In the wall of the trench the pit had a maximum width of ca. 40 cm at an elevation of 99.43 m. At 99.22 m the base of the feature was rounded and about 10 cm wide. Its uppermost extent occurred at 99.54 m, but this portion had been truncated by various disturbances. Matrix in the pit was a dark grayish brown (10YR4/2) silty sand interspersed with small rounded pea gravels. In plan view, at an elevation of ca. 99.44 m, the feature was somewhat rounded but relatively indistinct, measuring ca. 50 cm north-south. Its east-west extent, to the edge of the backhoe trench, was ca. 18 cm.

A cross section of F-8 revealed it had been filled with what appeared to be naturally deposited sediments which contained pea gravels, a piece or two of FCR, flecks and small chunks of charcoal, and minor amounts of debitage. Two Plain Brownware sherds and an unburned Pocket mouse mandible were recovered from the feature, but all of these likely entered the pit by accident. Nothing in the cross section was particularly enlightening. However, excavation of the feature revealed the presence of relatively large pieces of charred wood that seemed to extend outside of the pit. About half of this charred wood was in the feature and the other half out of it, but there was no conclusive evidence that it represented a single fragment that had partially disintegrated. A sample of this wood collected as CS-46 and submitted for chronometric analysis through the radiometric technique provided corrected and calibrated dates of A.D. 1680–1740, A.D. 1810–1930, and A.D. 1950–1960 (Beta-221015), with the second of these the most statistically viable at 71 percent (Reimer et al. 2004). These data suggest F-8 dates to the Alamito or Presidio phase, although based on a 27 percent probability it could date to the Conchos phase. Two matrix samples were collected from the northern portion of F-8, one from the area above CS-46 (SS-7) and the other from below it (SS-8).

The backhoe trench profile, cross section cut, and excavation of F-8 failed to firmly establish whether or not this was a cultural feature. Further efforts in Test Unit 8 revealed F-8 overlay an interment (Burial 5) that had been placed in a La Junta phase burial pit (F-14) beneath a pithouse floor (F-13b). This answered questions about the origin of the fibula fragment initially discovered in the backhoe trench wall, as rodents had been quite active within the burial pit, yet questions remain about F-8. It was never clearly

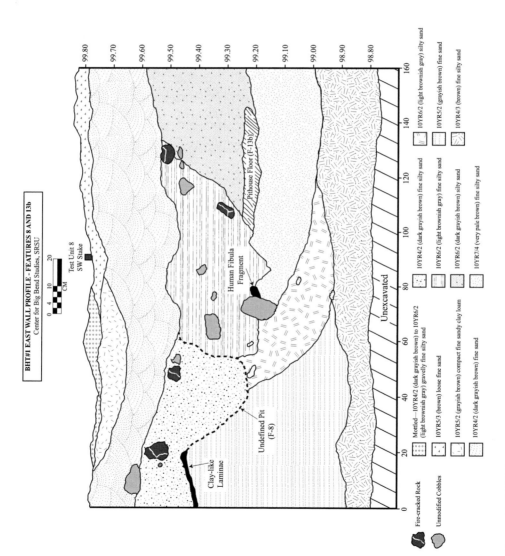

Figure 25. BHT #1 east wall profile showing F-8 (undefined pit) and F-13b (pithouse floor).

definable and yielded nothing to indicate an explicit function, but had a crude pit shape in both the plan view and profile. It is possible that it represented a cavity of sorts formed after the pithouse had been abandoned and collapsed; however, the charred wood dated from it clearly post-dated the structure. Taking this into account, it is possible the upper portion of the pithouse was still an open depression when the wood and F-8 fill were deposited, perhaps as an intentional manmade pit or perhaps as a fortuitous pit. Due to these uncertainties, F-8 is classified as an undefined pit.

Feature 9

A small scattered hearth uncovered several centimeters below the surface of Test Unit 8 was designated F-9. Visible on its upper surface were four or five obvious pieces of FCR with maximum dimensions of 8–14 cm, but within most of this exposure was a pavement of unmodified gravels (cobbles and pebbles) with maximum dimensions of 2–8 cm. At this point there were uncertainties about whether or not this somewhat circular anomaly represented a hearth. However, after removal of the stones, ca. 75 percent of which proved to be burned to one degree or another, the sediment below was found to be oxidized. Careful brushing of this surface provided an oval shape.

The upper exposure of concentrated gravel and FCR was roughly centered in the test unit and measured ca. 75 x 80 cm, with the slightly longer axis in an east-west direction. The oxidized area at the base of the hearth was appreciably smaller, measuring ca. 22 x 32 cm, the long axis in a north-south direction. In plan view, the oxidized area occurs below the southeastern edge of the upper portion of the feature, which suggests at least a degree of disturbance. Upper stone eleva-

tions were around 99.74 m, and the oxidized sediment occurred from ca. 99.69–.68 m.

Found within or near the edge of the feature, from elevations of 99.71–.69 m, were five ceramic sherds: three Plain Brownwares, a Polished Plain Brownware, and a Majolica. Uncovered at similar elevations just outside the F-9 edge were a unifacial tool with a spokeshave bit, a trimmed chip, a ground stone fragment, and hematite-stained sediment. Also found within the feature were several human bone fragments which had been displaced from Burial 5 below, apparently through bioturbations.

Two charcoal samples (CS-22 and CS-23) were secured from just outside the oxidized area at elevations of 99.69 m. One of these (CS-23) was submitted for chronometric analysis and provided corrected and calibrated dates of A.D. 1510–1600, A.D. 1620–1670, and A.D. 1780–1800 (Beta-221011). Of these, the first two are the most statistically viable at ca. 50 percent and 40 percent, respectively (Reimer et al. 2004). These dates, in tandem with the stratigraphic setting and the ceramics in or near association, indicate the hearth likely was constructed and used during the Concepcion phase.

Feature 10

An undefined pit exposed in BHT #5 was designated F-10. Located at the southern end of Third Street, BHT #5 was excavated to provide a window into the deposits in this area of the site. Revealed within both the north and south walls of the trench was evidence of a pit of some sort, but time considerations for the project prevented any excavation. The south wall was profiled and the upper edges of the pit were documented at elevations of 98.98 m on the east side and 99.02 m on the west side, about 65–70 cm below ground surface (Figure 26). The pit had been excavated into a

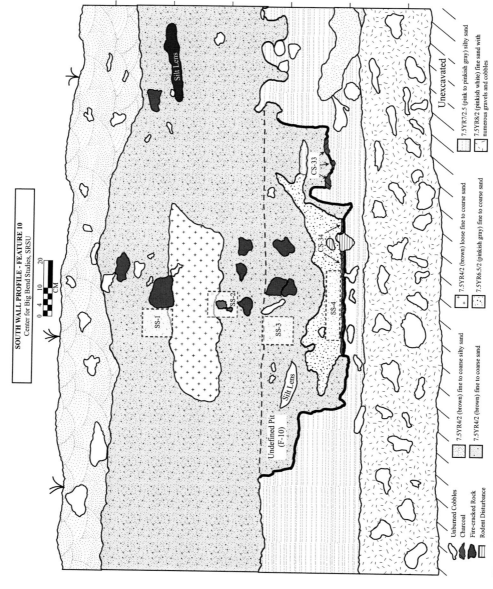

Figure 26. BHT#5 profile showing F-10 (undefined pit).

relatively undisturbed silty sand deposit that had a pinkish gray to pink hue (7.5YR7/2 to 7.5YR7/3). Bioturbations had disturbed the upper portion of these sediments in places, especially on the western side of the pit.

Width of the pit at its upper surface is ca. 1.25 m and overall depth is ca. 30 cm. However, the pit is stepped down on both the eastern and western sides, each of these appearing somewhat differently. The edge of the pit angles in slightly (ca. 4 cm) on the eastern side, dropping ca. 12 cm to an elevation of 98.86 m. From there it extends ca. 20 cm westward (dropping 2 cm) where it drops again, this time ca. 16 cm to the eastern base of the pit (at ca. 98.70 m). The western side of the pit is similar, but somewhat different. Although its upper corner is disturbed, when intact it seems to have angled straight down about 24 cm to an elevation of ca. 98.78 m. From there it extends ca. 22 cm eastward, dropping only a couple of centimeters across this exposure. At this point the profile reveals a straight up rise of ca. 7 cm, which seems to represent a niche of some sort that contains several small pockets or lenses of charcoal. From the eastern corner of the niche, the pit edge can be traced to the east again for about 4 cm before angling sharply downward for ca. 14 cm to an elevation of ca. 98.69 m. This is the bottom of the pit on its western side. The base of the pit has a width of about 72 cm and is truncated in places, appearing somewhat disturbed on both the eastern and western edges. A ca. 50 cm segment of it is relatively undisturbed and is lined with a thin (1 cm thick) charcoal lens.

Pit fill is moderately compact across this exposure, occurring as both a distinct amorphously shaped lens directly above the floor and a broader zone that dominates the profile. The amorphously shaped lens is a pinkish gray (7.5YR6.5/2) fine to coarse sand. Containing charcoal flecks and small chunks and appreciable pea gravels, this de-posit has thin stratified layers suggestive of slow, rather than rapid, filling. The remainder of the pit, including almost all of its upper portion, contains a more homogenous de-posit characterized as a brown to dark brown (7.5YR4/2) fine to coarse sand. Fire-cracked rock, charcoal flecks and small chunks, and cobbles up to 15 cm in maximum diameter occur throughout this broad and deep deposit that seems to be representative of an exten-sive midden.

Two matrix samples (SS-3 and SS-4) were recovered from the pit fill, one from each of the two sediments described above. Charcoal samples were collected from both the floor of the niche (CS-33) and the base of the pit (CS-34). Although neither of these have been submitted for analysis, the depth of F-10 suggests it dates to the La Junta phase.

Feature 11

In Test Unit 8, immediately and almost direct-ly below F-9, was a second hearth that was designated F-11 (Figure 27). Although these

Figure 27. View of the upper portion of F-11 (hearth).

two features were somewhat intertwined, they appeared to be separate and distinct from one another. Like F-9, the burned stones comprising F-11 were scattered, although this hearth appeared to have contained about three to four times the number of stones. Unlike F-9, there was no definitive sediment oxidation at the base of the feature.

Upper dimensions of the scattered FCR were roughly 75 x 100 cm, the long axis in an east-west direction, although there was no visible distinction between sediments inside and outside of this boundary. Upper elevations of the feature stones varied between 99.69–.68 m and the base occurred around 99.65 m.

Three artifacts were found amongst the feature stones and may have been associated with this hearth. A complete end scraper with a spokeshave fashioned on the exhausted scraper bit was found under a piece of FCR at an elevation of 99.68 m, and three Plain Brownware ceramic sherds were uncovered from 99.65–.64 m at the base of the feature. Unburned faunal remains from a large mammal were recovered from immediately below the feature between elevations of 99.64–.62 m. Only very small charcoal flecks were found within this scattered hearth, so no chronometric samples were secured.

Feature 12

A remnant of a rock wall, likely the remains of a structural foundation of some sort, was uncovered in Test Unit 7 and designated F-12. Test Unit 7 was originally positioned to uncover Burial 4 and F-7 (burial pit), both of which were exposed in the west wall of BHT #1. However, upper stones of F-12 were exposed 10–15 cm below the surface and found to extend into the east and south walls of the unit (Figure 28). Since only a small portion of F-12 was excavated, the data provided below is sketchy and incomplete.

The majority of the exposed portion of this feature was comprised of small vesicular basalt boulders, the largest having maximum dimensions of ca. 22 cm. A variety of other stones were also used in its construction,

Figure 28. View of F-12 (stone wall remnant) at an elevation of ca. 99.51 m.

Figure 29. Charcoal-stained sediments on the southeast side of F-12 (stone wall remnant).

small boulders of other stones (also up to 22 cm in maximum dimension) and cobble-sized basalt and non-basalt stones. Overall wall height was about 35 cm, the top of the uppermost stones had elevations of ca. 99.72 m and the base of the lower stones occurred between ca. 99.38–.36 m (see Figure 24). Several of the larger stones occurred at the base of the feature, where sediments varied from a very loose, light brownish gray (10YR6/2) sandy silt to a more consolidated dark brown (7.5YR3/2) sandy silt, the latter confined to areas southeast of the wall. The darker sediments extended up to 10 cm below the base of the wall and contained a profuse amount of charcoal (Figure 29).

The exposed portion of the wall measured ca. 1.25 m in length and was relatively straight, oriented at a ca. 55°/235° (magnetic north) angle. Stones of all sizes were documented on both sides of the wall, up to 60 cm away from the intact portion, and at differ-

ent elevations, suggesting that portions collapsed as it was slowly buried by alluvial and aeolian deposits. The lowest collapsed stones were on the southeast side of the wall and had basal elevations of ca. 99.31 m, about 5 cm below the lower and larger stones comprising the base of the wall. Considering this, and the fact that sediments northwest of the basal stones were quite loose, it is theorized that the interior of this wall would have been to the southeast where the charcoal-stained sediments were concentrated.

As the excavation proceeded downward a variety of artifacts, FCR, and charcoal were uncovered along or within the F-12 stones. As the feature was being exposed, these were considered to be "associated." Given the eventual basal depth of the feature, it is unlikely that any of these date to the same time that the wall was constructed and used. Only unmodified debitage was recovered from elevations corresponding to the lower portions of the wall. Included amongst the debris along the wall above this were a depleted bifacial core (99.67 m), a few sherds of Plain Brownware pottery (at various elevations), and two large Red-on-Brown sherds that conjoin. One of the conjoined sherds was recovered from ca. 35 cm southeast of the wall (99.49 m) and the other from ca. 45 cm northwest of it (99.41 m).

Charcoal, charcoal-stained sediments, and pockets of ash were documented along the wall and amongst the collapsed stones and several areas contained heavy concentrations of this residue. Nine charcoal samples (CS-26, CS-30, CS-32, CS-36, CS-38, CS-40, CS-41, CS-42, and CS-45) were collected and one of the lower of these (CS-42; 99.40 m) was submitted for chronometric analysis. It provided corrected and calibrated dates of A.D. 1640–1680, A.D. 1730–1810, and A.D. 1930–1950 (Beta-221013), the first (35 percent) and second (47 percent) of these the most statistically viable (Reimer et al. 2004). Thus, this wall appears to date to the latter portion of the Concepcion phase, the Conchos phase, or the first portion of the Alamito phase.

Rock based structures have not been previously documented in the La Junta villages, so the morphology and function of F-12 cannot be understood based on previous work. Since only a small portion of the wall was uncovered additional excavation will be needed to address this situation. However, given the lack of a definitive living surface and associated debris, and the presence of abundant charcoal, it is possible F-12 represents the remains of a ramada of some sort.

Feature 13

A portion of a pithouse was uncovered in Test Unit 8 and designated F-13. It contains two sub-features, F-13a and F-13b, the former a layer of puddled adobe or surface backing for

the pithouse, and the latter the prepared house floor. Only a small portion of this structure was uncovered in the test unit, thus the data presented below is incomplete and should be used accordingly.

F-13a is an angled or slanted, 3–4 cm thick layer of puddled adobe first uncovered at the eastern edge of the test unit (Figure 30). This layer slants to the east into the wall and is interpreted as a backing for the pithouse, which likely approximates the ground surface when the structure was originally constructed. The western edge of this backing occurs at an elevation of ca. 99.65 m and seems to represent the interior edge of the pithouse. This edge is somewhat irregular or wavy in plan view, varying in width (east-west) from ca. 24–32 cm. This could be related to the excavation and/or differential erosion, or perhaps sloppy construction. This sub-feature was cross sectioned in two places, which revealed

Figure 30. View of F-13a (puddled adobe backing) showing two cross section cuts.

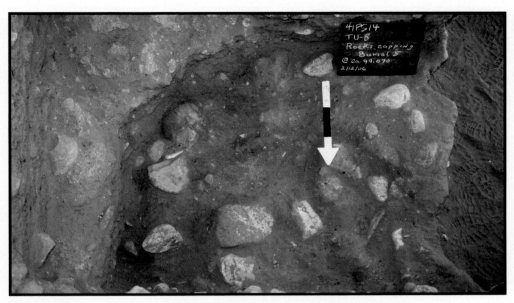

Figure 31. View of F-13b (pithouse floor) and upper exposure of F-14 (burial pit).

a light pinkish gray (7.5YR6/2 to 7.5YR7/2) compact loamy sand matrix intermixed with poorly sorted gravels and some cultural debris, including small pieces of FCR up to 2.5 cm in maximum diameter. A sample of this puddled adobe was collected from one of the cross sections and designated SS-9. In addition, a small charcoal sample (CS-35) was extracted from it during the cross section excavations. This is the first pithouse sub-feature of this type reported from the district. Although its function is unknown, the outward slant may indicate it was a "rainwater deflector" of some type, designed to keep water from running into the pit.

The pithouse floor (F-13b) first became visible below and immediately west of F-13a at elevations varying from ca. 99.31–.26 m. The floor appeared as an undulating and patchy, eroded puddled adobe surface with thicknesses that varied from 2–6 cm and was similar in color to F-13a. Cut into F-13b was a burial pit designated F-14, which contained Burial 5 and encompassed much of the test unit (Figure 31). As a result, the floor in the unit was only exposed east, southeast, and

northeast of the burial pit. Another exposure occurs in the eastern wall of BHT #1 about 10–55 cm south of Test Unit 8. Here there is a small, 45-cm wide remnant of the floor with a top elevation of 99.24 m (see Figure 25). Its northern edge was truncated by the burial pit. Since the southern end of this exposure does not appear to have been disturbed, it may mark the southern extent of F-13. No diagnostic artifacts were recovered from the floor of this pithouse.

Pithouse fill was mottled throughout and contained a hodgepodge of materials, including FCR, unburned cobbles, small pieces of puddled adobe, charcoal chunks (see F-8 discussion) and flecks, faunal remains (rabbit, rodent, even-toed ungulate, and medium to large unidentified mammal—only a large mammal bone fragment was burned), and a variety of artifactual materials: a Toyah arrow point, a probable Perdiz arrow point blade fragment, assorted debitage, an El Paso Brownware sherd, a Polished Redware sherd, five Plain Brownware sherds, and a Polished Plain Brownware sherd. In addition to CS-46 collected from part way into F-13 (see F-8

Figure 32. Burial 5 articulated within F-14 (burial pit).

discussion), two discrete charcoal samples (CS-39 and CS-44) were recovered from F-13 fill.

Although charcoal was recovered from the fill, there was appreciably less of this residue and it was much smaller than was seen in the lower floor area of F-5 (unknown structure). Burned daub was lacking in the fill, although several small pieces were recovered from nearby Test Unit 1. Furthermore, the complex stratigraphy interpreted as roof and wall fall in F-5 was completely lacking. These data, in tandem with the eroded appearance of the house floor, may indicate that after abandonment portions of the F-13 superstructure were salvaged. In such a scenario, the floor could have potentially been exposed to the elements and become eroded prior to the structure being filled.

Cortical bone from Burial 5 was submitted for radiometric analysis rather than any of the aforementioned charcoal samples due to contextual issues. Presented below, it provided a La Junta phase date which effectively dates the pithouse.

Feature 14

The burial pit for Burial 5, an intrusive interment within F-13 (pithouse), was designated F-14. Small pieces of human bone identified in the east wall of BHT #1 just south of F-8 prompted placement of Test Unit 8. While F-8 proved to be a small pit, excavation of the test unit also uncovered F-9 (hearth), F-11 (hearth), and a portion of F-13 (pithouse).

The burial pit had been excavated into a prepared adobe floor (F-13b) that had been partially eroded before the pithouse was filled. The level of the floor was ca. 99.31 m and this marks the upper level of the pit. The base of the pit was at an elevation of 98.94

m. The burial pit was not clearly outlined, and this may be related to the eroded nature of the pithouse floor. Matrix in the pit was a grayish brown to brown (10YR5/2–5/3) fine sandy loam interspersed with rounded gravels and pebbles. The interment had been covered with approximately 25 stones, mostly cobbles varying from 8–21 cm in length, although several pieces of FCR were also present (see Figure 31). Basal elevations of these stones varied from 99.12–.01 m, with most falling between 99.09–.06 m. The interment lay immediately beneath the stones (Figure 32). Exact dimensions were not discernible, but from the location of the covering stones and skeletal elements it appears the pit was roughly circular with a diameter of approximately 1.0 m. Two very fragmentary untyped arrow points were recovered from the fill, a triple-notched specimen and a corner notched specimen. Due to their fragmentary appearances and missing pieces, they were probably introduced into the pit within backfill rather than as mortuary offerings; a sherd of El Paso Polychrome recovered in the pit above the covering stones likely entered F-14 in a similar manner.

Three small charcoal samples (CS-49, CS-53, and CS-54) were recovered from the F-14 pit fill. While all of these were recovered in close proximity to various skeletal elements, cortical bone from the interment was chosen for radiometric analysis using the AMS method. This analysis provided a corrected and calibrated date of A.D. 1160–1290 (GX-32611-AMS), indicating the interment dates to the early to middle portion of the La Junta phase.

Mortuary Contexts and Human Remains

This chapter presents details of the mortuary sample recovered during excavations at the Millington site, and osteological and chemical analysis of the human remains, in combination with individuals recovered during the 1938–1939 excavations at Millington. The analysis includes discussion of the mortuary contexts, identification of each individual's age and sex as completely as possible, description of completeness of the remains and the effects of taphonomic processes, and discussion of any pathological conditions observed on the remains. Discussion of the Millington skeletal sample, and any trends or patterns observed therein, includes all observable individuals recovered from Millington. Additionally, this chapter presents the results of stable carbon and nitrogen analyses conducted on a subsample of remains, providing information about diet among the Millington occupants.

Skeletal Analysis Methodology

The human remains from the Millington site were catalogued by means of a system based on the recommended standards for osteological data collection (Buikstra and Ubelaker 1994). This includes an inventory of portions of skeletal elements present, observations of taphonomic changes, skeletal and dental pathology, and age and sex indicators. Metric and nonmetric data for skeletal elements and dentition are recorded where possible in order to provide comparative data for fu-

ture regional and chronological compilation of larger samples. Fragmentation and poor preservation of this sample prevent the use of metric and nonmetric data for stature estimation and assessment of populational affiliation.

All human remains were inventoried by fragment, recording to the greatest extent possible the portions of each skeletal element present through the use of osteological landmarks. Taphonomic alteration of each skeletal element, which often affects the presence and completeness of elements, was also identified and recorded during the inventory process.

The determination of sex for adult individuals is based primarily on pelvic indicators, and secondarily on cranial indicators, and trends in stature and robusticity. While pelvic and cranial indicators are considered the most secure traits for differentiating males and females, it is recognized that these traits overlap considerably, and the extent of overlap varies among populations. At a population level, discriminant function analyses are often performed on metrical data such as diaphyseal diameters of long bones, diameters of the femoral head, and measurements of the hand and foot bones. These methods vary in proven accuracy and populational applicability, require complete or nearly complete skeletal elements, and are meaningful only if utilized on samples of representative size in comparison to an appropriate reference sample. For these reasons, the sex determinations given in this report rely on the observation of pelvic and cranial indicators. It is recognized that the quantity of sex indicators observable for each individual directly affects the reliability of sex determination (Meindl et al. 1985), and the maximum number of indicators allowed by fragmentation and surface preservation were recorded for each individual in the sample.

Estimation of age at death for adult individuals is based on the accumulation of developmental and degenerative skeletal changes, the timing of which becomes more variable with increasing age. Standards have been developed for the estimation of adult age based on developmental changes on the auricular surface of the os coxae and secondarily, on cranial suture closure (Buikstra and Ubelaker 1994). In addition, degenerative changes, most of which can be classified as osteoarthritis, accumulate throughout the skeleton with advanced age. Due to variation

in the timing of these changes, and the lack of ability to correlate average rates of change with known ages at death for regional archaeological populations, estimation of adult age in samples such as this one are understood to be both broad and relative. In archaeological samples, older individuals are usually underrepresented due to these inherent biases (Cox 2000:63–64).

The estimation of age at death for subadults, based on developmental processes, can be completed with more accuracy and reliability than adult age estimation. While growth and development are influenced by populational affiliation, sex, health, and environmental factors, the ongoing processes of development and maturation are much more regular in subadults than the degenerative changes upon which estimation of adult age relies. The appearance, growth, and fusion of ossification centers, and the mineralization and eruption of deciduous and permanent teeth, can provide an age estimate with a range of a few years, or in very young individuals, a few months. Where possible within this sample, bone size of the subadult individual was observed to confirm age estimates derived from dental development and epiphyseal fusion sequences. The standard for timing of appearance and fusion of epiphyses used in this osteological analysis is taken from Scheuer and Black (2000), and the dental developmental sequence is based on Ubelaker (1989: Figure 71).

Pathological conditions expressed on the skeleton can indicate insults to the individual during life, including heritable pathologies, disease, nutritional disorders, trauma, and disturbances to the metabolic or endocrine systems. Degenerative skeletal changes provide information about activities during the individual's life and the aging process. A small number of pathologies become manifest on bone, and many of these only when chronic, limiting the abilities of paleopathological analysis in the documentation of health in an ancient population. However, the range of pathologies that are expressed provide evidence of internal and external factors influencing ancient health, and allow inter- and intrapopulational assessment of health status.

The recording procedures for pathological conditions within this sample follow the standards presented in Buikstra and Ubelaker (1994), which aim to document the observable changes to the bone in a manner that is maximally descriptive and facilitates comparison among samples. In addition, when specific diagnosis is possible, it is presented. The majority of pathological conditions documented in this sample are degenerative changes to articular and attachment surfaces, correlated with advanced adult age. In addition, periostosis, evidence of nonspecific infection or insult to the periosteum and associated bone, is present among these remains. Patterns of porosity on the parietal and occipital bones of the cranium were observed in this sample, and may be evidence of porotic hyperostosis, a cranial porosity caused by iron deficiency anemia in childhood. However, without a larger populational sample among which to determine patterns of incidence of this pathology, this diagnosis remains tentative.

The 2003/2006 Skeletal Sample

Burial 1: Test Unit 2, Feature 1

Burial 1 is the interment of a subadult individual in an intrusive burial pit feature, designated F-1. The western extent of this feature is defined by eight stones, 6 cm to 14 cm in length, situated upright just outside the border of the pit. While incomplete due to removal of much of the pit feature and burial during excavation of the backhoe trench, the largest pit dimensions of the preserved portion of Feature 1 are 30 x 30 cm, at an eleva-

tion of 99.29 m. The burial pit matrix is light brown (7.5YR6/3) sandy silt with scattered rounded gravels, and is clearly defined from surrounding matrix. It was clearly visible beginning at a depth of 15 cm below modern ground surface, at an elevation of 99.55 m. The base of the preserved portion of the pit lies at 99.14 m.

This individual is represented by portions of the right cranium and mandible, cervical vertebrae, right clavicle, scapula and humeral head, sternum and right ribs, and unsided hand bones (Table 2). The backhoe trench removed the majority of this burial, excepting the upper portion of the individual and hand elements, which were positioned around the mandible and neck. No other direct data on burial position was recovered due to backhoe disturbance, although it is likely that the individual was in a flexed position with the cranium to the west or southwest. Bioturbation has resulted in the deposition of small human bone fragments outside of the pit feature, many of these in clearly defined rodent burrows. Taphonomic processes have resulted in fragmentation, longitudinal cracking and minor to moderate loss of cortex on most of the remains, although observation for indicators of age and pathological conditions remains possible.

Eight permanent teeth were recovered in situ (Table 3). These include the maxillary right premolars and molars, and mandibular right molars. The maxillary and mandibular right third molars are unerupted, in a developmental stage with one-quarter of the root length complete.

Remains that can be assigned to this individual were collected from the backhoe trench and resulting backdirt piles during initial visitation of the backhoe trench in 2003. These remains can be securely identified with the subadult interred in Burial 1 based on size and developmental stage, contextual location, and non-overlapping occurrence of

Table 2: Skeletal Inventory of Burial 1 Remains

Element	Side	Completeness	Element	Side	Completeness
Frontal	L, R	85%	Ribs	L	---
Parietal	L, R	70%		R	10%
Occipital	L, R	45%		Unsided	35%
Temporal	L	40%	Humerus	L	30%
	R	10%		R	30%
	Unsided	25%	Radius	L	15%
Sphenoid	L, R	---		R	25%
Zygomatic	L	---		Unsided	10%
	R	90%	Ulna	L	---
	Unsided	20%		R	---
Maxilla	L, R	55%	Carpals	L	15%
Palatine	L, R	95%		R	15%
Mandible	L, R	60%	Metacarpals	L, R	25%
Clavicle	L	30%	Hand Phalanges	L, R	45%
	R	25%	Femur	L	---
Scapula	L	---		R	---
	R	30%		Unsided	15%
Sternum	L, R	30%	Tibia	L	---
Patella	L	---		R	10%
	R	35%	Fibula	L	---
Sacrum	L, R	---		R	---
Os Coxae	L	---		Unsided	10%
	R	---	Tarsals	L	---
Cervical Vertebrae		95%		R	---
Thoracic Vertebrae		15%		Unsided	10%
Lumbar Vertebrae		---	Metatarsals	L, R	---
			Foot Phalanges	L, R	---

Table 3: Dental Inventory of Burial 1

Maxillary Dentition	Presence	Mandibular Dentition	Presence
RM3	X	RM3	X
RM2	X	RM2	X
RM1	X	RM1	X
RP4	X	RP4	
RP3	X	RP3	X
RC	X	RC	
RI2		RI2	
RI1		RI1	
LI1		LI1	
LI2		LI2	
LC	X	LC	
LP3		LP3	X
LP4		LP4	X
LM1	X	LM1	X
LM2	X	LM2	
LM3		LM3	X
		Anterior root	X
		Molar Root	X

element portions. They include fragments of cranium, cervical and thoracic vertebrae, ribs, left clavicle, leg and foot, and arm and hand bones (see Table 2). Dentition from the Burial 1 individual collected in 2003 includes the maxillary left first and second molars, left and right canines, and mandibular left first and third molars, left and right first premolars, and left second premolar. Two anterior tooth roots and one molar root were also recovered (see Table 3).

Additional backdirt screening in 2006 resulted in the recovery of portions of the cranial vault and mandible, ribs, radius, distal fibula, and bones of the hand and foot (see Table 2).

Age indicators available for this individual include overall size of skeletal elements, epiphyseal fusion, and developmental stage of the dentition. The neural arches of the cervical vertebrae are fused to the centra, but epiphyses of the centra are unfused. The coracoid, subcoracoid, acromion, and glenoid epiphyses of the right scapula are unfused, as is the lateral epiphysis of the right clavicle. The single sternebra recovered and the tubercle epiphysis of the right first rib are unfused. One right rib head is also present and unfused. Fusion has not begun on the proximal and distal tibial epiphyses. The bases of the metacarpals and hand phalanges show no fusion, while heads are either completely or nearly completely fused. This skeletal developmental stage indicates an early adolescent, less than approximately 15 years of age (Scheuer and Black 2000).

The developmental stage and attrition patterns on the dentition correlate with estimation of age from skeletal elements. The mandibular and maxillary permanent premolars and first and second molars show moderate attrition. The third molars are unerupted, and show partial root development. This evidence results in a dental age of 13 years +/- 36 months, or an early adolescent.

A nonspecific infection is evident in the form of slight porosity on the parietals and occipital of the cranial vault, healed at time of death. The superior articular facet of the first cervical vertebra shows marginal lipping, indicating slight active osteoarthritis as the result of a localized injury. The maxillary canines, left first and second molars and mandibular first premolars and first molars show slight calculus deposition at the cervicoenamel junctions.

Burial 1 is thus the interment of an early adolescent within a pit feature, in unknown burial position and orientation. Many of the remains attributed to this individual were recovered from disturbed context in and adjacent to the backhoe trench. The individual displays little skeletal and dental pathology, limited to a slight nonspecific pathology on the cranial vault, an injury affecting the first cervical vertebra, and slight calculus on the dentition.

Burial 2: Test Unit 3, Feature 2

Burial 2 is the interment of an adult male in an intrusive bell-shaped burial pit (F-2) that was disturbed during excavation of the backhoe trench. A possible clay pit lining became visible at an elevation of 99.52 m, and matrix to the east of it was distinguishable in color and texture from matrix outside of the pit. Only the upper portion of the pit contained this possible lining, which ceased at an elevation of 99.39 m with pit matrix and human remains continuing below this. The pit matrix is dark gray with charcoal flecking. Four stones were set upright to the immediate west of the possible pit lining, defining the western edge of the feature. While portions

of the pit and burial were removed during excavation of the backhoe trench, the maximum preserved east-west dimension of F-2 was 19 cm, at an elevation of 99.28 m. The base of Feature 2 was excavated between the elevations of 99.10 m and 99.03 m. Bioturbation resulted in the deposition of small bone fragments outside of the pit matrix. Many of these were located in clearly defined rodent burrows.

Skeletal remains recovered in situ include portions of the legs and feet, pelvis and lower vertebral column, ribs, and fragments of the left lower arm and hand (Table 4). The individual was interred in a tightly flexed position on the left side, with pelvis and femur oriented to the south of the ribs and vertebral column, suggesting that the head was oriented to the north or northeast. The distribution of the skeletal elements recovered reflects the bisection of the flexed interment by the backhoe. These remains have been affected by some fragmentation, longitudinal cracking and in some cases slight cortical erosion, although all elements remain observable for age and sex indicators and pathological conditions.

The only identified dentition recovered from the in situ remains is the mandibular left second incisor. This tooth is heavily worn. A heavily worn unidentified anterior tooth and a maxillary left premolar were also recovered (Table 5). More complete identification of this dentition is prevented by the extent of attrition, which has removed most of each tooth crown.

A small collection of skeletal remains belonging to this individual was made in 2003, and consists of bone fragments found loose at the base of the trench below the in situ remains. These include radius, fibula, rib, and vertebral fragments (see Table 4).

Excavation of adjacent backdirt piles in 2006 resulted in the recovery of the majority of the cranium and mandible, cervical and

Table 4: Skeletal Inventory of Burial 2

Element	Side	Completeness		Element	Side	Completeness
Frontal	L, R	85%		Humerus	L	15%
Parietal	L, R	90%			R	---
Occipital	L, R	85%			Unsided	25%
Temporal	L	40%		Radius	L	100%
	R	40%			R	---
Sphenoid	L, R	---			Unsided	20%
Zygomatic	L	---		Ulna	L	100%
	R	---			R	10%
Maxilla	L, R	10%			Unsided	20%
Palatine	L, R	---		Carpals	L	50%
Mandible	L, R	15%			R	---
Clavicle	L	---		Metacarpals	L	20%
	R	---			R	---
Scapula	L	---		Hand Phalanges	L, R	50%
	R	---		Femur	L	85%
Sternum	L, R	---			R	15%
Patella	L	---		Tibia	L	30%
	R	---			R	40%
Sacrum	L, R	30%		Fibula	L	90%
Os Coxae	L	75%			R	---
	R	50%		Tarsals	L	75%
Cervical Vertebrae		15%			R	75%
Thoracic Vertebrae		65%		Metatarsals	L	80%
Lumbar Vertebrae		40%			R	90%
Ribs	L	25%		Foot Phalanges	L, R	65%
	R	30%				
	Unsided	10%				

thoracic vertebrae, and arm and hand fragments (see Table 4). A maxillary premolar and mandibular premolar, both with severe dental attrition, were also recovered (see Table 5).

Determination of the sex of this individual is based on markers on the left os coxae. The ventral arc, subpubic concavity, and ischiopubic ramus ridge all score as male (Buikstra and Ubelaker 1994). The greater sciatic notch, incompletely preserved, scores as probable male. These pelvic indicators confirm that the individual is male. This determination is supported by markers on the cranium excavated from backdirt in 2006. The right mastoid, left and right supraorbit-

Table 5: Dental Inventory of Burial 2

Maxillary Dentition	Presence	Mandibular Dentition	Presence
RM3		RM3	
RM2		RM2	
RM1		RM1	
RP4		RP4	
RP3		RP3	
RC		RC	
RI2		RI2	
RI1		RI1	
LI1		LI1	
LI2		LI2	X
LC		LC	
LP3		LP3	
LP4		LP4	
LM1		LM1	
LM2		LM2	
LM3		LM3	
Left Premolar	X	Anterior tooth	X
Premolar	X	Premolar	X

al margins, and supraorbital ridge all score as probable male (Buikstra and Ubelaker 1994).

Estimation of the individual's age derives primarily from examination of the pubic symphysis, and is corroborated by evidence of degenerative joint changes and dental attrition. Cranial suture closure, often utilized as supporting evidence for age estimations, is not observable on the cranial elements excavated from backdirt in 2006. The left pubic symphysis is complete, and 30 percent of the right pubic symphysis is present. These score as stages 3–5 in the Todd system and 3–4 in the Suchey-Brooks system (Buikstra and Ubelaker 1994), resulting in an age estimate of 25–40 years. Dental attrition on the few teeth present is heavy, which supports the pelvic age estimate. Degenerative joint changes are present throughout the skeleton,

as described below. Overall, these indicators of age suggest that the individual was a middle adult, probably 30–40 years of age.

Skeletal pathologies observed for this individual include degenerative joint changes, localized infection, and nonspecific infection. Slight marginal lipping and osteophyte development are present on the bones of the legs and feet, lower left arm and hand, and a few rib fragments, with more pronounced changes visible on the vertebrae and sacrum (Table 6). The patterns of degeneration on this individual's joints are moderate, and do not represent advanced age.

The left fibula displays localized periostosis on the distal third of the diaphysis, in an area 1.5 cm in length. This pathology is characterized by porosity and irregular bone deposition, in an advanced stage of healing, and represents an infection accompanying a localized minor injury. A small unsided tibial diaphysis fragment displays slight healed periostosis, and may be related to the infection affecting the left fibula.

Nonspecific infection is evidenced on the left ulna and the cranial vault. Slight periostosis, characterized by porosity and osteophytic activity in a 4.5 cm-long area around midshaft, is present on the left ulna. This pathology was healed at time of death. Slight healed porosity is located on the parietals of the cranial vault.

Evidence of dental pathology is primarily restricted to calculus, due to near complete removal of tooth crowns by attrition. The mandibular left second incisor displays severe calculus, the anterior tooth root shows moderate calculus, and the maxillary left premolar is affected by slight calculus. The maxillary and mandibular premolars excavated from backdirt display similar patterns of moderate calculus. These bands of calculus are all situated on the tooth roots below the cervicoenamel junction, indicating moderate periodontal disease. The mandibular

Table 6: Degenerative Changes on Skeletal Elements of Burial 2

Skeletal Element	Side	Articular or Attachment Surface	Surface Erosion or Porosity	Marginal Lipping or Spicules	Osteophytes	Facet Shape Change
Cranium		spheno-occipital synchondrosis			X	
Radius	L	head	X	X	X	
Ulna	L	trochlear notch	X		X	
Ulna	L	distal			X	
Lunate	L	facet		X		X
Hand Phalanges	L, R	base		X		
Hand Phalanges	L, R	head		X		
Rib	R	head		X	X	X
Cervical Vertebrae		3 centra	X	X	X	X
Thoracic Vertebrae		7 centra	X	X	X	
Thoracic Vertebrae		7 facets		X		X
Lumbar Vertebrae		2 facets		X		
Sacrum		promontory	X	X		
Femur	L	head		X		
Tibia	R	distal		X		
Talus	L, R	calcaneal facets		X		
Calcaneus	L, R	sustenaculum tali		X		
Cuneiforms	L, R	facets		X		
Cuboid	L, R	facets		X		
Navicular	L, R	facets		X		
Metatarsals	L, R	base		X		
1st Metatarsal	R	head		X		
1st Proximal Foot Phalanx	R	head	X	X	X	

premolar recovered from backdirt in 2006 displays a banded brown hypocalcification on the small portion of preserved crown. This pathology indicates a nonspecific health insult in childhood.

In summary, Burial 2 contained the remains of an adult male, approximately 30–40 years of age at death. While this burial was impacted by excavation of the backhoe trench, remains that can be attributed to this individual were recovered in 2003 and excavated from adjacent backdirt in 2006. Pathologies evident on these remains include degenerative joint changes characteristic of middle adult individuals from this population, a slight localized infection on the left fibula, and nonspecific infection on the cranial vault and the left ulna. While severe dental attrition precludes the observation of tooth crowns for developmental enamel defects in most cases, a single instance of hypocalcification is present. The dentition has also been affected by calculus deposition, in a pattern on the tooth roots indicating moderate periodontal resorption.

Burial 3: Test Unit 1, Feature 3

The remains designated as Burial 3 are poorly preserved and disarticulated human skeletal elements situated near the base of a fire-cracked rock sheet midden. The associated matrix is dark grayish brown (10YR3/2) fine loamy sand, with lighter mottling due to rodent disturbance. The minimum number of individuals represented by the burial is one. While it is likely that these remains represent an interment, possibly disturbed in antiquity by activity associated with the midden, their disarticulated nature prevent determination of the relative importance of the backhoe trench excavation and poor preservation as taphonomic factors affecting the absence of many skeletal elements.

Human bone was located between the elevations of 99.46 m and 99.27 m. Each skeletal element recovered lacks all cortex and morphological integrity, disintegrating into powder upon excavation or cleaning. Thus, many elements remain incompletely identified, and observations of age, sex and pathology are not possible. Most of the remains collected are portions of long bone shafts, some identified in situ as humerus, fibula, and ribs. The human remains can thus only be attributed to an adult individual, as poor preservation prevents the recovery of any further observations.

Burial 4: Test Unit 7, Feature 7

Burial 4 is the intrusive interment of an adult individual in a tightly flexed supine position adjacent to and below F-12. The cranium, removed during excavation of the backhoe trench, was originally oriented to the west. F-7, the associated burial pit, is defined by sediment that is distinct from surrounding matrix. The burial pit matrix is pale brown (10YR6/3) loose sandy silt with small angular and sub-rounded gravels. The pit outline was visible at 99.20 m and its base was located at 98.84 m, with a maximum intact east-west dimension of 57 cm at 99.00 m and a maximum north-south dimension of 67 cm at 99.20 m. The base of F-7 consists of gravel and small cobbles. Human bone is present between the elevations of 99.20 m and 98.84 m. Rodent activity has displaced smaller skeletal elements and fragments.

Postcranial remains recovered in situ are nearly complete, with the upper right arm and shoulder and the majority of the cranium absent due to disturbance by backhoe activity. The remains are friable and fragmented, with extensive longitudinal cracking and moderate to severe cortical erosion that impacts the ability to fully observe some age and sex indicators and pathological conditions.

Table 7: Skeletal Inventory of Burial 4

Element	Side	Completeness		Element	Side	Completeness
Frontal	L, R	25%		Ribs	L	50%
Parietal	L, R	35%			R	50%
Occipital	L, R	15%			Unsided	5%
Temporal	L	---		Humerus	L	95%
	R	---			R	70%
Sphenoid	L, R	---		Radius	L	95%
Zygomatic	L	---			R	95%
	R	---		Ulna	L	95%
	Unsided	10%			R	85%
Maxilla	L, R	30%		Carpals	L	80%
Palatine	L, R	30%			R	80%
Mandible	L, R	35%		Metacarpals	L	85%
Clavicle	L	75%			R	30%
	R	---		Hand Phalanges	L, R	40%
Scapula	L	95%		Femur	L	95%
	R	---			R	90%
Sternum	L, R	95%		Tibia	L	75%
Patella	L	90%			R	80%
	R	100%		Fibula	L	75%
Sacrum	L, R	90%			R	70%
Os Coxae	L	70%		Tarsals	L	70%
	R	85%			R	70%
Cervical Vertebrae		10%		Metatarsals	L	80%
Thoracic Vertebrae		80%			R	85%
Lumbar Vertebrae		80%		Foot Phalanges	L, R	35%

Although fragmented and variably preserved, postcranial remains are represented by the majority of most skeletal elements (Table 7). Cranial elements recovered in situ include only small portions of the maxilla and mandible, reflecting removal of the superior majority of the cranium during the creation of the backhoe trench.

Maxillary and mandibular dentition was recovered in situ (Table 8). Severe dental attrition has inhibited the ability to completely identify all dentition. Maxillary dentition includes the left second molar and three anterior teeth, all characterized by severe attrition removing most or all of the crown. Mandibular dentition includes the right canine, right second molar, three premolars, and an incomplete incisor, all also affected by severe attrition removing all or most of the crown.

Skeletal elements and dentition that can be assigned to Burial 4 were recovered in 2003 from the base of the backhoe trench. These include portions of the upper right humerus, ribs, and cranium (see Table 7). The

Table 8: Dental Inventory of Burial 4

Maxillary Dentition	Presence	Mandibular Dentition	Presence
RM3		RM3	
RM2		RM2	X
RM1		RM1	
RP4		RP4	
RP3		RP3	
RC		RC	X
RI2		RI2	
RI1		RI1	
LI1		LI1	
LI2		LI2	
LC		LC	
LP3		LP3	
LP4		LP4	
LM1		LM1	
LM2	X	LM2	X
LM3		LM3	
Anterior tooth	3	Premolar	3
		Incisor	X
		Anterior root	X

mandibular left second molar and an unidentified anterior tooth root were also recovered (see Table 8). Additional exploration of the trench backdirt resulted in the recovery in 2006 of additional portions of the cranium and vertebrae (see Table 7).

Indicators of sex are present on the right and left os coxae. The subpubic concavities and right ventral arc show characteristics that suggest female sex. The right greater sciatic notch, however, is considered a stronger indicator of sex and scores as probable male. The individual is thus considered to be of probable male sex.

The right os coxae has been used as the primary source for age estimation, with supporting evidence from degenerative joint changes and dental attrition. The right pubic symphysis scores as stage 6 in the Todd system and stage 4 in the Suchey-Brooks system (Buikstra and Ubelaker 1994), suggesting a middle adult of the approximate age at death of 35–40 years. Degenerative joint changes throughout the skeleton, described below, and severe dental attrition support a middle adult age.

Skeletal pathologies observed on the postcranial remains include degenerative joint changes and nonspecific infection. The left and right parietals of the cranial vault exhibit slight porosity, healed at time of death. Degenerative joint changes are extensively distributed throughout the postcranium (Table 9), but the majority of osteoarthritic activity is limited to slight lipping of articular margins. Pronounced osteoarthritis is present in the thoracic and lumbar vertebrae, left ribs and foot phalanges.

Table 9: Degenerative Joint Changes on Burial 4 Skeletal Elements

Skeletal Element	Side	Articular or Attachment Surface	Surface Erosion or Porosity	Marginal Lipping or Spicules	Osteophytes	Facet Shape Change	Eburnation
Sternum		manubrium	X				
Sternum		facets		X			
Radius	R	head	X	X			
Ulna	R	trochlear notch			X		
Ulna	R	proximal		X			
Hand Phalanges	L, R	base		X			
Hand Phalanges		head		X			
Ribs	L	tubercle		X		X	
Ribs	L	head	X	X	X	X	
Ribs	R	head		X	X	X	
Cervical Vertebrae		1 facet				X	
Thoracic Vertebrae		8 centra		X	X		
Thoracic Vertebrae		10 facets		X		X	
Lumbar Vertebrae		1 centrum		X			
Lumbar Vertebrae		11 facets		X	X	X	
Sacrum		promontory		X		X	
Sacrum	R	facet		X			
Femur	L	head		X	X		
Femur	L	distal	X	X			
Femur	R	head		X			
Patella	L	facet		X	X		
Patella	R	facet		X	X		
Tibia	R	plateau	X	X			
Tibia	R	distal		X			
Fibula	R	distal		X		X	
Talus	R	head		X	X		
Navicular	L	facets		X			
First Metatarsal		head		X			
Foot Phalanges		head		X		X	
Foot Phalanges		base		X	X	X	X

Elements of the lower legs and feet have been affected by periosteal reactions. The right tibia displays slight periostosis on the distal diaphysis, characterized by woven bone deposition and observable along a 2 cm length where cortex is preserved. The right fibula evidences a similar periosteal reaction, consisting of woven bone deposition and porosity along a 4 cm length around midshaft. An area 3 cm in length on the left fibula displays periostosis in the form of irregular cortical surface and porosity, resulting in changes to the morphology of the interosseous crest. This pathological reaction is more superior on the diaphysis than that present on the right fibula, and thus does not strictly represent a bilaterally symmetrical pathology. All incidences of periostosis on this individual were completely or nearly completely healed at time of death. An unsided proximal foot phalanx exhibits arthritic reaction to localized trauma, characterized by lateral displacement of the bulk of the head, and irregularity and lipping of head margins.

All dentition associated with Burial 4 displays moderate calculus below the cervicoenamel junction. The positioning of the calculus bands indicates periodontal resorption. The mandibular left second molar shows severe calculus lingually and distally on the root, indicative of dehiscence and associated abscess. Carious lesions are present on the distal cervicoenamel junction of the maxillary left second molar and anterior cervicoenamel junction of the mandibular right second molar. The right mandibular canine, one of the only teeth with sufficient crown present to allow observation, shows two linear enamel hypoplasias indicating a nonspecific insult to the individual's health between the ages of four and five years.

Burial 4 is thus the flexed pit interment of a probable male middle adult. The majority of the burial was intact upon excavation, and portions of the cranium and other skeletal elements impacted by backhoe disturbance were recovered from the trench base and from backdirt in 2003 and 2006. This individual was affected by slight degenerative joint changes throughout the skeleton, concentrated in the legs and feet, and more advanced joint degeneration in the vertebrae, ribs, and feet. Nonspecific infections, healed or nearly healed at time of death, are evident in the two most common locations, the cranial vault and lower legs. Dental attrition is severe, and calculus deposition and an abscess of the mandibular left second molar illustrate periodontal disease and accompanying resorption. Two molars exhibit carious lesions, and linear enamel hypoplasias are present on the mandibular right canine. Thus, this individual was affected both by pathologies related to middle adult age and by nonspecific and localized insults to health during both childhood and adulthood.

Burial 5: Test Unit 8, Feature 14

Burial 5 is the intrusive interment of an adult individual below the floor (F-13b) of a pithouse. The individual was placed in grayish brown to brown (10YR5/2 to 5/3) fine loamy sand, with rounded gravels and pebbles, beginning at an elevation of 99.31 m directly below the floor. Large cobbles were placed directly over the individual. The outline of the burial pit was not clearly distinguishable during excavation. Articulated skeletal elements lay between the elevations of 99.07 m and 98.94 m, with occasional small fragments recovered from higher elevations in association with rodent burrows. The individual was interred in a supine position with the head to the southeast, facing northeast. The arms were extended along the sides, and the legs were flexed to the individual's left below the pelvis. The remains recovered in situ represent nearly all cranial and postcranial elements. Taphonomic processes have resulted in fragmentation and minor cortical erosion, although all observations of age and sex indicators and pathologies remain possible.

All major skeletal elements are represented by a majority of each element (Table 10). Elements of the hands and feet and the right patella are absent. Only one tooth, the maxillary right first premolar, was recovered (Table 11). The left alveolum of the maxilla indicates the antemortem loss of all left maxillary molars, premolars, and canine, suggesting that this individual probably retained little dentition at time of death. Other max-

illary and mandibular alveolum portions are not preserved, prohibiting a complete detailing of antemortem tooth loss.

Remains recovered from the eastern side of the backhoe trench in 2003, and recorded as deriving from a backdirt pile approximately 2 m north of Burial 3, can be attributed to this individual. They include the right first metacarpal, fragments of right and left tarsals, and unsided distal tibia and fibula fragments (see Table 10). Preservation, non-overlapping occurrence of skeletal portions, degree of gracility, and evidence of degenera-

Table 10: Skeletal Inventory of Burial 5

Element	Side	Completeness		Element	Side	Completeness
Frontal	L, R	95%		Ribs	L	70%
Parietal	L, R	95%			R	60%
Occipital	L, R	95%		Humerus	L	85%
Temporal	L	95%			R	85%
	R	95%		Radius	L	90%
Sphenoid	L, R	65%			R	85%
Zygomatic	L	50%		Ulna	L	75%
	R	50%			R	45%
Maxilla	L, R	90%		Carpals	L	---
Palatine	L, R	95%			R	15%
Mandible	L, R	70%		Metacarpals	L, R	70%
Clavicle	L	60%		Hand Phalanges	L, R	15%
	R	40%		Femur	L	80%
Scapula	L	40%			R	70%
	R	70%		Tibia	L	35%
Sternum	L, R	80%			R	25%
Patella	L	95%			Unsided	5%
	R	---		Fibula	L	80%
Sacrum	L, R	45%			R	70%
Os Coxae	L	60%			Unsided	10%
	R	45%		Tarsals	L	10%
	Unsided	5%			R	40%
Cervical Vertebrae		85%			Unsided	25%
Thoracic Vertebrae		95%		Metatarsals	L, R	45%
Lumbar Vertebrae		95%		Foot Phalanges	L, R	10%

Table 11: Dental Inventory of Burial 5

Maxillary Dentition	Presence	Mandibular Dentition	Presence
RM3		RM3	
RM2		RM2	
RM1		RM1	
RP4		RP4	
RP3	X	RP3	
RC		RC	
RI2		RI2	
RI1		RI1	
LI1		LI1	
LI2		LI2	
LC		LC	
LP3		LP3	
LP4		LP4	
LM1		LM1	
LM2		LM2	
LM3		LM3	

tive joint changes of the same character as the Burial 5 remains recovered in situ all support the assignation of these backdirt remains to the Burial 5 individual.

The right os coxae possesses preserved sex indicators, and forms the primary source for determination of sex for this individual. Cranial sex indicators are used secondarily. The right subpubic concavity and ischiopubic ramus ridge score as female, with the right ventral arc scoring as probably female. The left and right supraorbital margins of the cranium score as probably female, while glabella and the nuchal crest are indeterminate sex indicators on this individual. The individual is therefore considered as probably female.

Age estimation is based on the right pubic symphysis, with supporting evidence from degenerative joint changes. Cranial sutures are not sufficiently preserved to assist in estimation of age. The right pubic symphysis scores as stage 10 in the Todd system

and stage 6 in the Suchey-Brooks system (Buikstra and Ubelaker 1994), indicating that the individual was a middle adult between the approximate ages of 45–55 years. Degenerative joint changes, present throughout the skeleton and described below, support a middle adult age estimate.

This individual was affected by degenerative joint changes, expressed slightly in the arms and legs and more pronounced on the ribs and vertebral column (Table 12). Slight expressions of nonspecific and specific infection are present on the cranium and left arm. Healed porosity is present on the superior squama of the frontal and occipital, and the left and right parietals near the sagittal suture. A healed infection is located in the left maxillary sinus. This is expressed as porosity with some areas of coalescence. The single tooth recovered displays slight calculus at the cervicoenamel junction.

In addition, a healed fracture is present on the left ulna and radius. This is characterized by a periosteal reaction including irregularity of cortical surface, and alteration of diaphyseal morphology on the inferolateral left ulna. The distal epiphysis displays marginal lipping and osteophyte development that appears to be related to the trauma. The left radius displays a fracture callous consisting of a periosteal reaction and shaft expansion on the proximal diaphysis. Additionally, the ulnar notch of the left radius shows bony growth and slight displacement of the rim, indicating alteration of the articulation with the distal ulna. While the radial pathology is located more superior on the diaphysis than

the ulnar pathology, it is likely that these two healed fractures are related. The ulna and radius are fractured more commonly than other elements in clinical and archaeological samples (Lovell 1997:166), and the causes of injury are varied and primarily accidental. The locations of the fractures on this individual do not suggest that they are the result of interpersonal violence.

Burial 5 is thus the nearly complete interment of a probable female middle adult below a pithouse floor. Like other middle adults in this sample, this individual was affected by degenerative joint changes throughout the skeleton which were more pronounced on the ribs and vertebrae. Healed porosity is pres-

Table 12: Degenerative Joint Changes on Burial 5 Skeletal Elements

Skeletal Element	Side	Articular or Attachment Surface	Surface Erosion or Porosity	Marginal Lipping or Spicules	Osteophytes	Facet Shape Change
Humerus	L	head		X		
Radius	L	head		X		
Radius	L	distal		X		X
Ulna	L, R	coronoid		X		
Ulna	L	distal		X	X	
Sternum		facet		X		
Metacarpal	R	base		X		
Ribs	L, R	tubercle	X	X		X
Scapula	L	acromion	X	X		
Cervical Vertebrae		5 centra	X	X	X	
Cervical Vertebrae		8 facets		X	X	X
Thoracic Vertebrae		10 centra		X	X	
Thoracic Vertebrae		32 facets	X	X		X
Lumbar Vertebrae		4 centra		X	X	
Lumbar Vertebrae		3 facets	X	X		X
Sacrum		promontory		X		
Tibia	L	plateau			X	
Fibula	L	proximal		X		
Talus	R	head		X		
Talus	R	trochlea		X		
Calcaneus	R	facets		X		

ent on the cranial vault. A healed infection is evident in the left maxillary sinus, and the left ulna and radius exhibit healed fractures. Only one tooth was recovered, with calculus deposited at the cervicoenamel junction, and preserved portions of maxilla indicate extensive antemortem tooth loss.

Isolated Human Remains Recovered During 2006 Excavations

Isolated human remains were recovered from non-mortuary contexts during excavation in Test Unit 6. The occurrence of these small fragments is not surprising, given the apparent density of interments in this area of the site and the frequency of rodent and other taphonomic disturbance. These remains likely indicate the presence of an interment in nearby unexcavated context.

Excavations in Test Unit 6 uncovered a complete right proximal foot phalanx at an elevation of 99.23 m and a complete unsided intermediate hand phalanx at an elevation of 98.98 m. Both bones were located in the northwestern quadrant of the unit, the latter within the jumbled zone of roof and wall materials of F-5, a pit structure. Extensive rodent disturbance in these areas of excavation is the most likely cause of the location of the human remains; phalanges were frequently observed to have been displaced, often upward, by rodent activity during excavation of the burials reported upon here. Two large side-by-side cobbles were discovered approximately 20 cm below the hand phalanx, which may represent the top of a burial feature. These cobbles were left in place and excavation was not continued below them, however, so any association of the human remains with this possible burial feature remains entirely speculative until further excavations can be undertaken.

Both phalanges show root etching and slight cortical erosion, but observation is not compromised by these taphonomic alterations. Both belong to an adult individual of indeterminate sex. Slight marginal lipping associated with joint degeneration is present at the head and base of both phalanges. This is accompanied by slight compression and osteophytic activity on the head of the right proximal foot phalanx. Other pathologies are absent on both bones. These degenerative changes are commonly observed among middle and older adults in the Millington sample, reflecting high levels of activity and age-related degeneration.

Unattributed Human Remains

Recovery of human remains from trench backdirt during 2003 site visitation and 2006 backdirt exploration included some remains that cannot be attributed specifically to one of the five excavated burials. These include postcranial fragments and dentition. The skeletal elements were recovered in 2003 from a backdirt pile located east of the backhoe trench and approximately 3 m north of Burials 1 and 4. Probable femur fragments, thoracic vertebral arch fragments, and carpal fragments from this backdirt location cannot be confidently assigned to one of the excavated individuals. Among these, one left inferior articular surface of a thoracic vertebra shows facet expansion associated with degeneration of the joint. One right rib shaft fragment was recovered from the base of the backhoe trench, approximately 2 m north of Burials 1 and 4, and remains unassigned.

During screening of trench backdirt associated with Burials 1 and 4 in 2006, teeth likely belonging to two subadult individuals were recovered. The first set of dentition includes eight teeth: the maxillary first molars and left second molar, and the mandibular deciduous second molars, right second incisor, right second premolar, and right first molar. The deciduous molars exhibit heavy attrition, with slight attrition and slight calculus deposition on the maxillary first molars and mandibular incisor. The mandibular right premolar is unerupted. This dentition suggests that the creation of the backhoe trench impacted the burial of a subadult, of the approximate age of 8–10 years +/- 24 months.

A second set of dentition includes six teeth: the maxillary second molars and right third molar, and the mandibular right second incisor, right second premolar and right second molar. All teeth exhibit slight wear, with attrition minimal on the third molar. Distal interproximal facets on the second molars are absent or only minimally formed, indicating that third molars were either unerupted or recently erupted. This, combined with minimal attrition patterns, suggests that the backhoe trench probably impacted the burial of a late adolescent, 17–19 years of age.

Slight calculus is present on the labial and lingual crown surfaces of the mandibular right second incisor. The maxillary second molars exhibit moderate calculus on the buccal crown surfaces. Calculus, caries, and abscess are absent on all other dentition. A single linear enamel hypoplasia is present on the mandibular right second incisor, formed at the approximate age of 3.3 years. Dental enamel defects are absent on the remaining dentition.

Analysis of Previously Excavated Human Remains from the Millington Site

Human skeletal remains recovered from mortuary contexts during the 1938–1939 excavations at the Millington site were analyzed in 2006 as a component of the osteological analysis associated with CBBS excavations. The previously excavated remains available for analysis are those curated at the Texas Ar-

cheological Research Laboratory of the University of Texas at Austin. These do not form a complete set of previously excavated remains, but include eight individuals recovered from six burials. Contextual information and results of the analysis of these individuals are presented in this section, as these individuals are incorporated into the Millington sample for discussions presented in subsequent sections of this chapter. Contextual data reported here are gathered from field notes and burial forms on file at the Center for Big Bend Studies. Burial numbers presented below were assigned during the 1938–1939 excavations, and should not be confused with those from the 2006 investigation.

Burial 3: House 7, Structure 15

One adult female individual was recovered from a post-abandonment interment resting on fill covering the floor of House No. 7. The individual was interred in supine flexed position, head south, with the arms crossed over the abdomen and the flexed legs angled to the individual's left. No associated artifacts or grave architecture are reported.

The skeletal remains are fragmented but display good cortical preservation, affected only by minor root etching. Some elements, particularly the right os coxae, have been treated with an unknown consolidant. Representation of skeletal elements is incomplete (Table 13), with foot elements present but the majority of the legs absent. The right os coxae is the only portion of the pelvis present. Small portions of hands, left and right arm and shoulder elements are present. The ribs and thoracic vertebrae are moderately well represented. Approximately 70 percent of the mandible and 30 percent of the cranium are present. In contrast, the dentition is nearly completely represented, lacking only the maxillary left first incisor and the mandibular right second and third molars.

Table 13: Skeletal Inventory of 1938 Burial 3

Element	Side	Completeness		Element	Side	Completeness
Frontal	L, R	25%		Ribs	L	30%
Parietal	L, R	25%			R	30%
Occipital	L, R	25%		Humerus	L	10%
Temporal	L	60%			R	---
	R	60%		Radius	L	---
Sphenoid	L, R	---			R	60%
Zygomatic	L	90%		Ulna	L	---
	R	80%			R	---
Maxilla	L, R	75%		Carpals	L	10%
Palatine	L, R	---			R	---
Mandible	L, R	70%		Metacarpals	L, R	75%
Clavicle	L	95%		Hand Phalanges	L, R	25%
	R	90%		Femur	L	10%
Scapula	L	20%			R	---
	R	10%		Tibia	L	---
Sternum	L, R	70%			R	---
Patella	L	---		Fibula	L	---
	R	---			R	---
Sacrum	L, R	---		Tarsals	L	5%
Os Coxae	L	---			R	10%
	R	85%		Metatarsals	L, R	95%
Cervical Vertebrae		10%		Foot Phalanges	L, R	35%
Thoracic Vertebrae		15%				
Lumbar Vertebrae		---				

Some pelvic and cranial sex indicators are preserved for this individual, but all are secondary. Right subpubic sex indicators tend toward male characteristics, but this tendency is slight. The right sciatic notch is fragmented and incomplete, and thus not observable as a sex indicator, but the preserved portion suggests a broad rather than narrow arc. The right supraorbital ridge and the mental eminence both score as female. Based on these indicators, and the overall gracility of the skeleton, this individual has been classified as possibly female.

The right pubic symphysis is observable for age estimation. Both the Todd and Suchey-Brooks systems place the individual in the range of 35 to 45 years at time of death. This middle adult age is supported by the presence of degenerative joint changes on the ribs, vertebrae, legs and feet.

Observable skeletal pathologies on this individual include cranial porosity, trauma and nonspecific infection on the ribs, and degenerative arthritic lipping. Like other Millington adults, this individual displays slight, healed cranial porosity on the left parietal and occipital squama. The left and right rib shafts evidence healed fractures, characterized by bony calluses, changes in shaft angle and morphology, and some associated porotic activity on the rib shafts near the sternal ends. This injury appears to have been accidental, rather than the result of violence.

A nonspecific infection appears on at least four right ribs, superior to the tubercles and on adjacent shaft fragments, and is unrelated to the rib trauma. This infection shows active portions and portions in the early stages of healing. As mentioned above, many observable joints are characterized by slight arthritic lipping, including vertebral body margins, rib tubercles, knee and foot joints. One thoracic vertebra shows more severe arthritic changes, characterized by severe compression of the vertebral body and moderate marginal lipping. Preservation does not allow observation that would distinguish whether this is an isolated case of traumatic osteo-

phytosis or a more widespread degenerative process in the thoracic spine.

The nearly complete dentition of this individual (Table 14) allows for the observation of dental attrition patterns and pathologies. Developmental defects of the enamel, including both hypoplasias and hypocalcifications, are present. The maxillary left first incisor, and the mandibular right second incisor and left canine, show series of hypoplastic pits across much of the labial enamel surfaces. Linear enamel hypoplasias are present on the maxillary left second incisor and mandibular left canine, indicating three episodes of childhood stress at the approximate ages of 2.9, 4.2, and 4.9 years. A banded brown hypocalcification is present on the maxillary right first incisor. Taken together, these enamel defects indicate significant nonspecific childhood stress.

This dentition is characterized by moderate attrition and slight to moderate calculus

Table 14: Dental Inventory of 1938 Burial 3

Maxillary Dentition	Presence	Mandibular Dentition	Presence
RM3		RM3	X
RM2		RM2	X
RM1	X	RM1	X
RP4	X	RP4	X
RP3	X	RP3	X
RC	X	RC	X
RI2	X	RI2	X
RI1	X	RI1	X
LI1	X	LI1	
LI2	X	LI2	X
LC	X	LC	X
LP3	X	LP3	X
LP4	X	LP4	X
LM1	X	LM1	X
LM2	X	LM2	X
LM3	X	LM3	X

deposition. Two interproximal carious lesions are present, on the distal cervicoenamel junctions of the maxillary right first molar and mandibular left second molar. There is, however, no evidence of abscessing or periodontal disease, and no observable antemortem loss. Thus, while diet has affected this individual's dentition, dietary-related dental pathologies are not severely expressed.

In sum, the individual recovered from Burial 3 of the 1938–1939 excavations is a middle adult possible female that was interred in a subfloor pit associated with a pithouse. Episodes of childhood stress are indicated by cranial porosity and dental defects. A slight nonspecific infection is manifest on the ribs, which also display healed fractures. Slight degenerative joint changes, and one more severe location of vertebral osteophytosis, are present in many joints throughout the skeleton. Carious lesions are present, but the caries process has not progressed into more severe dental pathologies.

Burial 5: Section IX-15, Block De

Burial 5, which contained two subadult individuals, was located in a relatively densely occupied area of the site near Structures 11 and 26. No grave architecture or artifacts are reported. One individual is recorded as interred in a loosely flexed position, on the right side, with the head northeast. It is not clear to which individual this refers, nor is the association of the two individuals with each other clear.

Individual A is represented by bones of the legs and feet, lower arms, and one cervical vertebra (Table 15). Those elements present show good cortical preservation, with occasional cortical erosion and longitudinal cracking. Root etching is occasionally present, but does not obscure observation for pathology. In addition to diaphyseal fragments, epiphyses of the tibia and humerus and me-

taphyseal surfaces of most elements present are observable, yielding an age estimate of three to four years at time of death. Only one tooth fragment, 80 percent of the crown of a permanent maxillary right molar, is present, making age and other observations on the dentition impossible.

No evidence of nonspecific infection or any other pathological condition is present on the remains present. The absence of the cranium prohibits observation for cranial porosity. Individual A of Burial 5 is thus a subadult of three to four years of age, represented primarily by long bone fragments, and lacking any pathologies on those skeletal elements present.

Individual B is an infant represented by portions of the majority of skeletal elements, with notable exceptions being the bones of the feet and hands (Table 16). The remains are occasionally cracked or fragmented, but display generally good cortical preservation. An unknown consolidant has been applied to the cranial vault. The mandibular deciduous dentition and the maxillary deciduous first incisors, as well as a permanent maxillary canine cusp tip, are present (Table 17). Observation of skeletal development and epiphyseal fusion stages, as well as dental development, yields an age estimate of six months +/- three months.

This individual evidences an active, systemic bilateral nonspecific infection. This infection is manifest as periostosis on the diaphyses of the tibiae, humerii, radii and ulnae. The bilateral distribution, presence along the majority of the tibial diaphysis length and the superior arm diaphyses, and the active condition of the pathology all suggest a systemic infection that likely contributed to the individual's death. The parietals and occipital of the cranial vault show slight active porosity, which may be related to the systemic infection or may be nutritional in nature. This individual lacks developmental defects of the enamel, which are less common on deciduous dentition. The second individual included in this interment is thus an infant, six months +/- three months of age at death, with a slight but systemic infection at time of death.

The presence of a third subadult individual is indicated by approximately 90 percent of a right tibial diaphysis, curated with the remains of Individual B. This tibia is smaller and less developed than those of Individual B, possibly representing a neonate. Active infection is present along the medial length of the diaphysis. As with the other two subadults in this interment, contextual information regarding associations or relation of this individual to the others recovered is absent.

Table 15: Skeletal Inventory of Individual A of 1938 Burial 5

Element	Side	Completeness	Element	Side	Completeness
Frontal	L, R	---	Ribs	L	---
Parietal	L, R	---		R	---
Occipital	L, R	---	Humerus	Unsided	10%
Temporal	L	---	Foot Phalanges	L, R	10%
	R	---	Radius	L	95%
Sphenoid	L, R	---		R	95%
Zygomatic	L	---	Ulna	L	---
	R	---		R	95%
Maxilla	L, R	---	Carpals	L	---
Palatine	L, R	---		R	---
Mandible	L, R	---	Metacarpals	L, R	30%
Clavicle	L	---	Hand Phalanges	L, R	5%
	R	---	Femur	Unsided	40%
Scapula	L	---	Metatarsals	L, R	100%
	R	---	Tibia	L	80%
Sternum	L, R	---		R	75%
Patella	L	---	Fibula	L	95%
	R	---		R	95%
Sacrum	L, R	---	Tarsals	L	65%
Os Coxae	L	---		R	70%
	R	---	Cervical Vertebrae		10%
Lumbar Vertebrae		---	Thoracic Vertebrae		---

Table 16: Skeletal Inventory of Individual B of 1938 Burial 5

Element	Side	Completeness		Element	Side	Completeness
Frontal	L, R	75%		Ribs	L	90%
Parietal	L, R	75%			R	95%
Occipital	L, R	75%		Humerus	L	90%
Temporal	L	50%			R	90%
	R	---		Radius	L	90%
Sphenoid	L, R	30%			R	90%
Zygomatic	L			Ulna	L	90%
	R	95%			R	90%
Maxilla	L, R	---		Carpals	L	---
Palatine	L, R	---			R	---
Mandible	L, R	85%		Metacarpals	L, R	20%
Clavicle	L	80%		Hand Phalanges	L, R	15%
	R	85%		Femur	L	---
Scapula	L	---			R	---
	R	60%		Tibia	L	90%
Sternum	L, R	60%			R	90%
Patella	L	---		Foot Phalanges	L, R	---
	R	---		Fibula	L	90%
Sacrum	L, R	---			R	90%
Os Coxae	L	75%		Metatarsals	L, R	---
	R	80%		Tarsals	L	---
Lumbar Vertebrae		95%			R	---
Cervical Vertebrae		45%		Thoracic Vertebrae		90%

Table 17: Dental Inventory of Individual B of 1938 Burial 5

Maxillary Dentition	Presence	Mandibular Dentition	Presence
rdm2		rdm2	X
rdm1		rdm1	X
rdc		rdc	
rdi2		rdi2	
rdi1	X	rdi1	
ldi1	X	ldi1	X
ldi2		ldi2	X
ldc		ldc	X
ldm1		ldm1	X
ldm2		ldm2	X

Burial 6: Section VIII-6, Block Bg

Burial 6 is reported as the interment of an individual in a cist, near the eastern extent of the 1938–1939 excavations. A sketch of the individual indicates that it was interred in a flexed supine position, with the head to the northwest. This sketch depicts a complete skeleton, although the only elements curated are four hand phalanges and ten fragmentary teeth. Excavation notes also indicate that this individual was associated with at least two infant interments, too poorly preserved for recovery. Observation of skeletal characteristics is limited to two proximal, one intermediate and one distal hand phalanges. The distal hand phalanx shows slight lipping on the basal margin. Most of the anterior maxillary dentition, and the mandibular right third molar are present (Table 18). These teeth, moderately worn, exhibit slight calculus deposits at the cervicoenamel junction, which are not positioned to indicate periodontal disease.

The maxillary right canine shows hypoplastic pitting near the cervicoenamel junction. Carious lesions are present on the maxillary right third premolar and a fragment representing approximately 15 percent of a maxillary molar. While very little of this individual is present among the curated remains, degenerative joint changes indicate that the individual is most likely an adult of at east 30 years of age, and dental pathologies follow the typical tendencies toward childhood stresses and the decay process that are exhibited in the rest of the Millington sample.

Burial 7: Section VII-8, Blocks Ai and Aj

Burial 7 is an interment located to the northwest of Burial 6, in the eastern sector of the Millington site. The skeletal remains of two individuals are curated as recovered from Burial 7, one adult male and one child. Indi-

Table 18: Dental Inventory of 1939 Burial 6

Maxillary Dentition	Presence	Mandibular Dentition	Presence
RM3		RM3	X
RM2		RM2	
RM1		RM1	
RP4	X	RP4	
RP3	X	RP3	
RC	X	RC	
RI2		RI2	
RI1	X	RI1	
LI1	X	LI1	
LI2	X	LI2	
LC	X	LC	
LP3		LP3	
LP4		LP4	
LM1		LM1	
LM2		LM2	
LM3		LM3	

vidual A, the primary individual in the interment, was placed in a supine flexed position, with the arms over the abdomen and the head to the northwest. No information is available about the position or orientation of the child included in this interment. No associated grave architecture or artifacts are reported.

The remains of Individual A, the adult male, represent the majority of skeletal elements (Table 19), with the notable exceptions of the cranium and all dentition but one tooth. The remains are fragmented, and have been affected by slight to severe cortical erosion. Most of the elements show pronounced lon-

gitudinal and some multidirectional cracking, staining, and occasional rodent gnawing. The only tooth present is the maxillary right first incisor, showing moderate attrition and slight calculus deposition at the cervicoenamel junction. An unidentified tooth root fragment is also present.

The right sciatic notch indicates that this individual is male. Skeletal and dental indicators that would allow for the construction of an age estimate are either absent or too poorly preserved to observe, and therefore the individual is only categorized as an adult. The extensive distribution of degenera-

Table 19: Skeletal Inventory of Individual A of 1939 Burial 7

Element	Side	Completeness		Element	Side	Completeness
Frontal	L, R	---		Ribs	L	90%
Parietal	L, R	---			R	90%
Occipital	L, R	---		Humerus	L	90%
Temporal	L	---			R	60%
	R	---		Radius	L	10%
Sphenoid	L, R	---			R	95%
Zygomatic	L	---		Ulna	L	55%
	R	---			R	25%
Maxilla	L, R	---		Carpals	L	50%
Palatine	L, R	---			R	35%
Mandible	L, R	---		Metacarpals	L, R	65%
Clavicle	L	65%		Hand Phalanges	L, R	20%
	R	75%		Femur	L	30%
Scapula	L	40%			R	30%
	R	45%		Tibia	L	65%
Sternum	L, R	65%			R	50%
Patella	L	60%		Foot Phalanges	L, R	40%
	R	---		Fibula	L	40%
Sacrum	L, R	40%			R	45%
Os Coxae	L			Metatarsals	L, R	65%
	R	30%		Tarsals	L	70%
Lumbar Vertebrae		90%		Thoracic Vertebrae		90%
Cervical Vertebrae		30%				

tive joint changes, described below, suggest a middle or old adult age.

A bilateral healed infection is visible on the humeral diaphyses of Individual A. It is characterized by slight woven bone activity. The bilateral distribution of this periostosis suggests that the infection was systemic, although more common locations for the manifestation of systemic infections, such as the tibial diaphyses, are highly eroded and not consistently observable. The individual is also affected by degenerative joint disease, distributed extensively throughout the axial and appendicular skeleton. Observable appendicular joints are characterized by minor osteophytic lipping at joint margins, and sometimes porosity of the articular surface. Articular surface porosity ranges from slight to coalescing macroporosity. Changes in the axial skeleton tend to be more pronounced, ranging from slight to severe marginal lipping and facet expansion of rib and sternum articulations and vertebral bodies and facets. The most severe expression is in the lumbar spine, with ankylosis of three lumbar vertebrae. The individual also shows severe bilateral arthritic changes associated with cloacae in the proximal foot phalanges. The right trapezoid of the hand evidences expansion of the dorsal surface in association with cloacae. These arthritic manifestations suggest that the individual may have suffered from an inflammatory disease.

Individual A can be categorized as an adult male, with a possible systemic infection and arthritic changes suggestive of inflammatory disease. Indicators of childhood stress on the cranium and dentition are absent for this individual, as are indicators of diet and dental disease.

Individual B is represented by approximately 20 percent of the cranial vault, the left coronoid process of the mandible, one unidentified epiphysis fragment, and mixed deciduous and permanent dentition. The as-sociation of this individual, incompletely excavated, with Individual A is unclear.

One deciduous tooth, the maxillary left first deciduous incisor, and five maxillary and mandibular permanent teeth are present. The developmental stage of the dentition indicates that Individual B was five years +/- 1.5 years of age at time of death. The portion of the cranial vault present lacks porosity or any other pathology. The dentition lacks developmental defects of the enamel. No other pathological conditions are observable for this individual.

Burial 8: Section VI-14

Burial 8 was recovered from the north-central area of the 1938–1939 excavations, in the area of Structures 7 and 20. It contained an adult individual, interred in a tightly flexed supine position with the head to the north. Subadult cranial and dental remains are also present among the curated remains of the adult. No associated grave architecture or artifacts are reported.

The primary individual in this interment is represented by small portions of the majority of skeletal elements (Table 20). The skeletal remains are poorly preserved, characterized by fragmentation, longitudinal cracking, and moderate to severe cortical erosion. This obscures observation of several elements, particularly the cranial vault. It has also resulted in the absence of age or sex indicators, and this individual can therefore only be classified as an adult of indeterminate sex. The dentition of this individual is represented by a single tooth, the mandibular right second molar. Attrition is severe, and has removed most of the tooth crown.

Unsided fragments of fibula and tibia evidence slight healed periostosis. Few other elements are observable for pathology, preventing the diagnosis of this infection as systemic or more localized. Slight to moderate

Table 20: Skeletal Inventory of 1939 Burial 8

Element	Side	Completeness		Element	Side	Completeness
Frontal	L, R	15%		Ribs	L	40%
Parietal	L, R	15%			R	40%
Occipital	L, R	15%		Humerus	L	30%
Temporal	L	---			R	20%
	R	---		Radius	L	10%
Sphenoid	L, R	---			R	---
Zygomatic	L	---		Ulna	L	---
	R	---			R	30%
Maxilla	L, R	---		Carpals	L	10%
Palatine	L, R	---			R	---
Mandible	L, R	5%		Metacarpals	L, R	---
Clavicle	L	---		Hand Phalanges	L, R	5%
	R	---		Femur	Unsided	20%
Scapula	L	5%		Tarsals	L	---
	Unsided	5%			R	---
Sternum	L, R	10%		Metatarsals	L, R	---
Patella	L	---		Foot Phalanges	L, R	---
	R	---		Fibula	Unsided	10%
Sacrum	L, R	---		Tibia	Unsided	20%
Os Coxae	L	5%		Thoracic Vertebrae		10%
	R	---		Lumbar Vertebrae		5%
Cervical Vertebrae		---				

degenerative changes are present throughout the skeleton, most pronounced in the vertebrae. These are characterized by marginal lipping and occasional porosity of articular surfaces in the appendicular skeleton, and moderate to severe marginal lipping, coalescing porosity, and facet expansion on the vertebrae and ribs.

One subadult cranial vault fragment and a maxillary left deciduous second molar are present among the adult remains from Burial 8. The molar shows a diffuse brown hypocalcification covering approximately 60 percent of the crown, which is worn. Age determination of this individual is not possible with such limited remains.

Burial 8 thus contained an adult individual and possibly a subadult. Poor preservation and lack of many skeletal elements or portions thereof prevent detailed observation, but it is possible to report a nonspecific infection and degenerative joint disease on the adult remains, and developmental enamel defects on the subadult dentition.

Burial 9: House 14, Structure 5

Burial 9 is the interment of a child in a pit below the floor of Structure 5. The individual was interred in a tightly flexed supine position with the head to the south. No associated artifacts are reported. Curated remains include only the cranium and dentition, although the majority of both of these are present (Table 21). Dental development indicates that this child was five years +/- 1.5 years of age at time of death.

The cranial vault exhibits slight to moderate cortical erosion and occasional longitudinal cracking, but remains observable for pathology, which is absent. Fragments of mandible, excluding the alveolum, are also present and lack pathology. Maxillary and mandibular dentition is present, including mixed deciduous and permanent dentition as is typical of this age. This individual exhibits no calculus or caries, but several developmental enamel defects. Linear enamel hypoplasias are common on the anterior permanent dentition, specifically the maxil-

Table 21: Dental Inventory of 1939 Burial 9

Maxillary Dentition	Presence	Mandibular Dentition	Presence
RM2		RM2	X
RM1		RM1	X
RP4		RP4	
RP3		RP3	X
RC		RC	
RI2	X	RI2	X
RI1		RI1	X
rdm2		rdm2	
rdm1	X	rdm1	X
rdc	X	rdc	X
rdi2		rdi2	
rdi1	X	rdi1	
ldi1		ldi1	
ldi2		ldi2	X
ldc	X	ldc	
ldm1	X	ldm1	
ldm2		ldm2	X
LI1		LI1	X
LI2	X	LI2	X
LC		LC	X
LP3		LP3	X
LP4		LP4	X
LM1		LM1	X
LM2		LM2	

lary right second incisor, mandibular first and second incisors, and mandibular left canine. Two to three hypoplastic lines are present on each tooth, indicating six to seven episodes of stress between the approximate ages of 2.3 years and 4.6 years. Diffuse brown hypocalcifications are present on the maxillary left deciduous canine, and the mandibular right deciduous canine, right deciduous first molar, and left deciduous second molar, indicating nonspecific stress earlier in the individual's life, during development of the deciduous dentition. This individual shows the most extensive distribution of developmental enamel defects in the Millington sample, suggesting multiple stress episodes and compromised health status for most or all of the individual's life.

Metric and Nonmetric Data

The gathering of metric and nonmetric data on the skeletal and dental remains in this sample is inhibited by the fragmentation and cortical erosion of skeletal elements, and fragmentation and severe attrition of the dentition. Consistent measurements and observations were not possible, prohibiting comparison of this sample with other better-preserved samples from adjacent regions. Similarly, the portions of skeletal elements necessary to determine stature are infrequently present in the sample, preventing the compilation of stature estimates for these individuals. All observations possible on this sample are presented in Tables 22–24.

Skeletal Analysis Discussion

In addition to the 13 individuals discussed above from mortuary contexts at Millington, some documentation of three additional individuals (Burials 1, 10, and 11) from the 1937–1939 excavations has been reviewed. This information can be combined in a discussion of the demographic profile and mortuary patterns of the Millington sample. The full sample thus consists of 16 individuals, distributed as shown in Table 25. While a

Table 22: Adult Cranial Metric and Nonmetric Data

Element	Measurement	1938 Bur. 3
Cranium	Mult. Infraorbital Foramina	L absent
Cranium	Zygomatico-facial Foramina	L 1 large R 2 small
Cranium	Tympanic Dehiscence	R absent
Cranium	Auditory Exostosis	R absent
Mandible	Mental Foramen	L 2
Mandible	Mandibular Torus	Absent
Mandible	Chin Height	38.18 mm
Mandible	Mandibular Body Height	34.81 mm
Mandible	Mandibular Body Breadth	12.05 mm
Mandible	Minimum Ramus Breadth	30.63 mm

Table 23: Adult Postcranial Metric and Nonmetric Data

Element	Measurement	Burial 2	Burial 4	Burial 5
Humerus	Epicondylar Breadth		57.83 mm	
Humerus	Max. Diameter Midshaft		19.01 mm	22.29 mm (R)
Humerus	Min. Diameter Midshaft		17.05 mm	16.79 mm (R)
Humerus	Septal Aperture		Perforation (R)	Absent
Radius	A-P* Diameter Midshaft	11.90 mm	11.07 mm	11.55 mm (R)
Radius	M-L* Diameter Midshaft	14.93 mm	14.07 mm	13.75 mm (R)
Ulna	A-P* Diameter	14.32 mm	12.93 mm	
Ulna	M-L* Diameter	13.98 mm	13.55 mm	
Femur	Max. Diameter Head		43.15 mm	
Fibula	Max. Diameter Midshaft	15.76 mm	16.32 mm	

* A-P is Anterior-Posterior, while M-L stands for Medial-Lateral.

Table 24: Subadult Postcranial Metric Data

Element	Measurement	1938 Bur. 5A	1938 Bur. 5B
Ilium	Length		39.22 mm R
Ilium	Width		37.82 mm R
Pubis	Length		21.44 mm
Clavicle	Length		51.74 mm R
Clavicle	Diameter		4.32 mm R
Humerus	Length		80.29 mm
Humerus	Diameter		7.94 mm
Radius	Length	92.87 mm	64.33 mm
Radius	Diameter	7.43 mm	4.80 mm
Ulna	Length	102.85 mm	71.21 mm R
Ulna	Diameter	7.50 mm	5.47 mm R
Femur	Length		99.32 mm
Femur	Diameter		8.55 mm
Tibia	Length		81.17 mm
Tibia	Diameter		8.20 mm
Fibula	Length		77.73 mm
Fibula	Diameter	8.00 mm	4.66 mm

Table 25: *Distribution of Millington Human Remains by Age and Sex*

	Adult	Adolescent	Child	Infant
Male	4			
Female	2			
Indeterminate	4	1	3	2

small sample cannot be measured or submitted to formal demographic analysis, it may be noted that irregularities or demographic characteristics suggesting a demographic profile deviating from that normally expected for a prehistoric sedentary or semi-sedentary population are absent in the Millington sample. Age estimates of adults suggest that these individuals were between 30 and 55 years of age at death, while children's deaths cluster between three and five years of age. Assessments of the typical ages at death of infants and adolescents are not possible with the current sample.

Osteoarthritis

Degenerative joint disease (DJD) is a progressive arthritic condition that forms part of the aging process. It is characterized by changes to joint surfaces including porosity, eburnation (polishing) and increased or flattened surface areas, and lipping or osteophyte development of joint margins. Osteoarthritis may be primary, which in most cases is interpreted as degenerative changes associated with aging, or secondary when associated with a joint injury or other condition. Vertebral arthritis is classified as osteophytosis when characterized by lipping and porosity of the vertebral bodies, and as vertebral osteoarthritis when affecting articular facets. The relationship of degenerative joint disease to chronic occupational stress or specific activities has not been consistently demonstrated (Jurmain 1977, 1991), and as a result this discussion takes expressions of DJD to

be generally correlated with aging rather than identifiable activities.

In accord with recommendations for data coding and compilation for the analysis of osteoarthritis (Aufderheide and Rodriguez-Martin 1998a; Bridges 1991, 1993; Brunson 2000; Rogers et al. 1987; Waldron and Rogers 1991), arthritis in this sample has been classified by severity and compiled by joint. The most severe expression on any surface comprising a joint has been taken as the representative severity for that joint, rather than averaging all expressions within a single joint. Since previous studies have varied in reporting incidence of osteoarthritis including minor expression, or limiting incidence to moderate or severe cases, the data for this sample are presented using both standards of incidence to provide maximum comparability.

Arthritic changes are observable and have been presented above for Burials 2, 4 and 5. Data is additionally available from three Millington adults from the Kelley excavations. The four adults in this sample for which age can be determined fall between the ages of 30 and 55 years. It is clear that at least slight DJD is present throughout the joints of individuals in this sample by middle age, with expression more severe in the axial skeleton (primarily the vertebral column) than the appendicular skeleton. The small sample discussed here prevents the use of statistical tests of similarities and differences noted.

When incidence of appendicular degenerative joint disease is viewed by percentage of individuals affected to any degree, all individuals in the sample are affected at the elbow, knee and ankle/foot joints (Table 26). The shoulder and hip joints have the lowest incidence, but at least half of the individuals in the sample show changes at these joints. When only moderate or severe DJD is included in the compilation of incidence by individual, the elbow is the most affected joint, followed by the knee and shoulder joints, affected in the majority of individuals. Incidence in the hip, ankle/foot and wrist/hand falls below 50 percent in this compilation. When incidence is calculated by joint rather than by individual, ranking of the affected joints changes slightly but results remain very similar. These results correlate with a summary consideration of arthritis in prehistoric American populations, where the elbow and knee are the most frequently affected regardless of subsistence economy (Bridges 1992:71). There is not a strong tendency in this sample for either the upper or lower extremity to be more severely affected.

The overall incidence of appendicular degenerative joint disease among the occupants of Millington is much higher than for Lower Pecos samples (Hartnady 1988 in Steele and Powell 1989; Marks et al. 1985; Reinhard et al. 1989), Archaic or Mississippian samples from the southeastern United States (Bridges 1991), and samples from Pecos Pueblo, New Mexico (Jurmain 1977).

Vertebral arthritis is prevalent in this sample, with moderate to severe osteophytosis affecting the cervical, thoracic, and lumbar regions in all individuals (Table 27). The incidence of osteoarthritis between the articular facets of the vertebrae is also high. When osteoarthritis of any severity is considered, incidence decreases from lower to upper regions of the spine. When only moderate to severe expression is considered, incidence is highest in the thoracic region, followed by the lumbar and then the cervical region. This pattern of incidence is expected, with osteophytosis more prevalent than vertebral osteo-

Table 26: Incidence of Arthritis in Appendicular Joints

By Individual	Minor-Severe	Moderate-Severe	By Joint	Minor-Severe	Moderate-Severe
Shoulder	60%	60%	Shoulder	43%	43%
Elbow	100%	80%	Elbow	89%	44%
Wrist/Hand	83%	33%	Wrist/Hand	82%	18%
Hip	50%	33%	Hip	40%	20%
Knee	100%	67%	Knee	100%	75%
Ankle/Foot	100%	50%	Ankle/Foot	91%	36%

Table 27: Incidence of Vertebral Arthritis

Osteophytosis	Total Incidence	Moderate-Severe Incid.	Osteoarthritis	Total Incidence	Moderate-Severe Incid.
Cervical	100%	100%	Cervical	75%	25%
Thoracic	100%	100%	Thoracic	80%	80%
Lumbar	100%	100%	Lumbar	100%	75%

arthritis (Maat et al. 1995:295), although the Millington sample shows comparatively high incidence (Bridges 1994; Marks et al. 1985; Reinhard et al. 1989). More detailed comparison of vertebral arthritis with other skeletal samples is prevented by the small size of the Millington sample.

There is no clear pattern in this sample of bilateral asymmetry as expressed in degenerative joint disease of the appendicular skeleton. Minor differentiation by sex includes less severely affected elbows but more severely affected wrist and hand joints in females. Females tend toward more common and more severe osteoarthritis of the wrist and hand in diverse populations (Waldron 1993:216). Degenerative joint disease of the lower extremities is more prevalent among males, with complete absence of affected hip joints in females and more severe knee and ankle/foot expression in males. Females show more severe osteoarthritis of the cervical vertebrae. While a much larger sample is required to assess the persistence and significance of these patterns, it is possible that such trends suggest more stress from walking in males (Brunson 2000:9; Larsen 2002:133) and different lifting, throwing and/or grinding activities between men and women.

Trauma

Skeletal trauma is characterized by mechanical insult resulting in damage to bone, such as fracture or dislocation. Healing or healed fractures can be recognized by the formation of a bony callous and/or remodeling around the fracture site, abnormal angling of a bone, or nonunion of two sides of a fracture (Adams and Hamblen 1992; Judd 2002:1258). Traumatic arthritis is a secondary condition that can accompany a healing or healed fracture, or the joints affected by such a fracture. Traumatic arthritis most commonly develops in the joints of the hips, legs and feet, followed

by the shoulder and elbow (Aufderheide and Rodriguez-Martin 1998b:105). The recording of skeletal trauma for the Millington sample includes notation of the location of the trauma by shaft segment or element portion, extent of healing, any secondary conditions such as osteoarthritis or infection, and any effects of the trauma on adjacent joints.

Subadults in the Millington sample, where observable, lack any indications of skeletal trauma. Five of six observable adults evidence at least one location of skeletal trauma, for an incidence of 83 percent in the adult sample. Trauma is most common in the lower leg and foot, with lower arm and rib fractures also present. Additionally, the adolescent individual recovered from Burial 1 shows active osteoarthritis in one superior articular facet of the first cervical vertebra, associated with localized trauma. In most cases in this sample, secondary conditions such as angulation or compression of epiphyses, traumatic arthritis, and cloacae indicating associated infection are present. All adult trauma shows evidence of healing, leaving the adolescent minor vertebral trauma as the only active trauma in the Millington sample. This indicates that skeletal trauma was not a primary cause of death.

Although the adult sample is small, represented by three males, two females and one individual of indeterminate sex, differentiation in location of trauma by sex is evident. All of the lower leg and foot trauma is present on male individuals, and conversely all male individuals in the sample display healed or healing trauma on the lower leg or foot. The two females exhibit fractures of the arm or the ribs. The individual of indeterminate sex is the one adult in the sample with no evidence of skeletal trauma. It is possible that the concentration of leg and foot trauma among males is related to habitual or occasional activities that put males at greater risk of accidental leg and foot injury. The instances of foot trauma, in particular, exhibit characteristics of fatigue fractures, most commonly manifested in the metatarsals and caused by repeated prolonged walking (Adams and Hamblen 1992:13).

The incidence of adult skeletal trauma in the Millington sample is much higher than in samples from surrounding regions (Marks et al. 1985; Reinhard et al. 1989; Steele and Powell 1989), although the prevalence of accidental trauma is similar to Lower Pecos populations. This is likely a combination of factors including differences in subsistence strategy and extent of sedentism, gendered activity patterns, and localized environmental conditions.

Cranial Porosity

Cranial porosity, particularly when present in bilaterally symmetrical patterns on the parietals and occipital, has been attributed to iron deficiency anemia in childhood. This condition is designated porotic hyperostosis, and may be accompanied by thinning of the cranial bone and expansion of the diploe. Cribra orbitalia, defined as porosity on the orbital roofs, is also taken as an indicator of anemia. It is, however, not present on the individuals in this sample.

The specific attribution of cranial porosity to iron deficiency anemia, as opposed to other combinations of nutritional disorder, parasitic infestation and/or infection, is not considered certain in the absence of diploic changes (Ortner and Eriksen 1997; Ortner et al. 1999; Rothschild 2002). Therefore, porotic hyperostosis is taken in this analysis to be a nonspecific indicator of nutritional stress, perhaps complicated by infection. The presence of such nutritional stress is often the result of a complex interaction between diet, seasonal availability, disease, and parasite load. While coprolite studies have shown that parasite load is very low in the West Texas

region (Sobolik 1994:256), diet and disease patterns are potential contributors to manifestations of cranial porosity.

Four adults, one adolescent, and three subadults in the combined Millington sample could be observed for cranial porosity. All adults, consisting of two females and two males, show slight healed cranial porosity in the typical bilateral pattern that indicates nutritional stress. The adolescent cranium shows the same healed porosity. A subadult of six months +/- three months, Burial 5 from the 1938–1939 excavations, shows active cranial porosity. Two subadults of approximately five years of age, Burials 7 and 9 from the 1938–1939 excavations, are the only individuals in the sample who show no cranial porosity. The incidence in the Millington sample is thus 75 percent, much higher than hunter-gatherer samples from adjacent regions (Marks et al. 1985; Reinhard et al.1989: Table 21) and more typical of maize agricultural populations. The absence of differences in the incidence of cranial porosity by sex and the frequency of this disorder within the Millington sample suggest that nutritional stress was widespread during childhood. The consistent bilateral patterning of the porosity and the healed state in adolescent and adult individuals further suggest that cranial porosity in this sample may be specifically indicative of childhood anemia.

Nonspecific Infection

Nonspecific infection is indicated by the presence of periostosis or osteomyelitis, the result of chronic infectious response. Periostosis, the result of inflammation of the periosteum, is characterized by irregular bone deposition. When active, woven bone is deposited over the existing cortex, which is then remodeled during the healing process through the deposition of lamellar bone. The condition is defined as osteomyelitis when the infectious response is also present in the medullary cavity of the bone, often accompanied by cloacae. Periostosis and osteomyelitis may be localized or may be distributed across several skeletal elements, indicating a systemic infection. The most common locations for evidence of non-specific infections are the tibiae, fibulae, cranium, and humerus (Ortner and Putschar 1981).The presence of periostosis or osteomyelitis on the bones indicates a subacute chronic infection, often not a direct cause of death. Acute infections will result in death of the host without accompanying bony response. Thus, nonspecific infection on the skeleton reflects a chronic condition, impacting the health of the individual but also indicating the individual enjoyed sufficient health to not be overcome by the infection.

Evidence of infection is described in the analysis of this sample by the nature of bony deposition, location of pathological bony response, and degree of healing. For long bone diaphyses, the segment of the diaphysis on which the infection is located has been carefully noted, in order to facilitate discussion of bilateral symmetry. Systemic infections often manifest in bilaterally symmetrical patterns. An infectious response is only considered bilaterally symmetrical in this analysis if it is present on the same segment of the diaphysis of both left and right sides of the same skeletal element.

The sample of individuals from Millington on which infection is observable includes six adults and two subadults. The incidence of infection on this sample is 88 percent, with only a single subadult individual lacking evidence of infection. This incidence is much higher than samples from adjacent regions (Marks et al. 1985; Reinhard et al. 1989). All adult individuals evidence some form of infection, healed or in the advanced stages of healing in all but one case. Most infections manifested on the adult individuals are slight, with 33 percent of adults showing moderate

severity of infection. Two individuals each are affected by infection on the bones of the arm or leg, and one individual each shows infection on the ribs and in the maxillary sinus. The slight rib infection is the only adult infection with portions active at time of death. Since all adult individuals from Millington manifest nonspecific infection, this sample is not appropriate for exploring sex differences in the incidence of infection. It is interesting to note, however, that the males in this sample show infection on the common sites of the arm and leg diaphyses, while infection in females is on the maxillary sinus and the ribs, locations which may have a more specific and less systemic originating cause.

The subadult evidencing nonspecific infection was recovered from Burial 5 of the 1938–1939 excavations, and was approximately six months of age at time of death. This is the most pronounced infection in the sample, bilaterally and systemically affecting the diaphyses of the arms and legs, active at time of death. One other adult evidences bilaterally symmetrical infection patterns, which tend to indicate a systemic infection. A total of five individuals in the sample are observable for bilateral symmetry, yielding an incidence of 40 percent bilaterality. Bilateral symmetry is not correlated with severity of infection.

Developmental Enamel Defects

Enamel defects indicate insults to health during development of the teeth, and are classified as nonspecific stress indicators. A variety of factors may cause developmental defects of the enamel, including malnutrition or undernutrition, infectious disease, and metabolic disorders (Goodman and Armelagos 1985:479–480). A disruption in formation of enamel matrix causes hypoplasias, and disruption of the mineralization process causes hypocalcification. Hypoplasias can be single pits, nonlinear or linear series of pits, or linear grooves on the tooth crown. Hypocalcifications are opacities that can be white, yellow, or brown, and are characterized by either diffuse or discrete boundaries. Linear enamel hypoplasias can be correlated with approximate age of formation based on their location on the tooth crown, and as such have been extensively used in studies of the timing of childhood stress in a given population.

To construct incidence of developmental enamel defects, scores have been compiled by tooth group, both because individuals in this sample are not represented by complete dentitions and because the susceptibility to defects varies by tooth. The anterior teeth are most susceptible, followed by premolars and then molars (Goodman and Armelagos 1985:480). The location of linear enamel hypoplasias has been correlated with an approximate age based on the methodology of Reid and Dean (2000).

Seven individuals in this sample have permanent dentition observable for developmental enamel defects. Six individuals can be examined for hypoplastic defects, and six for hypocalcifications. Of these, four individuals (67 percent) have hypoplastic defects and two individuals (33 percent) have hypocalcifications. One individual, an adult of indeterminate sex recovered from Burial 6 of the 1938–1939 excavations, has only a series of hypoplastic pits on the maxillary canine, lacking linear enamel hypoplasias. All other individuals with hypoplastic defects show at least multiple linear enamel hypoplasias on a single tooth, and most have defects on more than one tooth. Two individuals display a single banded brown hypocalcification each.

When quantified by tooth group, the enamel defects in this sample follow the typical pattern of primarily affecting the anterior dentition (Table 28). With the exception of one mandibular premolar with a hypocalcification, all defects in the sample are present on the maxillary and mandibular incisors and canines. All hypoplastic defects are confined to the anterior teeth. Due to the small sample size for each tooth group, relative incidences among tooth groups are not considered representative.

Linear enamel hypoplasias occur more frequently on teeth than hypoplastic pitting or hypocalcification (Table 29). In all but one case, each tooth displays multiple linear enamel hypoplasias, indicating multiple stress episodes during childhood. These stress episodes occur in this sample between the ages of two and five years, when children in most populations are susceptible to a variety of stresses due to environmental factors and weaning stress. Among the three individuals in the sample with linear enamel hypoplasias, Burial 4 shows only two stress episodes, at the approximate ages of 4.2 years and 4.9 years. The female recovered from Burial 3 during the 1938–1939 excavations shows three stress episodes, at the same ages as Burial 4 and additionally around 2.9 years of age. The most severely affected individual in the sample is the subadult recovered from Burial 9 of the 1938–1939 excavations, with linear enamel hypoplasias indicating six to seven stress episodes between the approximate ages of 2.3 years and 4.6 years.

Four enamel defects are present on the deciduous dentition (Table 30), all appearing on the dentition of the subadult recovered from Burial 9 of the 1938–1939 excavations, approximately five years old at time of death. All four of these defects are diffuse brown hypocalcifications.

While comparison of the incidence of dental enamel defects is inhibited by the lack of consistency in scoring and reporting methodologies, it appears that the Millington sample may have a lower incidence of all forms of defects than other samples from West Texas. The incidence of linear enamel hypoplasia in a compiled Lower Pecos sample is 86 per-

Table 28: Incidence of Dental Enamel Defects in the Permanent Dentition

Tooth	Observable Sample	Number Affected
M^3	2	0
M^2	4	0
M^1	3	0
P^4	4	0
P^3	4	0
C	4	1 (25%)
I^2	5	2 (40%)
I^1	4	2 (50%)
Max. P	1	0
Max. M	1	0
I_1	3	2 (67%)
I_2	6	3 (50%)
C	4	3 (75%)
P_3	5	0
P_4	4	0
M_1	7	0
M_2	4	0
M_3	4	0
Mand. I	1	0
Mand. P	4	1 (25%)
Anterior Tooth	1	0

Table 29: Incidence of Dental Enamel Defects by Defect Group

Tooth	Observable Sample	Hypoplastic Pitting	Linear Enamel Hypoplasia	Hypocalcification
Max. C	4	1 (25%)	0	0
I^2	5	0	2 (40%)	0
I^1	4	1 (25%)	0	1 (25%)
I_1	3	0	2 (67%)	0
I_2	6	1 (17%)	2 (33%)	0
Mand. C	4	1 (25%)	3 (75%)	0
Mand. P	12	0	0	1 (8%)

Table 30: Incidence of Dental Enamel Defects in the Deciduous Dentition

Tooth	Observable Sample	Number Affected
dm²	0	0
dm¹	0	0
d^c	2	1 (50%)
di²	0	0
di¹	4	0
di$_1$	1	0
di$_2$	2	0
d$_c$	2	1 (50%)
dm$_1$	3	1 (33%)
dm$_2$	3	1 (33%)

cent (Reinhard et al. 1989:Table 21), higher than the Millington sample. The sample from Seminole Sink, in contrast, shows a lower incidence of linear enamel hypoplasia, but over a slightly different age span, from three to six years of age (Marks et al. 1985). The significance of these differences among samples may only be elucidated with the compilation of a larger pithouse village sample.

Caries and Antemortem Tooth Loss

Dental caries is the manifestation of a disease process caused by bacterial development on tooth surfaces (Duray 1992:308). The hard tissues of the dentition are compromised by acids produced by bacterial processing of food components, particularly carbohydrates (Larsen 1987:375). While the development and incidence of caries has been associated with the sticky carbohydrates typically consumed by agricultural populations, a complex set of factors contributes to the development of caries. Dietary components, particularly refined carbohydrates, are essential factors (Larsen et al. 1991:179), but cultural factors such as food preparation methods and use of the teeth for activities unrelated to food con-

sumption, and dental factors such as crown morphology, spacing of the dentition in the arch, and developmental enamel defects are also important contributors. The posterior teeth of individuals who consume highly processed sticky carbohydrates as a dietary staple are the most susceptible to caries development. The involvement of the root may lead to abscess, or expansion of the infection into the alveolum, resulting in pathological reaction of the bone and sometimes resulting in antemortem loss of the affected tooth. In the Trans-Pecos region, the reliance on desert succulents is an important factor leading to typically high caries and antemortem loss rates, regardless of the contribution of maize agriculture to the subsistence economy.

Mineralized plaque deposits, or calculus, can be related to the infectious process of caries and antemortem tooth loss. Calculus is characterized as supragingival or subgingival. If subgingival, or below the gum line, calculus on archaeological dentition can indicate periodontal disease, which involves pathological resorption of the alveolum and contributes to antemortem loss. Periodontal resorption can also be the result of advanced age of an individual, so the entire complex of related dental pathologies must be assessed in diagnosing periodontal disease.

Calculus and carious lesions are scored for each observable tooth in the Millington sample, noting the location on the tooth. The incidence of caries is calculated by tooth group. While several calibration procedures are available to control for the effects of antemortem and postmortem tooth loss on caries frequencies (Duyar and Erdal 2003; Erdal and Duyar 1999; Lukacs 1995), these calculations are not meaningful on a small sample, especially given the lack of agreement among procedures on the treatment of teeth lost antemortem versus those lost postmortem. In this analysis, only teeth with sufficient crown present or those that can be observed as lost antemortem are scored, and there is no attempt to compensate for the postmortem loss of dentition.

Carious lesions are absent on both the deciduous and permanent dentition of subadults, and also absent on the dentition of the adolescent individual recovered from Burial 1. The subadults lack calculus, while the adolescent shows slight calculus deposits.

Three adults in this sample of five observable individuals exhibit carious lesions, indicating an incidence by individual of 60 percent. Each individual with caries has lesions on two observable teeth. Incidence calculated by total number of observable teeth is 10.5 percent, a high frequency typical of agricultural populations (Larsen 1987) and due primarily to desert succulent processing and consumption patterns. There are no sex differences in the presence or location of carious lesions in this sample. It is more meaningful to examine caries incidence by tooth group, due to differential susceptibility among groups. This data is presented in Tables 31 and 32. No anterior teeth in this sample have carious lesions. Six percent of premolars and 28 percent of molars show carious lesions. All caries in this sample are interproximal rather than occlusal, due both to rapid attrition and to the prevalence of sticky carbohydrates in the diet.

Calculus is present in slight to moderate expressions in all seven observable adults within the sample. There is no direct correlation of calculus with carious teeth or individ-

Table 31: Incidence of Caries on Permanent Dentition by Tooth Group

Tooth Group	Observable Sample	Number Affected
Maxillary Incisors	7	0
Mandibular Incisors	6	0
Incisors Total	13	0
Maxillary Canines	4	0
Mandibular Canines	3	0
Canines Total	7	0
Maxillary Premolars	9	1 (11%)
Mandibular Premolars	9	0
Premolars Total	18	1 (6%)
Maxillary Molars	8	3 (38%)
Mandibular Molars	10	2 (20%)
Molars Total	18	5 (28%)

Table 32: Incidence of Caries on Permanent Dentition by Tooth

Tooth	Observable Sample	Number Affected	Location
M³	1	0	
M²	3	1 (33%)	distal CEJ
M¹	3	1 (33%)	distal CEJ
P⁴	4	0	
P³	4	1 (25%)	mesial CEJ
C	4	0	
I²	3	0	
I¹	4	0	
Max. P	1	0	
Max. M	1	1 (100%)	interproximal
I$_1$	1	0	
I$_2$	4	0	
C	3	0	
P$_3$	2	0	
P$_4$	3	0	
M$_1$	3	1 (33%)	distal CEJ
M$_2$	4	1 (25%)	mesial CEJ
M$_3$	3	0	
Mand. I	1	0	
Mand. P	4	0	
Anterior Tooth	1	0	

CEJ=cervicoenamel junction.

uals with caries. Two individuals of five observable show calculus deposition low on the roots, indicating periodontal disease. Both of these dentitions are characterized by moderate calculus deposition, while the majority of dentitions lacking evidence of periodontal disease have slight deposition of calculus.

Antemortem tooth loss can only be evaluated for two adult females in this sample. In one of these individuals loss is severe, while in the other it is absent. The individual exhibiting extensive antemortem loss has been estimated to have been 45–55 years of age at death, 10 years older than the indi-

vidual with no antemortem loss. While this sample is too small to evaluate whether age is a factor in antemortem loss, other Trans-Pecos and Lower Pecos samples (Hartnady 1988; Marks et al. 1985; Steele and Powell 1989) show high frequencies of loss at earlier adult ages.

The male recovered from Burial 4, with moderate calculus deposition, periodontal disease, and two carious lesions, also has the only abscess observed in this sample, at the mandibular left second molar. This individual could not be evaluated for antemortem tooth loss. Three adults and one adolescent were observable for abscessing, yielding an incidence of 25 percent for individuals with abscesses in this sample. The nature of the Millington sample prevents the investigation of any correlations between caries frequency and antemortem tooth loss among individuals, as each adult individual in the sample tends, for reasons of preservation, to not be observable for at least one of these factors.

Stable Isotope Analysis

Stable isotope analysis of bone apatite and collagen was conducted at Geochron Laboratories on samples from six individuals interred at Millington. These analyses yielded signatures of carbon and nitrogen isotopes, which reflect diet over the last years of an individual's life. Results of stable carbon analysis indicate the relative dietary contributions of C_3 (trees and temperate grasses), C_4 (maize and amaranth), and CAM (many desert succulents) plants, all of which are readily available in the La Junta district. CAM plants, including desert succulents, vary in photosynthetic mode, with factors such as elevation, temperature and water availability affecting whether $\delta^{13}C$ values are more similar to C_3 or C_4 plants. CAM plants in the Big Bend region have been shown to be most similar to the C_4 pathway (Eickmeier and Bender 1976).

The carbon signatures on bone collagen and apatite yield different $\delta^{13}C$ values based on the differential incorporation of nutrients in each component. Bone collagen preferentially reflects the protein component of the diet. Animal protein, which contains all of the indispensable amino acids, contributes more to collagen than plant protein (Schwarcz 2000), meaning that low-protein plant foods, such as maize and desert succulents, are under-represented in collagen $\delta^{13}C$ values. Bone apatite more closely reflects total diet, although this process is neither total nor constant, given some uncertainty regard-

ing the fractionation of carbonates (Schwarcz 2000, 2006). Nevertheless, when collagen is taken as preferentially reflecting protein and apatite as more closely reflecting total diet, the comparison of the two $\delta^{13}C$ values provides complementary information regarding paleodiet.

The analysis of nitrogen isotopes on bone collagen provides a measure of the animal protein component of the diet. $\delta^{15}N$ values reflect the contribution of terrestrial, riverine, and marine animal proteins, as well as that of nitrogen-fixing plants such as legumes.

The sample for which isotopic analysis was possible includes three individuals from the 2006 excavations by the Center for Big Bend Studies, and three individuals from the 1937–1939 excavations under the direction of J. Charles Kelley (Table 33). Three of these individuals are adult males, two are adult females, and one is an adult of indeterminate sex. The bone collagen samples from Burials 7 and 8 yielded little collagen due to preservational factors, necessitating additional laboratory procedures and resulting in the possibly diminished reliability of these results.

The average $\delta^{13}C$ collagen value for the Millington sample is -16.7 ‰, and that of apatite is -7.9 ‰. These values fall well outside of the ranges of horticulturalists and agriculturalists focusing on maize, and also outside of groups relying on CAM plant staples. They are more congruent with mobile foraging populations incorporating a significant amount of C_3 plants such as wild grasses and tree nuts into the diet. The Millington average $\delta^{15}N$ value, omitting the unrealistically inflated outlying result of Burial 8, is 6.6 ‰. This indicates that nearly all of the animal protein in the diets of these individuals derived from terrestrial animals, and that riverine resources were only minimally exploited.

Table 33: Stable Isotope Values for Individuals Interred at Millington

Project	Individual	Sex	Date	δ13C collagen	δ13C apatite	δ15N collagen
CBBS	Burial 2	M	Late Prehistoric	-15.6	-7.6	8.2
CBBS	Burial 4	M	Late Prehistoric	-15.9	-7.6	5.5
CBBS	Burial 5	F	Late Prehistoric	-17	-8.9	7.4
Kelley	Burial 3	F	Late Prehistoric	-16.9	-8.0	7.6
Kelley	Burial 7	M	Late Prehistoric	-18.2	-6.9	4.3
Kelley	Burial 8	I	Late Prehistoric	-16.8	-8.1	17.3

The results of the stable isotope analysis of these six individuals from Millington deviate from those expected for a semi-sedentary population practicing agriculture. These values indicate a mixed diet with a greater contribution from C_3 plants than mobile groups of the eastern Trans-Pecos (Piehl in press), and greater terrestrial meat consumption than Late Archaic mobile groups in the region. The La Junta village results indicate that maize provided less than 25 percent contribution to the diet. This is in contrast to assumptions that have been based on archaeological, settlement pattern, and historic data that posit a significant degree of maize agriculture in La Junta village settings. The $\delta^{13}C$ collagen values for the La Junta village occupants lie closer to Archaic populations outside of the eastern Trans-Pecos or Lower Pecos regions, rather than incipient agriculturalists or those relying on maize agriculture. These combined data indicate a dietary pattern significantly different from that expected for the La Junta villagers, and suggest greater complexity in subsistence strategies. Neither maize nor desert succulents were dietary staples for these individuals, nor were they heavily exploiting nearby riverine resources. Historic accounts that mention maize agriculture, but also the frequent failure of agricultural efforts to provide substantial harvests (Kenmotsu 1994), suggest that occupants of the La Junta villages, while familiar with maize agriculture, did not consider it of primary importance in their subsistence regime and practiced opportunistic cultivation, reliant on floodwaters, that frequently failed.

Mortuary Practices

Mortuary practices provide information about cultural traditions and rituals, stratification and community organization, social inequality, and cultural origins. The sample of interments from Millington with known details of mortuary context (n=16) fits well with patterns observed for the La Junta district in general, not surprising considering that the Millington sample is the largest from any site in the district.

Pit interment is the most common form of burial at Millington in the La Junta phase, utilized for individuals of both sexes and all ages in the sample. Of the 16 interments discussed here, the only alternative form of burial is inclusion within a midden, of which two examples are currently known. These are Burial 3 of the 2006 excavations, and Kelley's Burial 7, containing an adult male and a child. All other interments for which grave type could be determined are pits, located in most determinable instances beneath or intruding into structural floors.

Marking stones or loose cobble cairns were found at the top of the pits in four interments, those of two males, one female, and one adolescent (CBBS Burials 1, 2, and 5 and Kelley's Burial 1). Burials 1 and 2 of the 2006 excavations included small pit defining stones on the western top border of the interment, a departure from the more recognizable practice of covering the interred with cobbles. The use of small marking stones is a practice documented at Millington during excavations by the CBBS that was previously unknown in the region.

All individuals for whom we have data (n=12) were placed in the pits in a flexed position. Most of these individuals were supine, with the exception of two adult males interred on their sides. A strong preference is shown for orientation of individuals with heads in the northern or southern quadrants of the interments, with one adolescent and one adult male oriented with heads to the west. Where sex has been determined on adult individuals, all males were interred with heads in the northern quadrant and all females were placed with heads in the southern quadrant. This is a previously unrecognized gendered mortuary pattern at Millington, which is consistent with other gendered patterns of mortuary ritual throughout the eastern Trans-Pecos (Piehl in press). None of the 16 Millington interments contain associated artifacts or other items that could be interpreted as mortuary goods.

The patterning present in mortuary practices at Millington shows strong cultural traditions, which dictated grave type and location, and position and orientation of individuals. The lack of associated goods and the use of gender as a primary factor of mortuary differentiation confirm archaeological and historical evidence of the relative lack of social stratification in this community, and ties with preceding and contemporary mobile cultural groups.

Conclusion

The Millington mortuary sample departs in many ways from expectations for the occupants of this La Junta district village. Hypotheses treating the degree of sedentism, diet and lifeway, and both diachronic and synchronic connections with other Trans-Pecos groups are all challenged by the results of the analyses reported in this chapter.

The combination of health and disease patterns with the dietary results obtained from stable isotope analysis make it clear that the Millington population was reliant on neither maize agriculture nor desert succulents. While there is archaeological and historic evidence that these practices took place, research to date has not approached the question of relative importance of these activities at Millington. Isotopic signatures and patterns of dental caries and antemortem loss differ substantially from results expected for significant dietary contribution of maize, succulents, or both. Dental enamel defects, cranial porosity, and nonspecific infection indicate both acute and chronic insults to health in childhood and adulthood at Millington. While these pathologies are nonspecific and by definition unattributable to a specific cause, malnutrition or undernutrition are undoubtedly major contributors to disease patterns in this group. More research is necessary before we will be able to comment on whether these patterns are due to episodes of food scarcity, perhaps during droughts, consistent nutritional inadequacies in the preferred diet, and/or other environmental factors that compromise buffering to health.

The settlement pattern and architectural data clearly indicate that Millington functioned as an aggregated village. In addition to the above-mentioned factors that rule out maize agriculture as the primary subsistence regime, however, there are a number of other lines of evidence in the human remains that contradict assumptions of sedentism. Patterns of arthritis and trauma, high in all adults and concentrated in the lower extremities of males, suggest high mobility across the rugged terrain of the eastern Trans-Pecos, particularly by males. This mobility pattern, which likely brought Millington occupants in contact with other cultural groups, may also in part explain the high levels of infection among Millington individuals. The village of Millington seems to have functioned more as a central gathering area, where groups of individuals based themselves while continuing to incorporate foraging and long-distance travel into their lives.

MATERIAL CULTURE

A total of 2,745 artifacts were recovered during the 2006 investigation at the Millington site. These consist of both materials from the surface (n=314) and cultural residue recovered during excavations at the site (n=2,431). All of the surface materials were provenienced with the TDS with the exception of six lithic material samples.

Materials Recovered from the Subsurface

A total of 2,431 artifacts were recovered from subsurface contexts during the investigation. These specimens consist of 32 bifaces, 4 unifaces, 115 pieces of edge-modified debitage, 2,020 pieces of unmodified debitage, 130 ceramic sherds, 110 glass specimens, and 20 metal items. Excluding radiocarbon and faunal samples, a total of 118 other materials were collected from the subsurface. Although some of these are technically not material culture, they are briefly described at the end of this section. Faunal materials are presented in Appendix II.

Bifaces

Specimens with any degree of workmanship on both faces are termed "bifaces." Thirty-two specimens recovered from the subsurface meet this definition and have been divid-ed into arrow points (n=21) and other bifaces (n=11).

Arrow Points

A total of 21 arrow points and arrow point fragments were recovered from the subsurface during the 2006 investigation at the Millington site (Figure 33; Table 34). Five are complete or almost complete. The arrow points consist of three Toyah (Figure 33a–c), three Toyah-like (Figure 33 d–f), four Fresno (Figure 33g–j), one Sabinal-like (Figure 33k), one Washita-like (Figure 33l), six untyped (Figure 33m–r), and three distal blade fragments (Figure 33s–u).

All three of the Toyah points are essentially complete, while the three Toyah-like points are fragmentary or unusual enough to preclude confident assignment within the

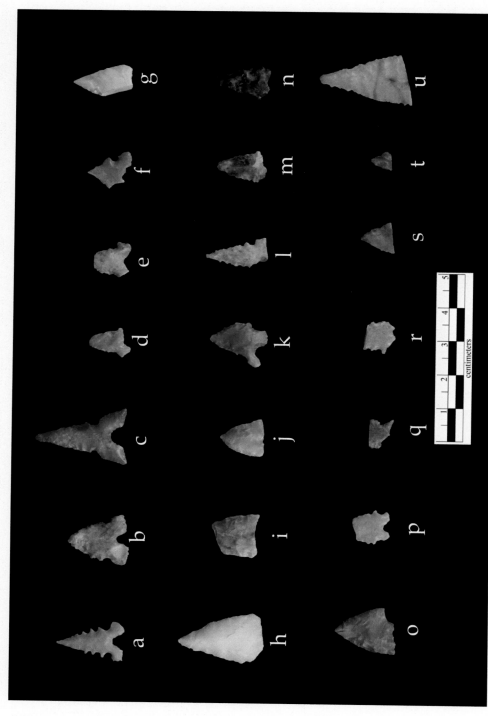

Figure 33. Arrow points recovered from the subsurface: (a–c) Toyah, (d–f) Toyah-like, (g–j) Fresno, (k) Sabinal-like, (l) Washita-like, (m–r) untyped, (s–u) distal fragments.

Table 34: Arrow Points – Subsurface

Lot #	Provenience	Level #	Elevation (m)	Type	Length (mm)	Max. Width (mm)	Max. Thick. (mm)	Neck Width (mm)	Basal Edge Width (mm)	Wt. (g)	Material	Description
3	Test Unit 1	3	99.60–.50	—	—	—	1.3	—	—	0.1	light grayish brown chert	Small distal blade fragment; relatively thin with odd cross section—plano-convex cross section on one edge and lenticular cross section on the other; alternately beveled on right edge of both faces; remnants of original flake facets on both faces (Figure 33s).
3	Test Unit 1	3	99.60–.50	—	—	9.2	2.5	5.6	—	0.3	variegated off-white/clear agate	Small, crude arrow point fragment; missing stem; blade-like arris on original dorsal face; small right angle barbs (Livermore-like, but much shorter); one barb intact, other broken; most workmanship confined to edges of both faces; convex blade edges; plano-convex in cross section; remnants of original flake facets on both faces (Figure 33m).
5	Test Unit 1	3–4 (wall clean-up)	99.60–.40	—	16.8	9.8	2.4	7.4	7.9	0.4	variegated pink/dark green moss agate	Complete, small stemmed arrow point; only missing tiny piece of blade tip; crude workmanship; short broad concave stem; side notched, but notches very shallow; plano-convex cross section; recurved blade edges; asymmetrical appearance; one right angle barb; the other edge is weakly shouldered; blade tip angles off to one side; remnants of original flake facets on both faces (Fig. 33n).
7	Test Unit 1	5	99.40–.30	Toyah-like	12.3	—	1.4	—	—	0.2	tan chert	Fragmentary triple notched arrow point; missing most of one notch and adjacent basal ear; crudely worked along most of edges of both faces; shallow intact notch; broad U-shaped basal notch; small triangular blade with concave edges beveled on right edge of both faces; intact basal ear pointed and angled down and outward; irregular lenticular cross section; remnants of original flake facets on majority of both faces (Figure 33f).

Table 34

Lot #	Provenience	Level #	Elevation (m)	Type	Length (mm)	Max. Width (mm)	Max. Thick. (mm)	Neck Width (mm)	Basal Edge Width (mm)	Wt. (g)	Material	Description
7-1	Test Unit 1	5	99.40	—	—	—	2.3	2.3	—	0.6	tan chert	Fragmentary triangular arrow point; missing lower portion of one blade corner and portion of what appears to have been a small, short stem; convex blade edges, although one only slightly; asymmetrical; plano-convex cross section; remnants of original flake facets on both faces (Figure 33o).
19	Test Unit 4	1	99.20-.10	Toyah-like	—	—	2.7	7.6	—	0.3	light gray chert	Fragmentary tripled notched arrow point; missing blade tip and portion of one basal ear; good workmanship; shallow side notches and broad V-shaped basal notch; moderately straight and slightly serrated blade edges; arrises extend down basal ears on both faces; lenticular cross section; due to size, blade may be reworked; remnants of original flake facet on one face (Figure 33e).
20-5	Test Unit 4	2	99.09	Sabinal-like	16.5	—	3.1	6.0	4.4	0.5	variegated brown chert	Fragmentary stemmed arrow point; missing one barb and tiny piece of distal blade; crudely worked on the edges of both faces, but minimal workmanship on stem; intact barb angles down and outward; stem contracts slightly; slightly convex base; wedge-shaped base in cross section; overall cross section varies from lenticular to plano-convex; blade edges slightly convex to straight; basally notched; large remnants of original flake facets on both faces (Figure 33k).

Table 34

Lot #	Provenience	Level #	Elevation (m)	Type	Length (mm)	Max. Width (mm)	Max. Thick. (mm)	Neck Width (mm)	Basal Edge Width (mm)	Wt. (g)	Material	Description
24	Test Unit 5	2	99.70–.60	Toyah	19.5	11.8	2.2	6.8	11.8	0.3	off-white/clear chalcedony	Complete triple notched arrow point; excellent workmanship; deep U-shaped basal notch and side notches of medium depth; blade edges strongly serrated, but otherwise straight; basal ears somewhat squared with boot shape; one ear is slightly larger and shaped somewhat differently resulting in slight asymmetry; lenticular cross section; blade tip sharply pointed; only tiny remnant of original flake facet on one face (Figure 33a).
24	Test Unit 5	2	99.70–.60	Toyah-like	—	—	1.9	6.4	—	0.2	light brown/tan chert	Small fragmentary arrow point; missing one basal ear and a portion of the other ear; blade tip rounded and reworked after impact fracture; very shallow, almost imperceptible side notches; basal notch broadly V-shaped; blade edges straight to very slightly convex; basal ears flair down and outward; lenticular cross section; crudely made with remnants of original flake facets on both faces (Figure 33d).
33	Test Unit 5	4	99.50–.40	—	—	—	1.8	—	—	0.1	light pink/clear chalcedony	Very small probable arrow point blade tip; relatively thin; plano-convex cross section; blade edges slightly recurved; alternately beveled on right edge of both faces; remnant of original flake scar on one face (Figure 33t).
36	Test Unit 6	1	99.79–.70	Toyah	17.1	14.8	2.5	10.1	14.8	0.5	variegated pink/gray chert	Complete; relatively well made and symmetrical, although blade and base slightly off-center; triple-notched with shallow side notches and deep, U-shaped basal notch; one blade edge slightly serrated; blade edges slightly convex; squared basal ears; lenticular cross section; remnants of original flake facets on both faces; burned (Figure 33b).

Table 34

Lot #	Provenience	Level #	Elevation (m)	Type	Length (mm)	Max. Width (mm)	Max. Thick. (mm)	Neck Width (mm)	Basal Edge Width (mm)	Wt. (g)	Material	Description
51	Test Unit 6; F-6	4	99.50–.40	Fresno	17.1	—	2.6	n/a	—	0.4	off-white chert	Fragmentary triangular arrow point; missing small portion of one basal corner, all of other corner, and portion of attached edge; crude workmanship—base possibly reworked; pointed blade tip; plano-convex cross section; relatively straight blade edges; remnants of original flake facets on both faces (Figure 33g).
64	Test Unit 6	7	99.20–.10	Washita-like	17.7	—	2.0	5.8	—	0.2	light pink chalcedony	Small side-notched arrow point; missing one basal corner; side notches of medium depth (ca. 1.4 mm); blade edges straight to slightly convex and slightly to moderately serrated; slightly concave base; plano-convex cross section; blade tip beveled on right edge of both faces; remnants of original flake facets on both faces (Figure 33).
64–4	Test Unit 6	7	99.14	Fresno	24.3	14.4	4.0	n/a	9.9	1.4	off-white chalcedony	Complete triangular arrow point; rounded basal corners; asymmetrical base with corners shaped differently; one blade edge straight, the other slightly convex; lenticular cross section; base straight and wedge-shaped in cross section; good workmanship; blade tip pointed and beveled on right edge of both faces; one face beveled on most of both edges; small remnants of original flake facets on both faces (Figure 33h).
79–2	Test Unit 6	11	98.79	Fresno	—	13.1	2.6	n/a	13.1	0.6	variegated brownish gray chert	Fragmentary triangular arrow point; missing distal portion of blade; asymmetrical appearance with one basal corner sharply pointed and the other rounded; concave base; one blade edge recurved, the other straight; plano-convex cross section; remnants of original flake facets on both faces (Figure 33i).

Material Culture   119

Table 34

Lot #	Provenience	Level #	Elevation (m)	Type	Length (mm)	Max. Width (mm)	Max. Thick. (mm)	Neck Width (mm)	Basal Edge Width (mm)	Wt. (g)	Material	Description
81	Test Unit 7; E wall profile	—	99.78–.17	Fresno	12.7	11.2	2.4	n/a	11.2	0.4	brownish tan chert	Complete triangular arrow point; appears to be a reworked distal fragment as basal edge is sinuous in cross section and crudely formed; recurved base; slight asymmetry with one basal corner pointed and the other slightly rounded; one blade edge convex, the other recurved; blade tip pointed; plano-convex to lenticular cross section; remnants of original flake facets on both faces. (Figure 33j)
92	Test Unit 8	3	99.60–.50	Toyah	26.1	16.4	3.3	7.6	16.4	0.9	variegated brown chert	Complete triple-notched arrow point; good workmanship; shallow side notches; deep U-shaped basal notch; large, pointed, and symmetrical basal ears; basal edge generally concave; blade edges relatively straight; lenticular cross section; blade tip alternately beveled on right edge of both faces; blade tip slightly rounded. (Figure 33c)
93	Test Unit 8	4	99.50–.40	probable Perdiz	—	—	2.5	—	—	0.9	light gray/tan chalcedony	Large arrow point blade fragment; missing stem, lower blade, and tiny portion of blade tip; slight serrations along both blade edges; both blade edges recurved; plano-convex cross section; remnants of original flake facets on both faces. (Figure 33u)
100	Test Unit 8; F-14	—	ca. 99.04	—	—	—	1.9	7.6	—	0.2	off-white chert	Fragmentary, very small, triple-notched arrow point; missing distal portion of blade and small portions of both basal ears; very shallow side notches; asymmetrical appearance with different sized and angled basal ears; slight serrations along both blade edges; plano-convex cross section; remnant of original flake facet on one face. (Figure 33p)

Table 34

Lot #	Provenience	Level #	Elevation (m)	Type	Length (mm)	Max. Width (mm)	Max. Thick. (mm)	Neck Width (mm)	Basal Edge Width (mm)	Wt. (g)	Material	Description
100-4	Test Unit 8; F-14	—	99.00	—	—	8.9	1.8	5.2	—	0.1	light pinkish gray chert	Fragmentary, very small arrow point; missing most of blade and one basal ear; expanding stem; corner notched; concave base; weak shoulders; intact basal ear very sharply pointed; good bifacial workmanship; lenticular cross section; tiny remnant of original flake facet on one face (Figure 33q).
117	BHT #1; W wall; F-6	—	no elevation; screening of controlled sediment from feature	—	—	—	2.1	7.8	—	0.2	off-white/tan fossiliferous chert	Fragmentary, small, triple-notched arrow point; missing distal portion of blade and both basal ears; very shallow side notches; slight to moderate serrations along intact blade edge; asymmetrical appearance with larger serration above basal ear on one edge; lenticular cross section; similar to Lot 100 specimen (Figure 33r).

type (Suhm et al. 1954:508; Suhm and Jelks 1962:291–292; Turner and Hester 1985:193). One of the Toyah-like specimens was recovered from a lower sheet midden in Test Unit 1 dated to the latter portion of the La Junta phase (A.D. 1290–1410). Although relatively few radiocarbon dates have been secured for Toyah points in the region, all indicate a ca. A.D. 1200–1400 time period of use (Cloud et al. 1994:125; Corrick 2000:8; Seebach 2007:51). Workmanship on these specimens varies from somewhat crude (i.e., asymmetrical and retaining original flake facets on one or both faces) to well made. As mentioned in the background chapter, Kelley (1957) has indicated that crudely manufactured specimens with Toyah shapes are associated with the Bravo Valley aspect, while well-made ones were by-products of the Livermore culture. However, since both varieties have been recovered from other La Junta sites (see Shackelford 1951, 1955 and Cloud et al. 1994) as well as from this investigation, additional efforts will be needed to sort out this interpretive issue.

Two of the four Fresno points are complete, although one of these is a reworked distal blade fragment. Three were recovered from F-5 (unknown structure), one of these from near the suspected floor of this late La Junta phase (A.D. 1290–1410) pit structure. These specimens have triangular shapes with concave and straight basal edges, straight, convex, and recurved blade edges, and pointed and rounded basal corners. These attributes suggest the primary distinction of this point is the triangular shape. Fresno points are, perhaps, one of the most poorly defined arrow points (Suhm et al. 1954:498; Suhm and Jelks 1962:273–274; Turner and Hester 1985:174). Triangular arrow points in a variety of sizes and shapes are widespread across the state and are found in adjacent regions as well, seemingly associated with a plethora of Late Prehistoric cultures. Although Fresno

points have been reported from La Junta sites (e.g., Shackelford 1951, Kelley 1957), much work remains to be done to understand regional variants of this type.

The Sabinal-like arrow point is missing one barb, but is sufficiently intact for this classification (Turner and Hester 1985:188). It was recovered from an undated midden-like deposit. Although Sabinal points are reported to be centered in south and southwest Texas, the author has observed points adhering to this type in the Big Bend region. However, this projectile is much smaller and more crudely manufactured than is common for the type and may be a completely unrelated form. Sabinal points are reported to date from ca. A.D. 1120–1250 (Turner and Hester 1985:188), a span which overlaps the earliest portion of the La Junta phase.

The Washita-like arrow point is missing one basal edge, but has intact attributes suggestive of this type (Turner and Hester 1985:195). Like several of the aforementioned arrow points, this specimen was recovered from F-5 structure fill. A characteristic point of the Washita focus of Oklahoma, this type is also commonly found in the Panhandle of Texas and on the Southern Plains. This specimen exhibits attributes uncharacteristic of Washita points—flake remnants on both faces and serrated blade edges—and may represent a crude copy of that type. Washita points appear in the southwestern portion of the Southern Plains by ca. A.D. 1200 during the transition from pit to surface houses (Hughes 1991:29), which coincides with beginning dates for the La Junta phase.

Five of the untyped arrow points are crudely/expediently manufactured, and none of these can be confidently assigned to any existing types. They have various shapes and sizes, and only one is complete. One specimen from Burial 5 fill (F-14) and another from F-6 (Figure 33p and r) are similar and distinct from the others, with attributes of both the Lott and Toyah types, yet are too small or fragmentary for classification within either category. Another specimen (Figure 33q), also from F-14, has a distinctively shaped basal ear reminiscent of those on Lott points, but is much smaller than points of that type. Lott points are concentrated in the western portion of the Southern Plains and date from ca. A.D. 1390–1500 (Turner and Hester 1985:182). Although the Burial 5 specimens appear to be fortuitous additions to the burial pit rather than grave furniture and the F-6 specimen was not recovered in situ, radiocarbon data from both of these features suggest the points date to the La Junta phase and predate the Lott type.

Three arrow point blade fragments were recovered during the investigation. One of these, found within pithouse (F-13) fill (Figure 33u), has several attributes suggestive of the Perdiz type (Suhm et al. 1954:504; Suhm and Jelks 1962:283–284; Turner and Hester 1985:187; Mallouf 1987; Cloud 2002). In the Big Bend, these points have been associated with both the Bravo Valley aspect (Kelley et al. 1940) and Cielo complex (Mallouf 1990, 1993, 1995, 1999), and based on radiocarbon dates from the eastern Trans-Pecos and Central and South Texas, are thought to date from ca. A.D. 1200–1750 (Prewitt 1983; Black 1986; Mallouf 1987).

Other Bifaces

In this analysis "other bifaces" refers to all specimens with workmanship on both faces that are not arrow points. Eleven specimens meet this general definition and four of these, based on presumed function, are classified as a beveled knife fragment, a drill/perforator fragment, a spokeshave, and a bifacial core. The fragmentary nature of the other specimens preclude functional assignments, thus they are classified simply as biface frag-

ments. Data on these specimens are provided in Table 35.

The beveled knife fragment was recovered from sediments removed from BHT #1 and thus only has a very general provenience. Beveled knives have been found in various settings in the Big Bend, including within assemblages of the Bravo Valley aspect (Kelley et al. 1940) and the Cielo complex (Mallouf 1990, 1999). They are widely distributed across the state, where they are frequently found with bison remains. The drill/perforator fragment was recovered from the upper fill of F-5 (unknown structure) dated to the La Junta phase. It is plano-convex in cross section and has only been minimally flaked on one face. It is crudely made and can be classified as an expediency tool. The specimen classified as a spokeshave is a crudely worked biface with two concave scraper bits of a size that suggests having been used to straighten arrow shafts.

Unifaces

Unifaces are defined as formal tools with unifacially shaped edges where most flake characteristics (i.e., platform, termination, etc.) have been removed. Only four specimens recovered from the subsurface are classified as unifaces. Functionally, these consist of two spokeshaves, a drill/perforator, and an end scraper/spokeshave. Data on these specimens is provided in Table 36.

One of the spokeshaves has a very wide (18.3 mm) and exhausted (>90°) bit, and would have been used on much larger pieces of wood than other spokeshaves found at the site. The drill/perforator, recovered from near the floor of F-5 (unknown structure), is an expediency tool exhibiting minimal wear. The end scraper/spokeshave was recovered from F-9 (hearth). The scraper bit is opposite the platform, extensively trimmed, and

Table 35: Other Bifaces from Subsurface

Lot #	Provenience	Level #	Elevation (m)	Max. Width (mm)	Max. Thickness (mm)	Weight (g)	Material	Description
2	Test Unit 1	2	99.70–.60	—	2.4	0.2	grayish tan chert	Small biface fragment; most of workmanship on one face; both ends broken; possible arrow point blade fragment.
2	Test Unit 1	2	99.70–.60	—	2.3	0.1	greenish brown fossiliferous chert	Small biface fragment; most of workmanship on one face; cursorily flaked; original flake remnants on both faces; possible arrow point distal/proximal fragment; unfinished.
48	Test Unit 6	3	99.60–.50	—	7.6	5.4	variegated tan fossiliferous chert	Fragmentary drill/perforator with adjacent spokeshave bit; fashioned protrusion with opposite end broken; small break on protrusion, but intact portion lightly smoothed and polished; spokeshave bit ca. 5.3 mm wide and characterized by step fractures, smoothing, and polish.
64	Test Unit 6	7	99.20–.10	—	3.4	0.9	translucent moss agate	Biface fragment—possibly a blade fragment; midsection; original flake remnants on both faces; one lateral edge bifacially trimmed w/pressure flakes; opposite edge unifacially flaked; use wear on both edges.
68	Test Unit 6	7 (compact soil)	99.20–.10	—	2.0	0.1	tan chert	Very small biface fragment; good bifacial workmanship on rounded protrusion that could have been arrow point shoulder.
80	Test Unit 6	11	99.76–.70	—	4.2	1.3	mottled gray-tan chalcedony	Biface fragment w/cursorily fashioned stem on one end; in early stage of reduction; most bifacial workmanship along one edge; rounded "stem" corners; twisted plano-convex cross section.
83-1	Test Unit 7	2	99.67	27.6	15.9	26.2	tan fossiliferous chert	Bifacial core; most of flake removals from both edges of one face; opposite face mostly cortex and more cursorily flaked; one end broken; depleted.
84	Test Unit 7	3	99.60–.50	—	9.3	2.8	variegated red and gray chert	Small core fragment; most of flake removals from edges on one face; opposite face mostly cortex and more cursorily flaked.
85	Test Unit 7	4	99.50–.40	26.8	11.4	11.8	variegated tan/off-white chert	Biface fragment; one end missing; remnant of original flake facet on one face; unfinished; two spokeshave bits (3.0 mm and 4.6 mm widths) along one edge moderately worn.
93	Test Unit 8	4	99.50–.40	—	4.3	0.7	light reddish brown chert	Biface medial fragment; only small portions of each lateral edge intact; possibly from finished tool, perhaps a knife.
105	BHT #1 (trench sediments)	—		—	6.2	8.0	orangish brown chert	Beveled knife fragment; extensively burned—potlids and crazing on both faces; alternately beveled blade fragment; mid-section—broken on both ends; moderately steep bevels on left edge of both faces; beveled edges worn from use; twisted appearance in cross section.

Table 36: Unifaces from Subsurface

Lot #	Provenience	Level #	Elevation (m)	Length (mm)	Max. Width (mm)	Max. Thickness (mm)	Weight (g)	Material	Description
9	Test Unit 1	7	99.20–.10	49.7	41.4	18.5	34.5	mottled grayish brown rhyolite	Spokeshave; complete; cortical flake fragment; distal end extensively trimmed and used as a large spokeshave; bit is ca. 18.3 mm wide and steep (>90°); exhausted or depleted.
79–1	Test Unit 6	11	98.80	29.2	—	4.9	2.4	reddish brown rhyolite	Drill/perforator; missing one lateral corner, but otherwise complete; plano-convex cross section; convex face cortex except where trimmed along edges; tear-drop shape with pointed end twisted and smoothed from apparent use as drill/perforator.
90–5	Test Unit 8	1	99.71	—	33.3	17.3	26.5	variegated brownish gray chert	Spokeshave; large cortical chip extensively trimmed around edges; one end broken; spokeshave bit formed by one large flake removal; step fractures and smoothed edge within bit from use.
91–1	Test Unit 8; F-11	2	99.68	35.7	42.4	14.8	21.9	purplish brown rhyolite	End scraper/spokeshave; complete; cortical flake fragment; extensively trimmed into scraper bit; bit is 35.9 mm wide and very steep (ca. 90°)—probably exhausted; a spokeshave bit (ca. 7.3 mm wide) occurs on the scraper bit and another (ca. 7.8 mm wide) occurs on a lateral edge—both are characterized by step fractures and worn edges.

exhausted. After the bit became too steep for further use, a portion of the edge was used as a spokeshave. Another like-sized spokeshave bit is on the lateral edge of this specimen.

Debitage

Debitage has been defined by Crabtree (1972:58) as the residual materials that result from lithic tool manufacture. These materials are pieces of stone removed from a larger mass (a core or partially finished tool) through the application of force. A total of 2,135 pieces of debitage were recovered during the Millington investigation. For the purposes of this analysis, debitage is divided into edge-modified and unmodified categories. There are 115 pieces of debitage that have had their edges modified and 2,020 unmodified specimens.

Edge-Modified Debitage

Edge-modified specimens have had one or more edges altered through intentional trimming and/or use. The 115 specimens of edge-modified debitage have 174 edges that have been modified to some extent. Edge alterations, based on the type of modification present, are divided into three categories: trimmed debitage, trimmed and utilized debitage, and utilized debitage. Trimmed pieces of debitage have been minimally chipped to form a working edge or edges, typically on a single face. These items differ from unifaces in that they have not been appreciably altered and show no signs of use. Specimens classified as trimmed and utilized have been minimally chipped to form a working edge or edges on one or more faces and also show signs of use (i.e., small uniform flake scars; rounded, smoothed, or polished edges). Some of these specimens have been used as informal spokeshaves, but the majority were probably used as expediency cutting or scraping tools.

Utilized pieces of debitage exhibit use wear along one or more edges. Unaltered when initially used, specimens in this category were probably used as cutting tools in most cases.

Of the 174 modified edges, 10 are trimmed, 67 are trimmed and utilized, and 97 are utilized. Each modified edge was also classified relative to its shape using the following categories: recurved, straight, convex, and concave. Recurved edges (n=63) are dominant, while the remaining edges are somewhat evenly divided—straight (n=37), concave (n=42), and convex (n=32). Straight, convex, and recurved edges were most likely used for cutting, whereas, concave edges could have been used as spokeshaves or for cutting when the concavity was relatively shallow.

The majority of these specimens were recovered from Test Unit 1 (n=26), Test Unit 6 (n=17), Test Unit 8 (n=32), and from BHT #1 backdirt (n=21). Test Unit 1 lies within several midden or midden-like deposits, the lowest dated to the La Junta phase and the uppermost one, based on 2-sigma possibilities, probably to the latter aboriginal occupations at Millington. Accordingly, the deposits in this unit span much of the overall chronology documented at the site. A cursory inspection of the edge-modified debitage from this unit indicates a general increase in size and in the numbers of expediency scrapers through time. Since the edge-modified debitage from Test Units 6 and 8 are mostly from F-5 (unknown structure) and F-13 (pithouse) fill deposits they provide little information in this regard. Similarly, the specimens recovered from BHT #1 deposits lack provenience and only provide general data on past activities at the site.

When this class of tools is viewed as a whole, it is apparent that cutting is the primary function represented and, in most cases, these items were used sparingly before being discarded. The small and very small size of many of the edge-modified pieces and preponderance of untrimmed edges is also striking, suggesting that simple expediency tools were needed for most tasks rather than formal tools. Even the edges that have been trimmed reveal very little work went into this effort. Additional data concerning these specimens is available upon request from the CBBS.

Unmodified Debitage

Unmodified debitage are lithic residue that do not appear to have been used or altered for use. The 2,020 pieces of unmodified debitage consist of 1,551 specimens large enough to provide meaningful data on chipped stone tool production and 469 pieces of micro-debitage. Specimens that could pass through 1/8-in mesh are considered micro-debitage. The larger specimens are separated into complete flakes, flake fragments, chips, and chunks.

A complete flake has both a platform and bulb of force at its proximal end and at least a fragmentary termination (e.g., feathered edge) at its distal end. Flake fragments have intact proximal ends, but lack terminations. Chips are portions of flakes that lack proximal ends—these specimens may or may not have intact distal ends. Chunks are fragments shattered during the detachment process that lack definable morphology. It is usually impossible to understand how a chunk was detached or what portion of a flake is represented.

Of the 1,551 pieces of debitage analyzed, 262 are classified as complete flakes, 330 as flake fragments, 538 as chips, and 421 as chunks. Each of these specimens is further separated into specimens with and without cortex. Only 35 percent of the analyzed specimens retain cortex. Since this collection was retrieved from a very small portion of the site, these data should be used with caution. A much larger investigation would be needed to attain more meaningful results.

The overwhelming majority of unmodified debitage is of some variety of chert, with agate, rhyolite, and chalcedony also well represented. Less common materials in the collection include mudstone, hornfels, quartzite, indurated sandstone, felsite, jasper, silicified wood, novaculite, opalite, and obsidian. Variation in color, grain-size, inclusions, texture, and density amongst these respective materials, often within the same class, is striking, testament to the complex geology of the area and the abundance of knappable materials within the Rio Grande gravels.

Ceramics

A total of 130 ceramic sherds were recovered from the subsurface (Figure 34). All but eight of these are prehistoric, and the majority of these (n=69) are classified as Plain Brownwares (Figure 34a–c). Other prehistoric categories used in the analysis are El Paso Brownware (n=8) (Figure 34d and e), Polished Plain Brownware (n=9), Polished El Paso Brownware (n=3), El Paso Polychrome (n=20) (Figure 34f–h), Polished Incised Brownware (n=1), Polished Red Slipped Earthenware (n=3) (Figure 34i), Red Slipped Earthenware (n=1) (Figure 34j), Red-on-Brown (n=5) (Figure 34k), White Slipped Earthenware (n=2) (Figure 34l), and Unidentified Polychrome (n=1). Historic categories consist of Black Pb Glaze (n=1) (Figure 34m), Galera Pb Glaze (n=1) (Figure 34n), Guanajuato Green Glaze (n=2) (Figure 34o), Majolica (n=3) (Figure 34p and q), and Soft Paste Porcelain (n=1).

The El Paso brownware tradition began as early as A.D. 200–400 and was remarkably stable until ca. A.D. 1000–1300, when bichrome and polychrome varieties made their appearance (Miller and Kenmotsu 2004:252–253). Recent chronometric dating of El Paso Polychrome associations indicates the type was developed sometime after A.D. 1200 and

Figure 34. Select ceramic sherds recovered from the subsurface: (a–c) Plain Brownware, (d and e) El Paso Brownware, (f–h) El Paso Polychrome, (i) Polished Red Slipped Earthenware, (j) Red Slipped Earthenware, (k) Red-on-Brown, (l) White Slipped Earthenware, (m) Black Pb Glaze, (n) Galera Pb Glaze, (o) Guanajuato Green Glaze, Majolica (p, q).

persisted until ca. A.D. 1450 (Miller 1996). While the Plain Brownware sherds likely represent what Kelley (2004) referred to as Concepcion and Conchos phase wares—Chinati Plain, Chinati Filleted Rim, Chinati Scored, Capote Plain, Capote Red-on-Brown, Conchos Plain, and Conchos Red-on-Brown—no attempt was made during the analysis to separate the collection into those types, since they were never formally defined. Additional typological work will be needed before these types can be confidently used. Notable within in the Red-on-Brown classification are two relatively large sherds found on either side of F-12 (collapsed stone wall) that conjoin (Figure 35). The historic sherds are primarily from Mexican ceramics, the lone exception the Soft Paste Porcelain specimen, a Euro-American ware. The ceramic findings are discussed much more in-depth in Appendix I of this report.

Glass

A total of 110 glass specimens were recovered from the subsurface during the investigation and all but one of these are fragmentary pieces of containers or undiagnostic shatter fragments. The lone exception is a small glass trade bead. Mostly recovered from upper levels of the test units, the fragmentary specimens are almost exclusively represented by small and very small curved pieces of glass. Brown (n=59) and colorless (n=39) fragments are dominant within this collection, with green (n=8), light green (n=1), purple (n=1), and milk glass (n=1) also represented. Most of these fragments lack signs of antiquity, but nine specimens appear to be older than the others based on the presence of pitting and/or patination. These consist of one green, three brown, and five colorless fragments. Two of these were recovered from the

Figure 35. Conjoined Red-on-Brown sherds in possible association with F-12.

same unit and level (Test Unit 4, Level 1) that yielded the glass trade bead.

The glass trade bead is a purple to red color and fairly symmetrical. It has a diameter of 3.6 mm, a hole diameter of 1.2 mm, a height or length of 2.7 mm, and weighs 0.05 g. The specimen is described using nomenclature from an extensive glass trade bead analysis of 106,354 specimens found at archaeological sites along the Arkansas, Red, Brazos, Sabine, Trinity, and Mississippi rivers in Texas, Oklahoma, and Lousianna (Harris and Harris 1967). It is a small sized, doughnut-shaped garter bead of simple construction. This bead most closely resembles two varieties of small red beads presented in that analysis, Nos. 51 and 87. The former was placed within the sub-period A.D. 1700–1836 and the latter in the sub-period A.D. 1740–1767 (Harris and Harris 1967:144, 147, 156–157, Figure 53), however, both of those were of compound construction and may be completely unrelated to the bead recovered in Test Unit 4.

Metal

Twenty metal artifacts were recovered from the subsurface. For the most part these are nondescript or relatively uninformative. Similar to the glass specimens, they were mostly recovered from upper levels of the units. The most informative of these specimens are a complete bullet and a cartridge casing fragment. The bullet is a non-military issued rimfired .44 caliber. It is unstamped and could be for either a pistol or rifle (Robert W. Gray, personal communication 2008). Forty-four caliber pistol and rifle cartridges were introduced in the late 1860s or early 1870s (Gillio et al. 1980:37). The fragmentary cartridge casing has a head stamp with the following information: Western, .410, Field, and 12 mm.

Other Materials Collected

Other materials that were collected from the subsurface during the investigation consist of 96 pieces of house residue and 22 stone or sediment samples.

House Residue

House residue collected consists of five puddled adobe samples, two pieces of wall plaster, 33 pieces of daub, nine burned dirt dauber nests, 43 probable superstructure (burned and partially burned wood) samples, one burned river cane fragment, and three burned fiber/filament samples. Almost all of these were recovered in apparent association with either F-5 (unknown structure) or F-13 (pithouse). The puddled adobe samples were taken from the F-13 ground-level backing and house floor (see F-13 description), whereas almost all of the other materials were secured from or in close proximity to F-5. The pieces of wall plaster were recovered from BHT #1 deposits, in the general area of F-13. With the exception of the puddled adobe backing from F-13, a new architectural element, and the mud dauber nests, the recovered house residue are materials typically used in the construction of the walls, roofs, and floors of La Junta pithouses (Kelley 1939, 1949, 1985, 1986; Kelley et al. 1940; Shackelford 1951, 1955).

The burned and partially burned wood samples are likely portions of the F-5 superstructure—walls and roof—while the burned river cane fragment and fiber/filament samples probably represent different layers of roofing materials. The latter occurred in angled exposures over relatively broad areas and may be burned grass residues (see Figure 19). In describing the roof of the first house excavated at Millington, Kelley (1939:226) stated "poles ranging slightly less than an inch in diameter had been laid rather loosely together across the framework of the house, then covered by two layers of reeds running in opposite directions across the poles, and then by a layer of grass, corn husks, etc." He also indicated that "beneath the roofing and in places still attached to it was a thick accumulation of fire-hardened "mud-dauber" nests" (Kelley 1939:226–227). Thus, the recent Millington findings generally mirror those reported previously from La Junta house excavations (Kelley 1939, 1949, 1951, 1985, 1986; Shackelford 1951, 1955).

La Junta villagers used dried mud or daub interlaced with grass or sticks to seal/ plaster their *jacal* superstructures. Multiple reed and sapling impressions occur on many of the hardened mud fragments recovered from La Junta houses, supplying further evidence of the wattle and daub construction technique. Several of the pieces of burned daub recovered in 2006 are of appreciable size, the largest measuring ca. 12 x 16 x 24 cm. Due to its size and the impressions on it,

this piece may have been from one corner of the superstructure. The pieces of wall plaster are smoothed and finished (Figure 36), but lack any evidence of paint as was found at one of the excavated houses at the Polvo site (Shackelford 1951, 1955). Although these fragmentary pieces were found in close proximity to F-13, excavations in Test Unit 8 failed to uncover any wall plaster within this pithouse.

Stone/Sediment Samples

Twenty-two samples of stone and sediment were collected during the course of the project. These include three pieces of hematite, a sample of hematite-stained sediment, and six possible stone manuports.

All of the hematite samples were recovered from Test Unit 8. The hematite stained sediment was found in the uppermost level, and the three pieces of unfaceted hematite were recovered from lower levels of the unit

Figure 36. Wall plaster from BHT #1.

above Burial 5. At the Shiner site, Kelley et al. (1940:76) found two pieces of red pigment on the floor of one of the excavated pithouses and above a burial. It was theorized that these pieces of stone, one of which was faceted by usage, may have had some connection with the interment. This situation is very similar to what was found during the recent Millington investigation and the same possibility should be considered.

Manuports are defined as unaltered items thought to have been carried onto a site by humans rather than occurring naturally. The recovered stones that are classified as possible manuports consist of two specimens from Test Unit 8 and four from BHT #1 backdirt. The Test Unit 8 specimens were found near the pithouse floor and within the Burial 5 grave pit (F-14). The former has a rounded spherical shape and a shallow, incomplete hole ca. 1.8 mm wide that could be either natural or man-made. This small piece of chalcedony is partially covered in cortex, weighs 0.35 g, and has a diameter that varies from 6.5–6.9 mm. While this specimen may be a stone bead preform, it is here classified as a possible manuport. The specimen recovered from the burial pit is also a spherical piece of chalcedony, but it lacks any vestiges of cortex and is unaltered. It has a diameter of 3.8–4.1 mm and weighs 0.1 g. The four specimens recovered from the backhoe trench consist of pieces of chalcedony, bubble agate, opalite, and an unknown material. Whether or not any of these were brought to the site by human hands remains unresolved.

Provenienced Surface Materials

A total of 314 items were collected from the surface and these consist of 55 lithic specimens, 10 shell specimens, 210 ceramic sherds, 13 glass specimens, and 26 metal specimens. As mentioned above, six of the lithic speci-

mens were collected as material samples and lack accompanying provenience data. These artifacts are briefly described below.

Lithic Specimens

The 55 lithic specimens collected from the surface of the Millington site consist of 20 arrow points, eight notched pebbles, eight other bifaces, two unifaces, seven pieces of edge-modified debitage (all are made of obsidian), four grinding implements, and six stone material samples.

Arrow Points

The 20 arrow points collected from the surface consist of 10 Perdiz (Figure 37a–j), one Toyah-like (Figure 37k), six Fresno (Figure 37l–q), two fragmentary untyped specimens (Figure 37r and s) and one Perdiz preform (Figure 37t). Dimensional and descriptive data for these specimens is provided in Table 37.

This collection is dominated by the Perdiz type (Suhm et al. 1954:504; Suhm and Jelks 1962:283–284; Turner and Hester 1985:187), an arrow point well-represented in the region (Mallouf 1987, 1990, 1999; Ing et al. 1996; Cloud 2002) which has also been associated with the Bravo Valley aspect since its inception (Kelley et al. 1940:Figure 4). Interestingly, not a single Perdiz point or definite fragment was recovered from the subsurface investigations herein reported. All but one of the 10 Perdiz points in the collection are fragmentary, but can be assigned to this distinctive type characterized by contracting stems, triangular blades, and well-barbed shoulders (Suhm et al. 1954:504). Also in the collection is a fragmentary Perdiz preform and a blade fragment that, based on several attributes, is probably from a point of this type. The other fragmentary untyped arrow point in this collection has some similarities to the Perdiz type, but its asymmetrical barbs

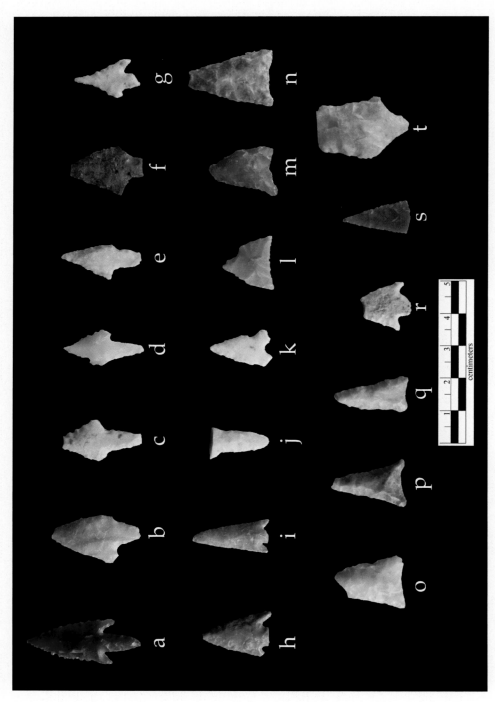

Figure 37. Arrow points recovered from the surface: (a–j) Perdiz; (k) Toyah-like; (l–q) Fresno; (r, s) untyped; (t) Perdiz preform.

Table 37: Surface Collected Arrow Points

Lot #	Type	Length (mm)	Max. Width (mm)	Max. Thickness (mm)	Neck Width (mm)	Basal Edge Width (mm)	Weight (g)	Material	Description
0–23	Fresno	—	11.3	3.4	—	11.3	0.9	tan chert	Fragmentary triangular arrow point; missing small portions of blade tip and one basal ear; very slight suggestion of side notches, likely a result of thinning; asymmetrical appearance; recurved blade edges; concave base; blade beveled on right edge of one face and both edges of the other; intact basal ear slightly rounded; remnant of original flake facet on one face (Figure 37q).
0–28	Fresno	—	14.6	4.7	—	14.6	1.2	dark tan/brown chert	Fragmentary triangular arrow point; missing blade tip; concave base; concave blade edges; lenticular cross section; basally thinned, with most of thinning on one face; all blade edges beveled, but steepest beveling on left edge of both faces; basal ears rounded, one a little more than the other (Figure 37p).
0–32	Perdiz	23.7	—	3.2	6.2	—	0.6	off-white chalcedony	Fragmentary stemmed arrow point; missing one shoulder and both barbs, with a nick in one blade edge; blade reworked; contracting stem; plano-convex cross section; blade beveled on both edges of one face; stem beveled on both edges of one face and one edge of opposite face; intact blade edge recurved and slightly serrated; base of stem pointed to slightly rounded; remnant of original flake facet on one face (Figure 37d).
0–36	Toyah-like	—	—	2.6	—	—	0.5	off-white chert	Fragmentary triple-notched arrow point; missing portions of both basal ears; asymmetrical appearance; shallow side notches and deep U-shaped basal concavity; slightly recurved blade edges; right edge blade beveling on one face; lenticular to plano-convex cross section; remnants of original flake facets on both faces (Figure 37k).

Table 37

Lot #	Type	Length (mm)	Max. Width (mm)	Max. Thickness (mm)	Neck Width (mm)	Basal Edge Width (mm)	Weight (g)	Material	Description
0–73	Perdiz	33.8	14.3	2.6	6.1	—	0.9	brown chert	Complete stemmed arrow point; symmetrical and very well made; contracting stem; strongly barbed; blade edges moderately serrated; stem base slightly rounded to pointed; lenticular cross section on stem and plano-convex cross section on blade; blade edges slightly convex; remnants of original flake facets on both faces (Figure 37a).
0–92	Fresno	—	17.3	4.5	—	17.3	1.9	mottled gray chert	Fragmentary triangular arrow point; missing blade tip; moderately thick; concave base; recurved blade edges—distal portion of blade likely reworked; basally thinned on both faces; lenticular cross section (Figure 37n).
0–130	Perdiz	—	10.4	2.4	4.4	—	0.5	light tan/gray chert	Fragmentary stemmed arrow point; missing stem and tiny portion of blade tip; plano-convex cross section; relatively straight blade edges except near tip where they are convex; very finely serrated blade edges; short pointed barbs; remnant of original flake facet on one face (Figure 37i).
0–147	Perdiz	—	—	3.0	6.7	—	0.5	pink fossiliferous chert	Arrow point stem fragment; missing remainder of point; relatively long contracting stem (14.2 mm); rounded stem base; stem edges slightly convex; lenticular cross section; remnant of original flake facet on one face (Figure 37j).
0–190	—	—	15.1	2.5	7.0	—	0.6	off-white chert	Fragmentary stemmed arrow point; missing blade tip and most of stem; asymmetrical appearance with one down turned, hooked barb and one outwardly flairing barb; lenticular cross section; both blade edges recurved; one face mostly covered with basal portion of cortex; remnant of original flake facet on one face (Figure 37r).
0–203	Perdiz	—	—	2.5	5.9	—	0.7	butterscotch chert	Fragmentary stemmed arrow point; missing most of stem and ends of both barbs; one blade edge convex and slightly serrated, other edge is recurved with distal portion likely reworked; plano-convex cross section; remnant of original flake facet on one face (Figure 37h).

Table 37

Lot #	Type	Length (mm)	Max. Width (mm)	Max. Thickness (mm)	Neck Width (mm)	Basal Edge Width (mm)	Weight (g)	Material	Description
0–207	Perdiz	—	—	2.9	6.6	3.1	0.7	tan chert	Fragmentary stemmed arrow point; missing blade tip and both barbs; contracting stem; straight stem base; small blade compared to stem—blade reworked; proximal end of stem plano-convex in cross section, while blade has plano-convex cross section; barb breaks small and indicative of reworked barbs before final breaks—one barb remnant at ca. 90° to long axis of point; recurved blade edges—one edge moderately serrated; remnant of original flake facet on one face (Figure 37c).
0–213	Perdiz	—	—	3.2	6.9	—	1.0	dark brown agate	Fragmentary stemmed arrow point; missing blade tip, both barbs, and a portion of stem; intact portion of stem contracts; both blade edges recurved, probably evidence of reworking; barb breaks indicate fairly large down and slightly outward angled barbs when intact; plano-convex cross section except near blade tip where it is lenticular (Figure 37f).
0–214	Fresno	19.7	15.5	5.6	—	14.6	1.5	light brown chert	Complete triangular arrow point; fairly thick for size; asymmetrical appearance with one basal ear and blade tip reworked; concave base thinned on both faces; more intact basal ear outwardly angled; lenticular cross section; both blade edges on one face steeply beveled; small remnant of original flake facet on one face (Figure 37m).
0–220	Fresno	—	*16.0	3.9	—	*16.0	1.2	off-white chalcedony	Fragmentary triangular arrow point; missing distal blade tip and small portion of one basal ear; good workmanship; concave base; one blade edge slightly concave, the other more recurved; lenticular cross section; basally thinned on both faces (Figure 37o).

Table 37

Lot #	Type	Length (mm)	Max. Width (mm)	Max. Thickness (mm)	Neck Width (mm)	Basal Edge Width (mm)	Weight (g)	Material	Description
0–223	Perdiz	—	—	3.1	7.3	—	1.1	tan fossiliferous chert	Fragmentary stemmed arrow point; missing one shoulder and barb, and small portions of blade tip, stem base, and other barb; contracting stem; slightly recurved blade edges; relatively short stem compared to blade; reworked blade, especially in area of missing shoulder; plano-convex cross section; remnants of original flake facets on both faces (Figure 37b).
0–236	Perdiz preform	—	19.7	3.2	9.9	—	1.9	tan/yellow fossiliferous chert	Fragmentary stemmed arrow point preform; missing distal portion of blade; crude workmanship and asymmetrical appearance; broadly contracting stem; both stem edges concave, but one only slightly; recurved blade edges; both shoulders rounded, but one barely formed; plano-convex cross section; remnant of original flake facet dominates one face (Figure 37f).
0–237	Perdiz	23.5	10.8	2.7	6.4	4.9	0.6	light pinkish tan fossiliferous chert	Fragmentary stemmed arrow point; missing one barb; other barb and shoulder also missing, but reworked; bulbous stem with slightly convex stem base; asymmetrical appearance; blade reworked; slightly convex and recurved blade edges; pointed and twisted blade tip with slight beveling; lenticular cross section; remnants of original flake facets on both faces that extend to base of stem (Figure 37e).
0–239	Perdiz	—	—	2.1	5.0	—	0.4	light tan fossiliferous chert	Fragmentary stemmed arrow point; missing one barb, about half of stem, and tiny portion of blade tip; intact portion of stem contracts; asymmetrical appearance when intact with different sized and shaped barbs; blade edges generally concave resulting in needle-like blade tip; very slightly serrated blade edges; plano-convex cross section; remnant of original flake facet on one face (Figure 37g).

Table 37

Lot #	Type	Length (mm)	Max. Width (mm)	Max. Thickness (mm)	Neck Width (mm)	Basal Edge Width (mm)	Weight (g)	Material	Description
0–240	probable Perdiz	–	–	1.9	–	–	0.34	brown chert	Arrow point distal blade fragment; broken in mid-blade; excellent workmanship; both edges slightly convex and very finely serrated; narrow and pointed blade tip (Figure 37s).
0–251	Fresno	15.0	16.5	2.3	–	16.5	0.5	light purplish tan chert	Fragmentary triangular arrow point; missing tiny piece of blade tip; distal portion of blade reworked; good workmanship; concave base; original blade edges relatively straight, now recurved from reworking; basally thinned on both faces; lenticular cross section (Figure 37l).

* estimate; missing tiny portion

and lack of a stem preclude confident placement within the type. The specimens classified as Perdiz and the probable Perdiz blade fragment were found in four loose clusters at the site (Figure 38).

Perdiz points are found throughout much of Texas and portions of northeastern Mexico and bridge the gap between the Late Prehistoric and Protohistoric periods (ca. A.D. 1200–1750) (Prewitt 1983; Black 1986; Mallouf 1987; Cloud 2002). Although their presence at village sites of the Bravo Valley aspect is well-documented (Kelley et al. 1940; Kelley 1949, 1957; Shackelford 1951; Cloud et al. 1994), there is no published data indicating direct association with any excavated house floors. Five specimens reported from early work at the Polvo site (41PS21) were all from surface contexts (Kelley 1949; Shackelford 1951), and although subsequent work at that site (Cloud et al. 1994) produced nine Perdiz points or fragments from the subsurface, none of those were recovered from pithouse contexts. Thus, this apparent pattern suggests that Perdiz points may not have actually been part of the tool kit used by the village occupants. If this possibility is correct, Perdiz points might have been left behind at the sites by regular visitors through time, perhaps people trading with the villagers. The clustered nature of the recovered Perdiz points at Millington is potentially supportive of such a possibility. The most likely outside traders in such a scenario would be people of the Cielo complex, whose arrow point assemblages were dominated by the Perdiz type (Mallouf 1990, 1999). The broken Perdiz preform indicates that points of this type were being manufactured on-site, but this adds little to the above hypothesis.

The Toyah-like point and Fresno arrow points recovered from the surface, like those from the subsurface, represent projectiles that have been previously associated with the Bravo Valley aspect (Kelley et al. 1940; Shackel-

ford 1951). Kelley originally coined the type names Piedras Triple Notched and Fresno Triangular for these specimens (Shackelford 1951; Kelley 1957). Both varieties are basically triangular points, the primary difference being the Toyah variants are side and basally notched.

Notched Pebbles

Notched pebbles were first recognized amongst the prehistoric debris along the Rio Grande and Río Conchos and interpreted as net sinkers by Sayles (1935, 1936). Kelley et al. (1940) included them as characteristic artifacts of all Bravo Valley aspect phases. Eight representative examples of this type of artifact were recovered; other specimens adhering to this classification were left at the site. These are generally flat river-worn pebbles and most have been bifacially notched on opposite ends. Very distinctive artifacts, notched pebbles occur regularly at sites along the Rio Grande and Río Conchos, but are lacking at sites away from the rivers. Thus, their presumed function as net weights used for fishing seems to be a reasonable hypothesis. Dimensional and descriptive data for these specimens is provided in Table 38.

Other Bifaces

Eight specimens collected from the surface are classified as other bifaces, specimens with workmanship on both faces that are not arrow points or notched pebbles. Four of these are finished tools or tool fragments that are classified as a spokeshave, a side scraper, a possible knife fragment, and a gouge. The other specimens are unfinished crudely worked bifaces that cannot be presumed to have been meant for a specific function. Dimensional and descriptive data for these specimens is provided in Table 39.

Spokeshaves, scrapers, and knives are regularly found within tool kits from La Junta

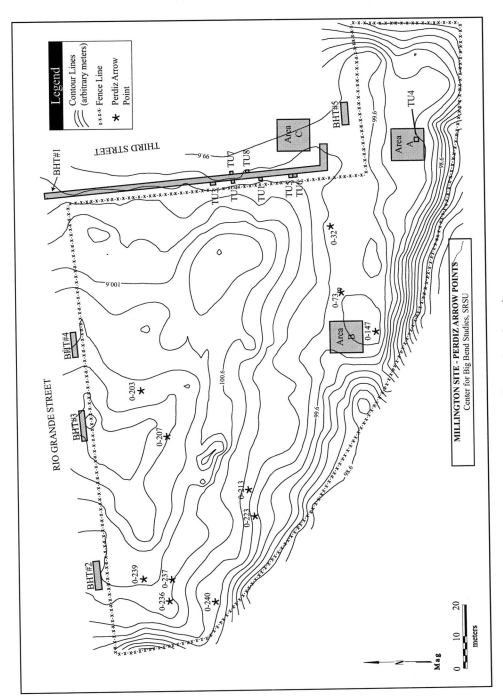

Figure 38. Distribution of Perdiz points and Perdiz preform collected from the surface.

Table 38: Surface Collected Notched Pebbles

Lot #	Length (mm)	Maximum Width (mm)	Maximum Thickness (mm)	Weight (g)	Material Type	Comments
0–25	69.3	67.8	22.3	140.5	gray unidentified igneous	No obvious signs of polish on faces.
0–120	58.1	53.6	16.2	65.7	yellowish tan unidentified (possibly indurated sandstone)	Some pecking on one face; no polish on faces.
0–137	47.4	38.7	21.0	61.3	gray unidentified igneous	Longitudinal scratches on both faces; slight polish in center of one face.
0–191	66.0	62.2	11.3	74.9	gray unidentified igneous	Edges pecked; no polish on faces.
0–204	77.4	55.3	16.3	102.2	reddish brown rhyolite	Some pecking, mostly on edges; natural polish on both faces.
0–212	64.3	51.0	20.0	87.8	dark gray unidentified igneous	Edges very scarred and battered; some pecking on faces; no polish on faces.
0–276	46.8	39.9	21.1	53.3	gray unidentified igneous	Edges well pecked; some pecking on faces; no polish on faces.
0–278	77.2	68.2	20.0	158.7	gray unidentified igneous	Unifacially notched on one end.

Table 39: Surface Collected Other Bifaces

Lot #	Length (mm)	Maximum Width (mm)	Maximum Thickness (mm)	Weight (g)	Material Type	Comments
0–26	43.9	26.7	9.0	11.0	brown–off white chert	Overall appearance of unifacial scraper, but bifacially worked and not a scraper; eight spokeshave bits (2.2–3.9 mm bit widths) around circumference.
0–86	47.6	43.3	6.4	14.2	light brownish gray chert	Subcircular blank; trimmed around edges of both faces; lenticular cross section; remnant of original flake facet dominates one face.
0–185	—	17.3	3.9	2.1	brown agate	Crude biface; plano–convex cross section with original flake facets on both faces; possible dart point blank or preform with parallel–sided stem, convex base, and weak shoulders.
0–196	—	25.0	9.0	14.3	tan chert	Elongated biface fragment; one end broken; lenticular cross section; possibly a blank or preform for a knife.
0–205	—	27.7	10.7	13.4	light gray fossiliferous chert	Side scraper worked bifacially; both lateral edges worn from use; plano–convex cross section; one end broken; convex and recurved edges.
0–233	—	—	7.9	6.4	brown and red agate	Midsection of finished biface; possible knife fragment based on dulling along one edge; both edges beveled on one face; lenticular cross section on one side, and plano–convex cross section on the other.
0–262	—	21.5	6.0	3.6	variegated purple–tan chert	Fragmentary biface; possibly an unfinished dart point fragment; plano–convex cross section; asymmetrical appearance; blade edges recurved and sinuous in cross section.
0–268	—	42.3	19.1	77.7	dense brownish gray unidentified igneous	Gouge; pebble worked bifacially on one end with other end missing; beveled bit with scooped appearance on one face, but bifacially worked; bit on opposite face shows flake scar damage from use; bit edge 29.6 mm long.

and the eastern Trans-Pecos, yet wood-working tools like gouges are somewhat unusual items in any regional assemblage. Although these tools have been documented amongst surface materials, they are infrequent. The Millington specimen has a worn scooped bit on one face fashioned from bifacial trimming and appears to have been used as a gouge.

Unifaces

Two unifaces were collected from the surface of the Millington site and are classified as an end scraper and a side scraper. The end scraper is complete with a convex ca. 35 mm-wide well-worn bit. The side scraper is fragmentary with one end broken. It has well-worn lateral edges with recurved and convex shapes, the latter exhausted with a bit angle exceeding 90–95°.

Edge-Modified Debitage

Seven specimens collected from the surface are classified as edge-modified debitage. These were collected exclusively because they are made of high grade obsidian. Due to the appearance of their cortex and/or color, they appear to represent two or three different source areas. Dimensional and descriptive data for these specimens is provided in Table 40.

Grinding Implements

Four grinding implements or implement fragments were collected from the surface. These consist of a mano, a probable mano, a mano fragment, and a stone bowl or portable mortar. All three of the specimens within the mano classification exhibit pecking in an attempt to rejuvenate their smooth and worn surfaces. The stone bowl/portable mortar is complete and a somewhat unusual specimen. Two slightly larger tuff stone bowls have been reported from the Polvo site, one in association with an adult burial and the other a fragmentary specimen painted with a band of red pigment (Shackelford 1951:62–63). The small size of the Millington specimen suggests it was used on a special kind of substance that was not in great demand. Dimensional and descriptive data for these specimens is provided in Table 41.

Lithic Material Samples

Six small pieces of debitage were collected from the surface as lithic material samples and were not provenienced. These materials consist of a banded opalite, a banded silicified wood, a moss agate, a red plume agate, a green chalcedony, and a variegated chalcedony.

Shell Specimens

Ten shell specimens were recovered from the surface. These consist of five mussel shell fragments, two marine shell beads (Figure 39a and b), and three marine shell fragments (Figure 39c–e). The beads are complete and in two forms, one with a discoidal shape and the other tubular. The discoidal bead is well made, has rounded edges, a diameter of 7.1 mm, a maximum thickness of 1.4 mm, and weighs 0.15 g. It contains a biconically drilled hole in its center that has a diameter of ca. 2.5 mm. The tubular bead is also well made and biconically drilled. Somewhat asymmetrical, it has a variable length of 3.6–4.7 mm, a diameter of ca. 8.0 mm, and weighs 0.2 g. Very thin-walled, it has a hole diameter of ca. 6.9 mm. The other marine shell artifacts are body whorl fragments.

The marine specimens most likely originated along the Pacific coast and came to La Junta through trade networks. In this scenario, they would likely have passed through Casas Grandes, a large redistribution center in northwestern Chihuahua during the Late Prehistoric period that specialized in certain items, one of which was marine shell

Tale 40: Surface Collected Edge-Modified Debitage

Lot #	Flake, Flake Fragment Chip, or Chunk	Platform Type	Number of Modified Edges	Shape of Modified Edges	Trimmed, Utilized, or Trimmed & Utilized	Length of Modified Edges (mm)	Weight (g)	Material
0–37	corticate flake fragment	ground	1	recurved	T & U	20.6	0.7	obsidian
0–193	decorticate chip	n/a	1	concave	U	1.2	0.6	obsidian
0–210	decorticate chip	n/a	2	convex	T & U	6.4	0.3	obsidian
				recurved	T & U	3.7		
0–222	decorticate chip	n/a	1	recurved	T & U	17.0	1.5	obsidian
0–225	corticate chip	n/a	1	convex	T & U	15.1	2.1	obsidian
0–245	corticate chip	n/a	4	recurved	T & U	13.6	3.2	obsidian
				straight	T & U	8.7		
				recurved	T	9.5		
				recurved	T & U	15.9		
0–257	secondary flake	ground	1	recurved	T & U	24.6	1.7	obsidian

Table 41: Surface Collected Grinding Implements

Lot #	Tool Type	Length (mm)	Maximum Width (mm)	Maximum Thickness (mm)	Weight (g)	Material Type	Comments
0–42	Mano	126.2	99.8	37.0	679.1	mottled tan indurated sandstone	Complete; two-sided; well-made with pecked and shaped vertical sides; oval shape in plan view; both sides flat, well-worn, and pecked to rejuvenate.
0–43	Mano Fragment	—	—	13.0	13.3	brownish red rhyolite	Very fragmentary; two-sided; both convex and flat to concave faces smoothed, polished, and pecked to rejuvenate.
0–123	Stone Bowl or Portable Mortar	66.2	63.2	37.4	183.6	dark grayish black vesicular basalt	Complete; about 10 mm deep and 40 mm wide circular hole or depression; depression ground smooth from apparent use.
0–206	probable Mano	119.4	81.8	20.4	280.6	tan indurated sandstone	Broken on two edges; presumed mano, but may have been small portable metate; single ground face flat, smoothed and polished, and pecked to rejuvenate; some pecking also on edge.

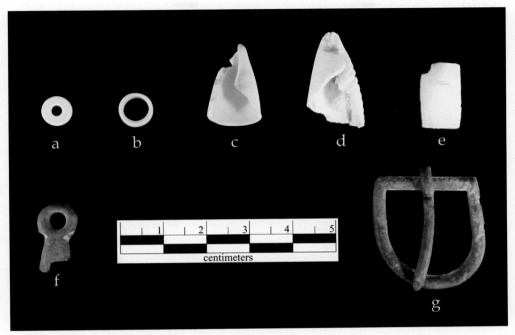

Figure 39. Select artifacts recovered from the surface. Marine shell: (a, b) beads, (c–e) whorl fragments. Cupreous metal: (f) fica, (g) buckle.

(Di Peso 1974a, 1974b; Di Peso and Fenner 1974). Casas Grandes flourished during the Medio Period (ca. A.D. 1150–1450) (Raves-loot 1988; Phillips 1989), and it was during that time that copious quantities of shell from the Pacific coast and other items from distant places were traded for, stored, and then re-distributed to cultural groups throughout the Southwest. In fact, almost four million shell artifacts were recovered from Medio Period sites during the Joint Casas Grandes Expedi-tion (Di Peso 1974b:401–403).

Ceramics

A total of 210 ceramic specimens were re-covered from the surface of the Millington site during the 2006 investigation. These consist of 66 prehistoric or native-made sherds (Figure 40) and 144 sherds made during the historic period by Spaniards and Mexicans, Euro-Americans, or others (Fig-ure 41). The prehistoric sherds consist of the following types and/or classifications: El Paso Polychrome (n=6) (Figure 40a and b), El Paso Brownware (n=1) (Figure 40c), Plain Brownware (n=21) (Figure 40d and e), Polished Plain Brownware (n=2) (Fig-ure 40f), Polished El Paso Brownware (n=1) (Figure 40g), Red-on-Brown (n=13) (Figure 40h–j), Red-on-White (n=7) (Figure 40k and l), White Slipped Earthenware (n=5) (Figure 40m), Red Slipped Earthenware (n=2) (Fig-ure 40n), Polished Red Slipped Earthenware (n=3) (Figure 40o), Smudged Brownware (n=1), Black-on-Yellow (n=1) (Figure 40p), Black-on-Red (n=1) (Figure 40q), Escondida Polychrome (n=1) (Figure 40r), and Black-on-White (Historic?) (n=1).

The sherds from historic times consist of the following types and/or classifications: Mexican ceramics—Majolica (n=66) (Figure 41a–e), Majolica? (n=1), Guanajuato Green Glaze (n=22) (Figure 41f), Galera Polychrome

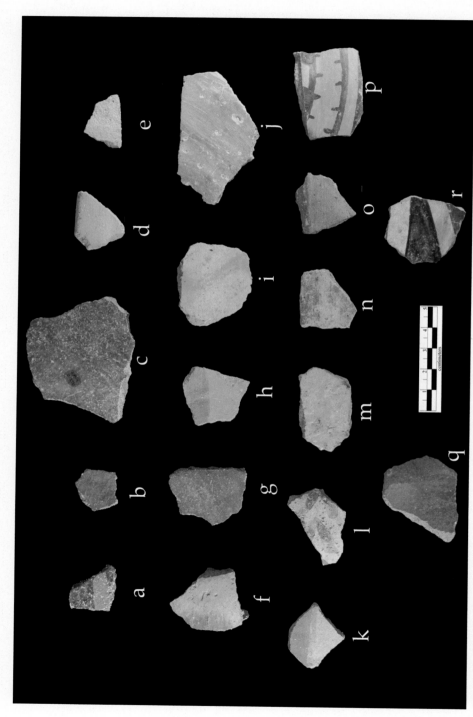

Figure 40. Select prehistoric ceramic sherds recovered from the surface: (a,b) El Paso Polychrome, (c) El Paso Brownware, (d, e) Plain Brownware, (f) Polished Plain Brownware, (g) Polished El Paso Brownware, (h–j) Red-on-Brown, (k, l) Red-on-White, (m) White Slipped Earthenware, (n) Red Slipped Earthenware, (o) Polished Red Slipped Earthenware, (p) Black-on-Yellow, (q) Black-on-Red, (r) Escondida Polychrome.

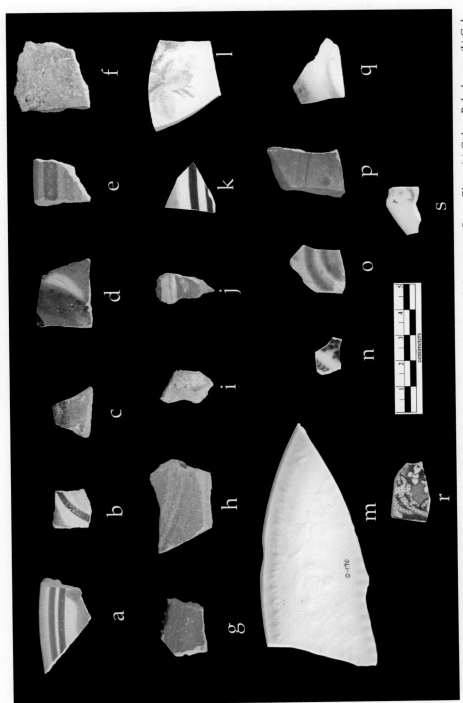

Figure 41. Select historic ceramic sherds recovered from the surface: (a–e) Majolica, (f) Guanajuato Green Glaze, (g) Galera Polychrome, (h) Galera Ware, (i) Presidios Green, (j) Sgraffiato Galera Tradition, (k) Annular/Mocha Ware, (l) Decalcomania Porcelain, (m) Feathered Edge Ware, (n) Flow-Blue, (o) Stoneware, (p) Salt Glaze Stoneware, (q) Sponge-Decorated, (r) Transfer Print, (s) Chinese Porcelain.

(n=3) (Figure 41g), Galera Ware (n=3) (Figure 41h), Presidios Green (n=4) (Figure 41i), and Sgraffiato Galera Tradition (n=1) (Figure 41j); Euro-American ceramics—Annular/Mocha Ware (n=5) (Figure 41k), Decalcomania Porcelain (n=1) (Figure 41l), Soft-Paste Porcelain (n=2), Feathered Edge Ware (n=1) (Figure 41m), Flow-Blue (n=1) (Figure 41n), Hotel Whiteware (n=1), Stoneware (n=3) (Figure 41o), Salt Glaze Stoneware (n=2) (Figure 41p), Sponge-Decorated (n=1) (Figure 41q), and Transfer Print (n=11) (Figure 41r); and Miscellaneous—Chinese Porcelain (n=1) (Figure 41s), Porcelain (n=4), Tile (n=2), and Unidentified (n=9).

Notable among the Plain Brownware specimens are two comal sherds (Figure 42). Their presence suggests the introduction of foodways that originated in central Mexico, perhaps via missionaries and/or soldiers. Discussion of the surface collected ceramics is provided in Appendix I of this report.

Glass

Thirteen glass artifacts were collected from the surface of the Millington site. These consist of three glass trade beads, one glass button, two milk glass fragments, four bottle fragments, and three ornamental fragments. The milk glass, bottle, and ornamental fragments are representative of common late nineteenth and early to mid twentieth century items and will not be further discussed here. The glass button is circular with a typical 4-hole pattern in the center. The glass trade beads provide much more meaningful data relative to the Spanish presence in the region and are individually described below.

One glass bead is blue, barrel-shaped, and patinated, with flat facets around the 2.0 mm wide hole on each end. These facets are ca. 5.5 mm wide. Relatively large and weighing 0.75 g, it is slightly out-of-round with a diameter of ca. 8.6 mm. It has a

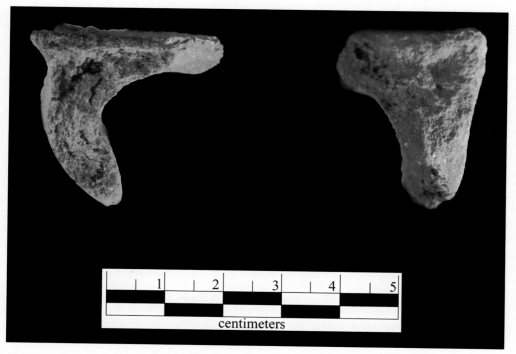

Figure 42. Comal sherds recovered from the surface.

height or length of 6.7 mm. When compared to specimens recovered from archaeological sites along the Arkansas, Red, Brazos, Sabine, Trinity, and Mississippi rivers in Texas, Oklahoma, and Lousianna (Harris and Harris 1967), it was found to be similar in size and shape, but not color, to what the researchers referred to as No. 52. This variety was placed in the sub-period A.D. 1700–1740 (Harris and Harris 1967:144, 156, Figure 52). Another of these is a tiny green, asymmetrical, doughnut-shaped seed bead. It is thin-walled, with a diameter of 2.7–2.9 mm and has a hole diameter of 1.4 mm. With a height or length of 1.9 mm, it weighs 0.1 g. It is similar in size, shape, and color to No. 83 in the Harris and Harris (1967:147, 156, Figure 52) study, which dates to ca. A.D. 1740–1767. The third specimen is a sky-blue color and multi-faceted, with an asymmetrical somewhat rounded appearance. Seventeen irregular, hexagonal to crudely triangular facets occur on its exterior. It has a diameter that varies from 5.3–6.3 mm, a height or length of 5.4 mm, and weighs 0.3 g. In the Harris and Harris (1967) study there is nothing quite comparable, although several types had similar numbers of facets (16–20) and these dated roughly from A.D. 1767–1836. However, the complete lack of patina on this specimen suggests it was manufactured much more recently.

Metal

Twenty-six metal artifacts were collected from the surface during the investigation: seven cupreous Spanish/possible Spanish items, eight cartridge casings, six buttons/ button fragments, one tin can lid, and four other assorted pieces of metal. The metal buttons/button fragments have different appearances and probably represent buttons for a variety of late nineteenth to mid twentieth century garments. The tin can lid is from a "25 oz." can of "Baking Powder" that appar-

ently cost "25¢." "KC" is embossed in the very center and around the edge and raised a little higher is "SAME PRICE TODAY AS 47 YEARS AGO" which, based on the date 1890 when the product was first produced, suggests a date between 1937–1940 (Rike and Rock 1989). The cupreous Spanish and possible Spanish specimens, all green from oxidation of the metal from which they were made, and the cartridge casings are described in more detail below.

The Spanish and possible Spanish items consist of a *fica*, a small buckle, a wire fragment, three pieces of sheet metal, and a small decorative fragment. These artifacts were somewhat clustered in the area of the site where the Spanish mission is suspected to have been located (Figure 43). *Ficas* were small jingling attachments the Spanish placed on *coscojos* or bridle decorations. This specimen is flattened with a circular hole in one end where it was attached and a protrusion on the other (Figure 39f). The latter is shaped like a hand with the index finger extended from a clenched fist. It has a length of 17.1 mm, a maximum width of 9.4 mm, a maximum thickness of 2.6 mm, and weighs 1.6 g.

The buckle is slightly deformed, and consists of two connected pieces that weigh 7.0 g (Figure 39g). The main piece is D-shaped and asymmetrical, and the tongue is slightly bent to one side and has a blunt point. It is ca. 30.4 mm long and about 2.7 mm wide. The main piece has maximum thicknesses that vary from 3.2–3.6 mm, depending upon which portion is being measured. There are several seams along portions of the main piece, indicating it was cast. Due to its size, this specimen likely was a horse trappings buckle rather than a small belt buckle.

The wire fragment is ribbed and twisted, the ribs or raised threads twisting around the long axis in a longitudinal direction. It weighs 0.1 g and has a maximum thickness of 1.9 mm.

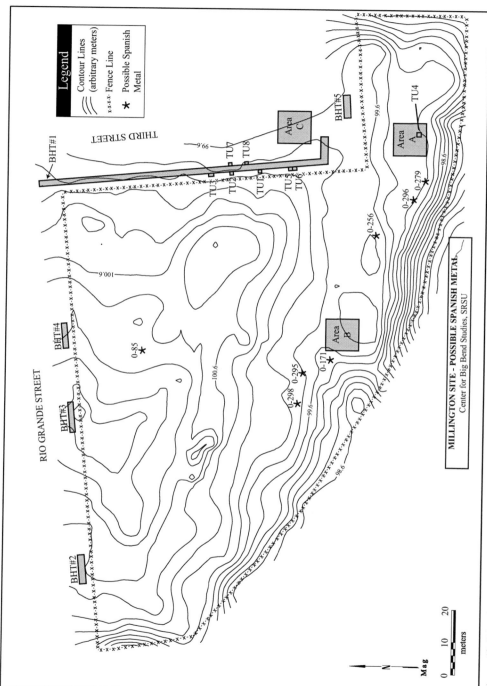

Figure 43. Distribution of cupreous metal artifacts collected from the surface.

All three sheet metal fragments are smashed or crimped and contain fashioned edges and/or grooves suggesting they are from finished items. Thicknesses vary from 0.4–0.5 mm. When complete, the most intact of these appears to have had a circular shape in plan view with a hole in the middle and a diameter of ca. 25.5 mm. The small item classified as a decorative fragment is square in cross section and appears to have been intentionally bent or shaped suggesting a decorative function. It is thicker at one end (1.6 mm) as well as more corroded—and tapers significantly at the other end just beyond the upward bend.

The eight cartridge casings are from the late nineteenth and early to mid twentieth centuries. Perhaps the oldest of these is a patinated and unstamped .50–.58 caliber cartridge fragment. It lacks any indication of a primer or firing mark, but probably was rim fired. Another patinated specimen is an unstamped .45 caliber carbine casing that has a single mark on the rim suggestive of rim-firing. Two patinated and unstamped rim-fired pistol cartridges that lack any indication of a primer also appear to have some antiquity. One of these has firing marks on opposing sides of the rim, and the other has a single mark. One center-fired .45 caliber cartridge, probably a .45–.55 casing, is stamped with 9/C/78/F reading in a clockwise manner from the left side. This indicates it was manufactured at the Frankford Arsenal in September 1878 for use in a carbine weapon (Reuland 1993:18). Two center-fired rifle or carbine cartridges date to the Mexican Revolution. They have head stamps of F/A/16/3 and F/A/15/5, indicating manufacture at the Frankford Arsenal in March 1916 and May 1915, respectively. The other cartridge is an unstamped pistol casing that is probably the most recent in this collection.

SUMMARY DISCUSSION

Undertaken after inadvertent damages from a water line trench in 2003, the 2006 Millington site investigation has reinvigorated scientific inquiry of the distinctive farming cultures that lived in the La Junta district. Although pioneering archaeologist J. Charles Kelley had unveiled many of the details of La Junta lifeways by the early 1950s, there ensued a long hiatus of focused research on these cultures. Kelley had conducted or supervised excavations at a handful of sites in the district in the 1930s and 1940s, allowing generation of a cultural construct for the district and various other hypotheses. However, as farsighted and ahead of its time as his work was, Kelley (1990) knew later in life that his La Junta efforts were dated and in need of revision. He likely would have relished the chance to use modern analytical field and laboratory techniques at a site in the district, especially the Millington site where he began his La Junta research (Kelley 1939). It was within this context that the 2006 project was conducted, and it was this investigation that first employed such techniques in the field and during the analysis while exploring the archaeological riches of the Millington site. Below is a brief summary of the more significant findings from the investigation.

Mortuary Data

Exposure of human burials prompted the 2006 investigation and it was from examining these findings that the most substantive data was generated. Human remains from five interments and skeletal elements from several other individuals were recovered during the investigation, and these recoveries prompted an effort to locate and analyze all previously recovered burials from La Junta, which include eight from Millington that are presented in this report. Disease and health patterns and dietary results from stable isotope analysis from these remains have challenged long-standing hypotheses concerning this village. These data argue that the Millington population did not rely on maize, desert succulents, or riverine resources, and indicate malnutrition and undernutrition contributed significantly to disease patterns observed in the group. Furthermore, patterns of

153

arthritis and trauma in the mortuary sample, especially for males, mirror patterns from hunter-gatherers of the region and are suggestive of high mobility across the rugged terrain of the eastern Trans-Pecos, contradicting most assumptions of sedentism. These data have been used to suggest Millington served more as a centralized gathering locale from which traditional foraging patterns and long-distance travel were conducted. This hypothesis fits well with historical data for La Junta groups, which have indicated high mobility for, among other purposes, bison hunting, and evidence that culturally distinct groups used La Junta as a central meeting place (Kenmotsu 1994a).

Kelley's previous hypotheses concerning Millington and the other La Junta villages posit an agricultural economy supplemented by typical hunter-gatherer foodstuffs, and a high degree of sedentism, with the exception of the transition between the La Junta and Concepcion phases when the area "may have been completely abandoned by pottery-making agriculturalists" (Kelley 1990:39). Kelley et al. (1940) offered that agricultural products of the Bravo Valley aspect consisted of corn, beans, and cucerbits, yet there is very little published data indicating maize or other agricultural crops were grown in the subsequent publications from La Junta archaeological investigations. Kelley's first efforts at Millington, during excavation of a house he thought dated to the Concepcion phase, provide the most data in this regard:

> On the floor of the house were burnt mesquite beans, an occasional charred corn-cob, a few corn husks and stalks, and miscellaneous fragments of burned and broken animal bones. A few fragments of fresh water mussel shell were found also. Mixed with the roof debris was an ear of corn, burned while still on the stalk, with the shucks still in place. (Kelley 1939:228)

The above reference to other apparent foodstuffs have been supplemented with more recent findings of fish bones from the Polvo site (Cloud et al. 1994) and from this investigation (see Appendix II). Although the number of fish bones recovered from these two investigations are meager, both excavations sampled relatively small areas of these respective sites. Furthermore, all La Junta village sites contain large numbers of notched pebbles thought to have been used as net sinkers in fishing endeavors. Copious quantities of burned rock occur regularly at the village sites, and are thought to be related to the use of earth ovens to process desert succulents. These data are based, in part, on assumptions that have yet to be verified through scientific means, or which only provide generic non-chronological data. Pertinent to this discussion is the fact that earth ovens, notched pebbles, etc. are visible cultural residue, biased and incomplete datasets due to the limitations of archaeological recovery. These features imply that certain foodstuffs were being eaten, but their importance in the diets of the La Junta people through time is difficult to assess without additional cultural clues.

Historical records also provide unreliable data about past village economies. Alvar Núñez Cabeza de Vaca apparently indicated La Juntans grew crops of beans, squash, and corn in A.D. 1535 (Bandelier 1905:151), and Luxán's account of the A.D. 1581–1582 Espejo *entrada* mentioned corn as part of the material goods at La Junta—at several different sites—but did not indicate whether or not this crop was being grown there (Hammond and Rey 1929:60–61). About a century later, in A.D. 1683–1684, the Mendoza-López expedition indicated corn and wheat crops were located on both sides of the Rio Grande at La Junta (Kelley 1952b:266–267). Late sixteenth century Spanish documents have indicated that a wide range of food crops were grown—wheat, corn, beans, other grains, squash, watermelons, and melons—and that other foodstuffs included tuna, mescal, fish, and game animals such as bison, deer, rabbits, mice, and snakes (Kenmotsu 1994a: 242–243). While these accounts provide some support for corn and other agriculture, and consumption of additional foodstuffs at La Junta during select times during the Protohistoric period, the account of Captain Joseph de Ydoiaga during his A.D. 1747–1748 *entrada* provides a little more detail. Through interviews with the inhabitants who lived at the Pueblo of San Cristóbal (Millington site) Ydoiaga indicated that agricultural yields were successful only infrequently due to droughts. He:

> asked whether they would have corn for the whole year; and they answered that many would not have enough, but that they would be helped by the wheat, which they were planting at the proper time as they had in the past; and they sustained themselves with some fish, *atole* [gruel-type beverage] from various seeds of plants, tunas, and other things from the hunt. (Madrid 1992:60)

These various accounts, albeit at select times over several hundred years, indicate that agriculture was attempted, that some corn was available, and that a variety of other foodstuffs were consumed, yet do not indicate a strong reliance upon any one in particular.

Thus, we have various lines of evidence about maize agriculture and other economic pursuits at La Junta. Chronometric data for the human remains recently analyzed are as limited as those from the historic accounts. Four of the six interments subjected to stable isotope analysis are at least relatively dated: two from the La Junta phase, one from the

transition between the La Junta and Concepcion phases, and one from the Concepcion phase. Represented similarly, only seven of the 13 interments in the skeletal analysis can be placed in La Junta chronology: four from the La Junta phase, two from the transition between the La Junta and Concepcion phase, and one from the Concepcion phase.

These data show the lack of a sound understanding of La Junta economies and lifeways throughout the ca. 600 year period of occupation. Past hypotheses have not been able to quantify the relative importance of potential foodstuffs in the diets of La Juntans. However, the skeletal data has, at least in the studied individuals, indicated fish, mescal, and corn, were not consumed in great enough quantities to influence isotopic make-up or health patterns. Much more research will be needed to address interpretive issues concerning the degree of sedentism, economies that were in place, and other related issues throughout the lengthy Bravo Valley aspect. Regardless, data obtained through the mortuary analysis have shed appreciable light on these research questions and opened the door to a more holistic and scientific approach to the study of La Junta lifeways.

Architectural Data

The 2006 investigation at Millington partially uncovered remains of three structures (F-5, F-12, and F-13) that, for the most part, cannot be neatly categorized within the existing La Junta architectural typology or framework (Kelley 1985). These structural remnants consist of a relatively deep pit structure of some type (F-5), a partially collapsed rock wall suspected to be a collapsed foundation (F-12), and a pithouse (F-13). In addition, an undefined pit (F-10) only documented in the walls of BHT #5 may represent some form of a pithouse. Our understanding of these features is severely limited since only small portions of each were excavated or uncovered. Radiocarbon data secured from the three assumed structures has provided chronological context. Both pit structures date to the La Junta phase (F-5—A.D. 1290–1410; F-13—A.D. 1160–1290) and the rock wall dates to later occupations at the site (A.D. 1640–1680—35 percent probability; A.D. 1730–1810—47 percent probability).

Due to being truncated by both F-4 (historic trench) and F-6 (ring midden/earth oven), the depth of the unknown pit structure (F-5) remains in question, although it appears to have at least been 90–100 cm deep. The definite pithouse (F-13) had a depth of ca. 35 cm. Pithouse depths uncovered during excavations at Millington in the 1930s have not been published, but some information in this regard does occur in Kelley's files. A partial list uncovered in his correspondence files provides pit depths for 11 of the 22 houses that were excavated. The shallowest was 40.6 cm, the deepest 177.8 cm, and the average 98.3 cm. Thus, F-13 would be the shallowest and F-5 would fall within the average on this abbreviated list.

Indications are that both F-5 and F-12 were burned at some point and this is consistent with evidence from many of the other excavated structures at the site. Apparent burned roof and/or wall fall, including large pieces of daub and mud dauber nests, were uncovered above the suspected level of the F-5 floor, and there was abundant charcoal near the base and on either side of F-12. In comparison, there was little in the way of masses of burned debris uncovered within F-13, only scattered charcoal amongst a few larger pieces. Since the burned residue of F-12 appeared markedly different than that of F-5, principally lacking daub, it is assumed that this structure had a completely different superstructure. It is possible F-12 was a

foundation of sorts for a ramada-like shade structure.

In-depth interpretation of the three partially uncovered structures is impossible at this point. These structures will need to be exposed to a much greater degree before confident assessments can be made concerning their morphologies, functions, and placements within the known architectural sequence of La Junta.

Material Culture Data

A total of 2,745 artifacts were recovered during the investigation, including 314 from the surface of the site. The materials collected from the surface represent the first systematic and provenienced collection of its type from Millington or, for that matter, from any of the La Junta villages. The provenienced artifacts provide a wealth of interpretive spatial data that will be useful in future investigations. As is often the case, arrow points and ceramic sherds in the collection provide some of the more significant data, however, most of the ones recovered from the subsurface lack associated radiocarbon data. Other artifacts recovered during the investigation, such as marine shell, cupreous metal, and glass trade beads have also provided important information.

Arrow points recovered from the subsurface include specimens classified as Toyah, Toyah-like, Fresno, Sabinal-like, and Washita-like. Many of these are crudely made and/or have asymmetrical appearances. Kelley (1957) has indicated that well-made Toyah points were a component of the Livermore phase and that crude and asymmetrical versions, what he called Piedras Triple Notched, were projectiles of the Bravo Valley aspect. He suggested that the former led to development of the latter (Kelley 1957:50), and this has been a long standing interpretive issue in the ensuing years. The Toyah and Toyah-like specimens recovered in the 2006 investigation, which consist of both well and crudely made and symmetrical and asymmetrical varieties, offer little toward resolution of this controversy. Appropriately derived collections from datable contexts, preferably house floors, will be needed to address this issue.

Almost equal numbers of arrow points were recovered from the subsurface (n=21) and surface (n=20). Unlike the subsurface points, the surface collection is dominated by arrow points of the Perdiz type. This apparent pattern has been used to suggest that the Perdiz specimens could have been left at the site by visitors or traders. If this possibility is correct, the most likely candidates would be coeval people of the Cielo complex, perhaps Jumano Indians, whose base camps occur nearby. Much more work will be needed to demonstrate the lack of Perdiz points in clear association with house floors and other features of the Bravo Valley aspect before this hypothesis can be adequately tested.

A wide range of prehistoric and historic ceramic sherds were recovered from both the surface and subsurface, and these specimens represent a significant class of artifacts. Most past collections from Millington and other La Junta villages that currently reside in repositories lack associated provenience data, hampering research efforts. Thus, the ceramics collected in 2006 will provide a fresh starting place from which to launch future analyses.

Kelley et al. (1940) indicated wares of the La Junta phase were predominantly trade items from the Southwest and this remains the accepted theory. While he never formally finished and published criteria for proposed Concepcion and Conchos phase types, his working drafts in this regard were recently published posthumously in order to assist ceramic researchers of the district (Kelley 2004). Furthermore, Kelley's hypotheses con-

cerning the origins of many of the ceramics found at La Junta have been verified through modern analytical means—i.e., petrographic and instrumental neutron activation analyses (Rodríguez-Alegría et al. 2004; Robinson 2004)—although additional efforts would be useful to better understand this subject.

The ceramic analysis presented in this report (see Appendix I) is based on a nontypological approach, especially in regard to the many plainwares that were recovered and which likely represent Kelley's proposed Concepcion and Conchos phase wares. Further analyses of these wares is clearly warranted before any of his proposed types can be confidently used by researchers. One method that might help sort out some of these plainware sherds temporally is luminescence dating by opically stimulated luminescence (OSL). Although this technique has not been universally accepted by researchers, there have been some promising results (Seymour 2003, n.d.).

Other significant material culture recoveries from the 2006 Millington investigation were of marine shell, cupreous metal, and glass trade beads. Marine shell artifacts recovered from the surface likely originated on the Pacific coast and passed through Casas Grandes, a major redistribution center in northern Mexico which corresponds temporally to the La Junta phase. These artifacts, mostly beads or bead preforms, along with ceramics from the Southwest, provide evidence of the apparent linkage that existed with Casas Grandes. On the other hand, cupreous metal artifacts and glass trade beads are materials linking Millington with Spanish activities at La Junta. Along with Spanish ceramics (e.g., Majolica), their distributions on the surface of the site have helped in approximating the area where the late seventeeth/early eighteenth century mission is suspected to have been located.

Geophysical Data

Two separate geophysical investigations were used at the site (see Appendixes III and IV), the first targeting three 10 x 10 m areas and the second revisiting one of these (Area B— the suspected location of the Spanish mission) and utilizing additional techniques. The first investigation located a number of sub-surface anomalies in all three areas and from their shapes, sizes, and depths, these likely are representative of various non-habitation pits, although an attempt to ground-truth one anomaly indicated it had a natural origin, perhaps a large boulder in the substata. The second investigation yielded evidence of three large, low-amplitude anomalies forming a partial square or rectangular pattern between ca. 12–36 cm below the surface. This anomaly is oriented northwest-southeast and has the potential to be a footing or remnant of the early Spanish mission. Excavation of this anomaly will be needed to confirm or refute this possibility.

Summary Statement

In sum, the 2006 Millington site investigation has served to revitalize research into the distinctive La Junta cultures, allowing several new possibilities and perspectives to be explored. Insights have been forthcoming concerning the architecture, mortuary customs, diet and health of the inhabitants. Several long-standing assumptions have been challenged, such as the degree of sedentism and the role that agriculture played in the diets of La Juntans, which further work in the district needs to address. While the results represents a relatively small step forward, further work planned by the CBBS at various La Junta sites, including at the Millington site, should facilitate a greater understanding of the cultures that lived in this remote location.

REFERENCES CITED

Adams, John Crawford, and David L Hamblen
>   1992   *Outline of Fractures: Including Joint Injuries.* Churchill Livingstone, Edinburgh, Scotland.

Albritton, Claude C., and Kirk Bryan
>   1939   Quaternary Stratigraphy of the Davis Mountains, Trans-Pecos Texas. *Bulletin of the Geological Society of America* 50:1423–1474.

Alex, Thomas C., Donald W. Corrick, and Frank A. García
>   1992   *A Report on the Archeological Survey for the Ross Maxwell Scenic Drive Highway Reconstruction Project, PRA-BIBE 15, in Big Bend National Park, Texas.* Unpublished draft report to the National Park Service, on file, Office of Resource Management, Big Bend National Park, Texas.

Antevs, Ernst
>   1955   Geologic-Climate Dating in the West. *American Antiquity* 20(4):317–335.

Applegate, Howard G., and C. Wayne Hanselka
>   1974   *La Junta de los Rios Del Norte y Conchos.* Southwestern Studies Monograph No. 41. Texas Western Press, University of Texas at El Paso.

Aufderheide, A. C., and C. Rodriguez-Martin
>   1998a   Degenerative Joint Disease and Degenerative Disease of the Spine. In *The Cambridge Encyclopedia of Human Paleopathology*, pp. 93–97. Cambridge University Press, Cambridge, England.

>   1998b   Traumatic Arthritis and Nonspecific Septic Arthritis. In *The Cambridge Encyclopedia of Human Paleopathology*, pp. 105–107. Cambridge University Press, Cambridge, England.

Bandelier, Adolph F.
    1890   Final Report of Investigations Among the Indians of the Southwestern United States. *Papers of the Archaeological Institute of America, American Series* 3, Part 1. University Press, Cambridge, Massachusetts.

Bandelier, Fanny (translator)
    1905   *The Journey of Alvar Nuñez Cabeza de Vaca and His Companions from Florida to the Pacific, 1528–1536.* Translated from a narrative by Alvar Nuñez Cabeza de Vaca. A. S. Barnes & Co., New York.

Barnes, Virgil E.
    1979   *Geologic Atlas of Texas, Emory Peak-Presidio Sheet.* Joshua William Beede Memorial Edition. Bureau of Economic Geology, University of Texas, Austin.

Beene, Debra L.
    1994   *Archaeological Investigations at Cuevas Amarillas (41PS201), Big Bend Ranch State Natural Area, Presidio County, Texas.* Unpublished Master's thesis, Department of Anthropology, University of Texas at Austin.

Black, Stephen
    1986   *The Clemente and Herminia Hinojosa Site, 41JW8: A Toyah Horizon Campsite in Southern Texas.* Special Report No. 18. Center for Archaeological Research, University of Texas at San Antonio.

Blair, W. Frank
    1950   The Biotic Provinces of Texas. *Texas Journal of Science* 2(1):93–117.

Booth, Robert K., Stephen T. Jackson, Steven L. Forman, John E. Kutzbach, E. A. Bettis, III, Joseph Kreig, and David K. Wright
    2005   A Severe Centennial-Scale Drought in Mid-Continental North Amreica 4200 Years Ago and Apparent Global Linkages. *The Holocene* 15(3):321–328.

Bridges, Patricia S.
    1991   Degenerative Joint Disease in Hunter-Gatherers and Agriculturalists from the Southeastern United States. *American Journal of Physical Anthropology* 85:379–391.

    1992   Prehistoric Arthritis in the Americas. *Annual Review of Anthropology* 21:67–91.

    1993   Effect of Variation in Methodology on the Outcome of Osteoarthritic Studies. *International Journal of Osteoarchaeology* 3:289–295.

    1994   Vertebral Arthritis and Physical Activities in the Prehistoric Southeastern United States. *American Journal of Physical Anthropology* 93:83–93.

Brunson, E.
   2000   Osteoarthritis, Mobility and Adaptive Diversity among the Great Salt Lake Fremont. *Utah Archaeology* 13:1–14.

Buikstra, J. E., and D. H. Ubelaker
   1994   *Standards for Data Collection from Human Skeletal Remains.* Arkansas Archeological Survey Research Series No. 44. Arkansas Archeological Survey, Fayetteville.

Butterwick, Mary, and Stuart Strong
   1976   A Vegetational Survey of the Colorado Canyon Area. In *Colorado Canyon*, edited by Don Kennard, pp. 71–87. Natural Area Survey No. 11. Lyndon B. Johnson School of Public Affairs, University of Texas at Austin.

Campbell, Thomas N.
   1970   *Archeological Survey of the Big Bend National Park, 1966–1967.* University of Texas at Austin. Submitted to the National Park Service. Copy on file, Big Bend National Park, Texas.

Castañeda, Carlos E.
   1976   *Our Catholic Heritage in Texas: 1519–1936.* Vols. I–IV. Reprinted. Arno Press, New York. Originally published 1936, Von Boeckmann-Jones, Austin, Texas.

Chipman, Donald E.
   1987   In Search of Cabeza de Vaca's Route Across Texas: An Historiographical Survey. *Southwestern Historical Quarterly* 91(2):127–148.

   1992   *Spanish Texas, 1519–1821.* University of Texas Press, Austin.

Cloud, William A.
   2001   *Archeological Testing at Sites 41PS800 and 41PS801, Presidio County, Texas.* Reports in Contract Archeology 2, Center for Big Bend Studies, Sul Ross State University, Alpine, and Archeological Studies Program Report 29, Texas Department of Transportation, Environmental Affairs Division, Austin.

   2002   The Rough Run Burial: A Semi-Subterranean Cairn Burial from Brewster County, Texas. *Journal of Big Bend Studies* 14:33–84.

   2004   *The Arroyo de la Presa Site: A Stratified Late Prehistoric Campsite Along the Rio Grande, Presidio County, Trans-Pecos Texas.* Reports in Contract Archeology 9, Center for Big Bend Studies, Sul Ross State University and Archeological Studies Program Report 56, Texas Department of Transportation, Environmental Affairs Division.

Cloud, William A., Robert J. Mallouf, Patricia A. Mercado-Allinger, Cathryn A. Hoyt, Nancy
A. Kenmotsu, Joseph M. Sanchez, and Enrique R. Madrid
    1994   *Archeological Testing at the Polvo Site, Presidio County, Texas.* Office of
           the State Archeologist Report 39. Texas Historical Commission and United
           States Department of Agriculture, Soil Conservation Service, Austin.

Corrick, Donald W.
    1992   Analysis of Toyah Arrow Points from Site 41BS188, Big Bend National
           Park, Brewster County, Texas. Department of Anthropology, Texas A&M
           University, College Station. Copy on file at Center for Big Bend Studies,
           Sul Ross State University, Alpine, Texas.

    2000   The Manufacture and Age of Toyah Arrow Points from Big Bend National
           Park, Texas. *Journal of Big Bend Studies* 12:1–12.

Cox, Margaret
    2000   Ageing Adults from the Skeleton. In *Human Osteology in Archaeology
           and Forensic Science*, edited by Margaret Cox and Simon Mays, pp.61–81.
           Greenwich Medical Media, London.

Crabtree, Don E.
    1972   *An Introduction to Flintworking.* Occasional Papers of the Idaho State Uni-
           versity Museum, No. 28. Pocatello, Idaho.

Dice, Lee R.
    1943   *The Biotic Provinces of North America.* University of Michigan Press, Ann
           Arbor.

Di Peso, Charles C.
    1974a   *Casas Grandes: A Fallen Trading Center of the Gran Chichimeca,* Vols.
           1–3. The Amerind Foundation, Inc., Dragoon and Northland Press, Flag-
           staff, Arizona.

    1974b   Introduction to Medio Period Shell Artifacts. In *Casas Grandes: A Fallen
           Trading Center of the Gran Chichimeca,* Vol. 6, pp. 401–408. The Amerind
           Foundation, Inc., Dragoon and Northland Press, Flagstaff, Arizona.

Di Peso, Charles C., and Gloria J. Fenner
    1974   Medio Period Shell Beads. In *Casas Grandes: A Fallen Trading Center of
           the Gran Chichimeca,* Vol. 6, pp. 408–434. The Amerind Foundation, Inc.,
           Dragoon and Northland Press, Flagstaff, Arizona.

Douglas, A. E.
    1935   *Dating Pueblo Bonito and Other Ruins of the Southwest.* National Geo-
           graphic Society, Pueblo Bonito Series, No. 1. Washington, D.C.

Duray, S. M.
    1992   Enamel Defects and Caries Etiology: An Historical Perspective. In *Recent Contributions to the Study of Enamel Developmental Defects*, edited by A. H. Goodman and L. Capasso, pp. 307–319. Journal of Paleopathology Monographic Publication 2. Edigrafital, Teramo, Italy.

Duyar, I., and Erdal, Y. S.
    2003   A New Approach for Calculating Dental Caries Frequency of Skeletal Remains. *Homo* 54:57–70.

Eickmeier, W. G., and M. M. Bender
    1976   Carbon Isotope Ratios of Crassulacean Acid Metabolism Species in Relation to Climate and Phytosociology. *Oecologia* 25:341–347.

Erdal, Y. S., and I. Duyar
    1999   Brief Communication: A New Correction Procedure for Calibrating Dental Caries Frequency. *American Journal of Physical Anthropology* 108:237–240.

Espejo, Antonio de
    1871   Testimonio Dado en Mejico sobre el Descubrimiento de 200 Leguas Adelante, de las Minas de Santa Bárbola, Governación de Diego de Ibarra. In *Colección de Documentos Inéditos Relativos al Descubrimiento, Conquista y Organización de las Antiguas Posesiones españolas de Améria y Oceanía*, edited by Joaquín F. Pacheco and Francisco Cardenas, vol. 15, pp. 101–135. M. Bernaldo de Quirós, Madrid, Spain.

Fenneman, Nevin, M.
    1931   *Physiography of Western United States*. McGraw-Hill Book Company, Inc., New York and London.

Gillio, David, Frances Levine, and Douglas Scott (Compilers)
    1980   *Some Common Artifacts Found at Historic Sites*. Cultural Resource Report No. 31, United States Forest Service, Southwestern Region.

Goodman, A. L., and G. J. Armelagos
    1985   Factors Affecting the Distribution of Enamel Hypoplasias within the Human Permanent Dentition. *American Journal of Physical Anthropology* 68:479–493.

Groat, Charles G.
    1972   *Presidio Bolson, Trans-Pecos Texas and Adjacent Mexico: Geology of a Desert Basin Aquifer System*. Report of Investigations No. 76. Bureau of Economic Geology, University of Texas at Austin.

Hammond, George P., and Agapito Rey (translators and editors)
    1929   *Expedition into New Mexico Made by Antonio de Espejo in 1582–1583, as Revealed in the Journal of Diego Pérez de Luxán, a Member of the Party.* Quivira Society Publications 1. Quivira Society, Los Angeles.

Harris, R. K., and Inus Marie Harris
    1967   Glass and Shell Trade Beads. In *A Pilot Study of Wichita Indian Archeology and Ethnohistory*, assembled by Robert E. Bell, Edward B. Jelks, and W. W. Newcomb, pp. 129–162. Final Report for Grant GS-964, National Science Foundation.

Hartnady, P. W.
    1988   *Premature Molar Tooth Loss in the Archaic Trans-Pecos Region of South Texas.* Unpublished Master's thesis, University of Arkansas.

Henry, Christopher D.
    1998   *Guidebook 27: Geology of Big Bend Ranch State Park, Texas.* Bureau of Economic Geology, University of Texas at Austin and Texas Parks and Wildlife Press.

Hickerson, Nancy
    1994   *The Jumanos: Hunters and Traders of the South Plains.* University of Texas Press, Austin.

Hilton, Evelyn Gill
    1986   Survey of Texas Big Bend's Prehistoric Indians and Their Pottery: Circa A.D. 1000–1500. *The Artifact* 24(4):50–85.

Hodge, Frederick Webb
    1911   The Jumano Indians. *Proceedings of the American Antiquarian Society*, n.s. 20:249–268.

Holliday, Vance T., and James E. Ivey
    1974   *Presidio-Ojinaga International Flood Control and Channel Relocation Project, Presidio County, Texas: An Evaluative Survey of the Archeological and Historical Resources.* Texas Archeological Survey Research Report 48. University of Texas at Austin.

Hughes, Jack T.
    1991   Prehistoric Cultural Developments on the Texas High Plains. *Bulletin of the Texas Archeological Society* 60:1–55.

Ing, J. David, Sheron Smith-Savage, William A. Cloud, and Robert J. Mallouf
    1996   *Archeological Reconnaissance on Big Bend Ranch State Park, Brewster and Presidio Counties, Texas, 1988–1994.* Occasional Papers No. 1. Center for Big Bend Studies, Texas Parks and Wildlife Department, Texas Historical Commission, and Sul Ross State University, Alpine, Texas.

Ivey, James E.
1990   *Presidios of the Big Bend Area.* Translated by Carlos Chavez. Southwest Cultural Resources Center Professional Paper No. 31. Division of History, Southwest Cultural Resources Center, National Park Service, Santa Fe, New Mexico.

Janes, Susan
1930   Seven Trips to Mount Livermore. *West Texas Historical and Scientific Society* 3:8–9.

John, Elizabeth A. H.
1991   Spanish-Indian Relations in the Big Bend Region during the Eighteenth and Early Nineteeth Centuries. *Journal of Big Bend Studies* 3:71–79.

Jones, Oakah L. Jr.
1988   *Nueva Vizcaya: Heartland of the Spanish Frontier.* University of New Mexico Press, Albuquerque.

1991   Settlements and Settlers at La Junta de los Rios, 1759–1822. *Journal of Big Bend Studies* 3:43–70.

Judd, M. A.
2002   Comparison of Long Bone Trauma Recording Methods. *Journal of Archaeological Science* 29:1255–1265.

Jurmain, R. D.
1977   Stress and the Etiology of Osteoarthritis. *American Journal of Physical Anthropology* 46:353–365.

1991   Degenerative Changes in Peripheral Joints as Indicators of Mechanical Stress: Opportunities and Limitations. *International Journal of Osteoarchaeology* 1:247–252.

Kelley, J. Charles
1939   Archaeological Notes on the Excavation of a Pithouse near Presidio, Texas. *El Palacio* 44(10):221–234.

1947   *Jumano and Patarabueye: Relations at La Junta de los Rios.* Unpublished Ph.D. dissertation, Harvard University, Cambridge, Massachusetts (See Kelley 1986 for published version).

1949   Archaeological Notes on Two Excavated House Structures in Western Texas. *Bulletin of the Texas Archeological and Paleontological Society* 20:89–114.

1951   A Bravo Valley Aspect Component of the Lower Rio Conchos Valley, Chihuahua, Mexico. *American Antiquity* 17(2):114–119.

1952a   Factors Involved in the Abandonment of Certain Peripheral Southwestern Settlements. *American Anthropologist* 54(3):356–387.

1952b   The Historic Indian Pueblos of La Junta de los Rios, Part 1. *New Mexico Historical Review* 27(4):257–295.

1953   The Historic Indian Pueblos of La Junta de los Rios, Part 2. *New Mexico Historical Review* 28(1):21–51.

1957   The Livermore Focus: A Clarification. *El Palacio* 64(1–2):44–52.

1985   Review of the Architectural Sequence at La Junta de los Rios. In Proceedings of the Third Jornada Mogollon Conference, edited by M. S. Foster and T. C. O'Laughlin. *The Artifact* 23(1 & 2):149–159.

1986   *Jumano and Patarabueye, Relations at La Junta de los Rios.* Anthropological Papers No. 77. Museum of Anthropology, University of Michigan, Ann Arbor.

1990   The Rio Conchos Drainage: History, Archaeology, Significance. *Journal of Big Bend Studies* 2:29–41.

1992   Introduction. In *Expedition to La Junta de los Rios, 1747–1748: Captain Commander Joseph de Ydoiaga's Report to the Viceroy of New Spain*, translated by Enrique Rede Madrid, pp. xi–xv. Office of the State Archeologist Special Report 33. Texas Historical Commission, Austin.

2004   Appendix IV: Preliminary Ceramic Type Descriptions from the La Junta Archeological District. In *The Arroyo de la Presa Site: A Stratified Late Prehistoric Campsite Along the Rio Grande, Presidio County, Trans-Pecos Texas*, by William A. Cloud, pp. 211–214. Reports in Contract Archeology 9, Center for Big Bend Studies, Sul Ross State University and Archeological Studies Program Report 56, Texas Department of Transportation, Environmental Affairs Division.

n.d.a   Reconnaissance of the Rio Grande: Fabens to Presidio, Texas. Manuscript on file, Center for Big Bend Studies, Sul Ross State University, Alpine, Texas.

n.d.b   Notes on file, Center for Big Bend Studies, Sul Ross State University, Alpine, Texas.

Kelley, J. Charles, and Ellen Abbott Kelley
    1990   *Presidio, Texas (Presidio County) Water Improvement Project, An Archaeological and Archival Survey and Appraisal.* Blue Mountain Consultants, Fort Davis, Texas.

Kelley, J. Charles, T. N. Campbell, and Donald J. Lehmer
    1940   The Association of Archaeological Materials with Geological Deposits in the Big Bend Region of Texas. *Sul Ross State Teachers College Bulletin* 21(3).

Kenmotsu, Nancy A.
    1994a   *Helping Each Other Out: A Study of the Mutualistic Relations of Small Scale Foragers and Cultivators in La Junta de los Rios Region, Texas and Mexico.* Unpublished Ph.D. dissertation, Department of Anthropology, University of Texas at Austin.

    1994b   Archeological Background. In *Archeological Testing at the Polvo Site, Presidio County, Texas,* by William A. Cloud, Robert J. Mallouf, Patricia A. Mercado-Allinger, Cathryn A. Hoyt, Nancy A. Kenmotsu, Joseph M. Sanchez, and Enrique R. Madrid, pp. 9–20. Office of the State Archeologist Report 39. Texas Historical Commission and United States Department of Agriculture, Soil Conservation Service, Austin.

    2001   Seeking Friends, Avoiding Enemies: The Jumano Response to Spanish Colonization, A.D. 1580–1750. *Bulletin of the Texas Archeological Society* 72:23–43.

    2005   Insights from INAA about Possible In-Migration of Groups to La Junta de los Rios, Texas. Paper presented at the 70th Annual Meeting, Society for American Archaeology, Salt Lake City, Utah.

Kenmotsu, Nancy A., and Barbara J. Hickman
    2000   Survey Report: FM 170 from approximately 0.268 mi. SE of the SE end of Alamito Creek Bridge to 1.067 miles SE of Redford, Texas. On file, Texas Department of Transportation, Austin.

Kenmotsu, Nancy A., and Mariah F. Wade
    2002   *American Indian Tribal Affiliation Study, Phase I: Ethnohistoric Literature Review.* Archeological Studies Program, Report No. 34, Texas Department of Transportation, Austin, and National Park Service, Amistad National Recreation Area, Del Rio.

Kennedy, Steve
    2004   Appendix III: Vertebrate Faunal Analysis of Materials from the Arroyo de la Presa Site (41PS800), Presidio County, Trans-Pecos Texas. In *The Arroyo de la Presa Site: A Stratified Late Prehistoric Campsite Along the Rio Grande, Presidio County, Trans-Pecos Texas,* by William A. Cloud, pp. 237–240. Reports in Contract Archeology 9, Center for Big Bend Studies, Sul Ross State University and Archeological Studies Program Report 56, Texas Department of Transportation, Environmental Affairs Division.

Larkin, Thomas J., and George W. Bomar
    1983   *Climatic Atlas of Texas.* Texas Department of Water Resources, Austin.

Larsen, Clark Spencer
    1987   Bioarchaeological Interpretations of Subsistence Economy and Behavior from Human Skeletal Remains. *Advances in Archaeological Method and Theory* 10:339–445.

    2002   Bioarchaeology: The Lives and Lifestyles of Past People. *Journal of Archaeological Research* 10:119–166.

Larsen, C. S., R. Shavit, and M. C. Griffin
    1991   Dental Caries Evidence for Dietary Change: An Archaeological Context. In *Advances in Dental Anthropology*, edited by M. A. Kelley and C. S. Larsen, pp. 179–202. Wiley-Liss, New York.

Lehmer, Donald J.
    1948   *The Jornada Branch of the Mogollon.* Social Science Bulletin 17. University of Arizona 19(2):9–99. Tucson.

Lovell, Nancy C.
    1997   Trauma Analysis in Paleopathology. *Yearbook of Physical Anthropology* 40:139–170.

Lukacs, J. R.
    1995   The 'caries correction factor': A new method of calibrating dental caries rates to compensate for antemortem loss of teeth. *International Journal of Osteoarchaeology* 5:151–156.

Maat, G. J. R., R. W. Mastwijk, and E. A. Van der Velde
    1995   Skeletal Distribution of Degenerative Changes in Vertebral Osteophytosis, Vertebral Osteoarthritis and DISH. *International Journal of Osteoarchaeology* 5(3):289–298.

Madrid, Enrique R. (translator)
    1992   *Expedition to La Junta de los Ríos, 1747–1748: Captain Commander Joseph de Ydioaga's Report to the Viceroy of New Spain.* Office of the State Archeologist Special Report 33. Texas Historical Commission, Austin.

Mallouf, Robert J.
    1981   Observations Concerning Environmental and Cultural Interactions During the Terminal Pleistocene and Early Holocene in the Big Bend of Texas and Adjoining Regions. *Bulletin of the Texas Archeological Society* 52:121–146.

    1985   *A Synthesis of Eastern Trans-Pecos Prehistory.* Unpublished Master's thesis, Department of Anthropology, University of Texas at Austin.

    1986   Prehistoric Cultures of the Northern Chihuahuan Desert. In *Invited Papers from the Second Symposium on Resources of the Chihuahuan Desert Re-*

gion, United States and Mexico, 20–21 October 1983, pp. 69–78. Chihua-huan Desert Research Institute, Alpine, Texas.

1987 *Las Haciendas: A Cairn-Burial Assemblage from Northeastern Chihuahua, Mexico.* Office of the State Archeologist Report 35. Texas Historical Commission, Austin.

1990 A Commentary on the Prehistory of Far Northeastern Chihuahua, the La Junta District, and the Cielo Complex. Translation of La Prehistoria del noreste de Chihuahua: Complejo Cielo y Distrito La Junta. In *Historia General de Chihuahua I: Geología Geografía y Arqueología*, edited by Arturo Marquez-Alameda. Universidad Autónoma de Ciudad Juárez y Gobierno del Estado de Chihuahua, Juárez, Mexico.

1993 Archaeology in the Cienega Mountains of Presidio County, Texas. *The Artifact* 31(1):1–44.

1994 The Natural Setting. In *Archeological Testing at the Polvo Site, Presidio County, Texas*, by William A. Cloud, Robert J. Mallouf, Patricia A. Mercado-Allinger, Cathryn A. Hoyt, Nancy A. Kenmotsu, Joseph M. Sanchez, and Enrique R. Madrid, pp. 4–8. Office of the State Archeologist Report 39. Texas Historical Commission and United States Department of Agriculture, Soil Conservation Service, Austin.

1995 Arroyo de las Burras: Preliminary Findings from the 1992 SRSU Archeological Field School. *Journal of Big Bend Studies* 7:3–39.

1999 Comments on the Prehistory of Far Northeastern Chihuahua, the La Junta District, and the Cielo Complex. *Journal of Big Bend Studies* 11:49–92.

2001 CBBS Documents Tall Rockshelter. *La Vista de la Frontera* 14(1):4.

2002 Archeologists Investigate Wolf Den Cave. *La Vista de la Frontera* 15(1):6.

2007 A Cave of Wonders: Return to Wolf Den. *La Vista de la Frontera* 18:1–3.

in prep The Livermore Phase and Late Prehistoric Adaptations in the Texas Big Bend.

Mallouf, Robert J., and Virginia A. Wulfkuhle
1989 An Archeological Reconnaissance in the Rosillos Mountains, Brewster County, Texas. *Journal of Big Bend Studies* 1:1–24.

Marks, M. K., J. C. Rose, and E. L. Buie
1985 Bioarchaeology of Seminole Sink. In *Seminole Sink: Excavation of a Vertical Shaft Tomb, Val Verde County, Texas*, edited by S. A. Turpin, pp. 75–118. Texas Archeological Survey, The University of Texas at Austin.

Meindl, R. S., C. O. Lovejoy, R. P. Mensforth, and L. Don Carlos
    1985   Accuracy and direction of error in the sexing of the skeleton: implications for paleodemography. *American Journal of Physical Anthropology* 68:79–85.

Miller, Miles R.
    1996   *The Chronometric and Relative Chronology Project.* Archaeological Technical Report No. 5. Anthropology Research Center and Department of Sociology and Anthropology, The University of Texas at El Paso.

Miller, Miles R., and Nancy A. Kenmotsu
    2004   Prehistory of the Jornada Mogollon and Eastern Trans-Pecos Regions of West Texas. In *The Prehistory of Texas*, edited by Timothy K. Perttula, pp. 205–265. Texas A&M University Press, College Station.

Newcomb, W. W. Jr.
    1961   *The Indians of Texas.* University of Texas Press, Austin.

Ortner, D. J., and M. F. Eriksen
    1997   Bone changes in the human skull probably resulting from scurvy in infancy and childhood. *International Journal of Osteoarchaeology* 7:212–220.

Ortner, D. J., and W. G. J. Putschar
    1981   *Identification of Pathological Conditions in Human Skeletal Remains.* Smithsonian Contributions to Anthropology No. 28. Smithsonian Institution Press, Washington, D. C.

Ortner, D. J., E. H. Kimmerle, and M. Diez
    1999   Probable Evidence of Scurvy in Subadults from Archaeological Sites in Peru. *American Journal of Physical Anthropology* 108:321–331.

Peabody, Charles
    1909   Reconnaissance Trip through Western Texas. *American Anthropologist*, n.s. 11:202–216.

Phillips, David A. Jr.
    1989   Prehistory of Chihuahua and Sonora, Mexico. *Journal of World Prehistory* 3:373–401.

Piehl, Jennifer C.
    in press Human Osteology and Mortuary Practices in the Eastern Trans-Pecos Region of Texas. Center for Big Bend Studies, Sul Ross State University, Alpine, Texas.

Powell, A. Michael, and Richard A. Hilsenbeck
    1995   A Floristic Overview of the Chihuahuan Desert Region. *Chihuahuan Desert Discovery*, 1995(Winter/Spring):4–14.

Prewitt, Elton
  1983   From Circleville to Toyah: Comments on Central Texas Chronology. *Bulletin of the Texas Archeological Society* 54:201–238.

Ravesloot, John C.
  1988   *Mortuary Practices and Social Differentiation at Casas Grandes, Chihuahua, Mexico.* Anthropological Papers of the University of Arizona 49. University of Arizona Press, Tucson.

Reid, D. J., and M. C. Dean
  2000   Brief Communication: The Timing of Linear Hypoplasias on Human Anterior Teeth. *American Journal of Physical Anthropology* 113:135–139.

Reimer, P. J., M. G. L. Baillie, E. Bard, A. Bayliss, J. W. Beck, C. J. H. Bertrand, P. G. Blackwell, C. E. Buck, G. S. Burr, K. B. Cutler, P. E. Damon, R. L. Edwards, R. G. Fairbanks, M. Friedrich, T. P. Guilderson, A. G. Hogg, K. A. Hughen, B. Kromer, F. G. McCormac, S. W. Manning, C. B. Ramsey, R. W. Reimer, S. Remmele, J. R. Southon, M. Stuiver, S. Talamo, F. W. Taylor, J. van der Plicht, and C. E. Weyhenmeyer
  2004   IntCal04 Terrestrial radiocarbon age calibration, 26 - 0 ka BP. *Radiocarbon* 46:1029–1058.

Reinhard, Karl J., Ben W. Olive, and D. Gentry Steele
  1989   Bioarchaeological Synthesis. In *From the Gulf to the Rio Grande: Human Adaptation in Central, South, and Lower Pecos Texas*, edited by Thomas R. Hester, Stephen L. Black, D. Gentry Steele, Ben W. Olive, Anne A. Fox, Karl J. Reinhard, and Leland C. Bement, pp. 129–140. Center for Archaeological Research, University of Texas at San Antonio, Texas A & M University, and Arkansas Archeological Survey, San Antonio.

Reuland, Walter P.
  1993   *Cartridges for the Springfield Trapdoor Rifles and Carbines, 1865–1898.* 2nd Edition. Heritage Concepts, Laramie, Wyoming.

Rike, Richard, and James Rock
  1989   *Historic Cans and Bottles: Identification and Contexts.* University of Nevada at Reno Historic Preservation Program.

Robinson, David G.
  2004   Appendix VI: Petrographic Analysis of Prehistoric Ceramics from Two Sties in the La Junta Archeological District, Presidio County, Trans-Pecos Texas. In *The Arroyo de la Presa Site: A Stratified Late Prehistoric Campsite Along the Rio Grande, Presidio County, Trans-Pecos Texas*, by William A. Cloud, pp. 227–235. Reports in Contract Archeology 9, Center for Big Bend Studies, Sul Ross State University and Archeological Studies Program Report 56, Texas Department of Transportation, Environmental Affairs Division.

Rodríguez-Alegría, Enrique, Michael D. Glascock, and Robert J. Speakman
    2004   Appendix V: Instrumental Neutron Activation Analysis of Ceramics, Soil Samples, and a Possible Tempering Agent from the La Junta Region, Trans-Pecos Texas. In *The Arroyo de la Presa Site: A Stratified Late Prehistoric Campsite Along the Rio Grande, Presidio County, Trans-Pecos Texas*, by William A. Cloud, pp. 215–226. Reports in Contract Archeology 9, Center for Big Bend Studies, Sul Ross State University and Archeological Studies Program Report 56, Texas Department of Transportation, Environmental Affairs Division.

Rogers, J., W. Tony, P. Dieppe, and I. Watt
    1987   Arthropathies in Palaeopathology: The Basis of Classification according to Most Probable Cause. *Journal of Archaeological Science* 14:179–193.

Rothschild, B.
    2002   Porotic Hyperostosis as a Marker of Health and Nutritional Conditions. *American Journal of Human Biology* 14:417.

Sauer, Carl
    1934   The Distribution of Aboriginal Tribes and Languages in Northwestern Mexico. *Ibero-Americana* 5.

Sayles, E. B.
    1935   *An Archeological Survey of Texas*. Medallion Papers 17. Gila Pueblo, Globe, Arizona.

    1936   *An Archeological Survey of Chihuahua, Mexico*. Medallion Papers 22. Gila Pueblo, Globe, Arizona.

Scheuer, Louise, and Sue Black
    2000   *Developmental Juvenile Osteology*. Academic Press, London.

Scholes, Frances V., and H. P. Mera
    1940   *Some Aspects of the Jumano Problem*. Contributions to American Anthropology and History, 34. Carnegie Institution Publication, No. 523. Carnegie Institution, Washington D. C.

Schwarcz, Henry P.
    2000   Some Biochemical Aspects of Carbon Isotopic Paleodiet Studies. In *Biogeochemical Approaches to Paleodietary Analysis*, edited by Stanley H. Ambrose and M. Anne Katzenberg, pp. 189–209. Kluwer Academic/Plenum Publishers, New York.

    2006   Stable Carbon Isotope Analysis and Human Diet. In *Histories of Maize: Multidisciplinary Approaches to the Prehistory, Linguistics, Biogeography, Domestication, and Evolution of Maize*, edited by J. E. Staller, R. H. Tykot, and B. F. Benz, pp. 315–321. Elsevier, Amsterdam.

Scuddy, James F.
 1976   Vertebrate Fauna of the Colorado Canyon Area, Presidio County, Texas. In *Colorado Canyon*, edited by Don Kennard, pp. 99–116. Natural Area Survey No. 11. Lyndon B. Johnson School of Public Affairs, University of Texas at Austin.

Seebach, John D.
 2007   *Late Prehistory Along the Rimrock: Pinto Canyon Ranch*. Papers of the Trans-Pecos Archaeological Program, No. 3. Center for Big Bend Studies, Sul Ross State University, Alpine.

Seymour, Deni J.
 2003   Protohistoric and Early Historic Temporal Resolution. Lone Mountain Report 560–003. Manuscript on file, Conservation Division, Diretorate of Environment, Fort Bliss, Texas.

 n.d.   The Implications of Mobility, Reoccupation, and Low Visibility Phenomena for Chronometric Dating. Manuscript submitted to *American Antiquity* and currently under review.

Shackelford, William J.
 1951   *Excavations at the Polvo Site in Western Texas*. Unpublished Master's thesis, Department of Anthropology, University of Texas at Austin.

 1955   Excavations at the Polvo Site in Western Texas. *American Antiquity* 20(3):256–262.

Sobolik, K. D.
 1994   Paleonutrition of the Lower Pecos region of the Chihuahuan desert. In *Paleonutrition: the Diet and Health of Prehistoric Americans*, pp. 247–264. Center for Archaeological Investigations, Southern Illinois University at Carbondale.

Soil Conservation Service
 1992   *General Soil Map: Presidio County, Texas*. Soil Conservation Service in cooperation with Texas Agricultural Experiment Station, National Cartographic Center, Fort Worth, Texas.

Steele, D. G. and J. F. Powell
 1989   An Osteological Examination of Prehistoric Hunters and Gatherers of the Southern Desert and Semi-Arid Regions of North America. Paper presented at the Archaic Symposium, Lajitas, Texas.

Stuiver, Minze, Paula J. Reimer, Edouard Bard, J. Warren Beck, G. S. Burr, Konrad A. Hughen, Bernd Kromer, Gerry McCormac, Johannes van der Plicht, and Mark Spurk
 1998   INTCAL98 Radiocarbon Age Calibration, 24,000–0 cal BP. *Radiocarbon* 40(3):1041–1083.

Suhm, Dee Ann, and Edward B. Jelks
    1962   *Handbook of Texas Archeology: Type Descriptions.* Texas Archeological Society Special Publication 1 and Texas Memorial Museum Bulletin 4. Austin.

Suhm, Dee Ann, Alex D. Krieger, and Edward B. Jelks
    1954   An Introductory Handbook of Texas Archeology. *Bulletin of the Texas Archeological Society* 25.

Swift, Roy L., and Leavitt Corning Jr.
    1988   *Three Roads to Chihuahua: The Great Wagon Roads that Opened the Southwest, 1823–1883.* Eakin Press, Austin.

Talma, A. S., and J. C. Vogel
    1993   A Simplified Approach to Calibrating ^{14}C Dates. *Radiocarbon* 35(2):317–322.

Thornbury, William D.
    1965   *Regional Geomorphology of the United States.* John Wiley & Sons, Inc., New York, London, and Sydney.

Turner, Ellen Sue, and Thomas R. Hester
    1985   *A Field Guide to Stone Artifacts of Texas Indians.* Texas Monthly Press, Austin.

Ubelaker, Douglas H.
    1989   *Human Skeletal Remains: Excavation, Analysis, Interpretation.* 2nd edition. Taraxacum, Washington, D. C.

Van Devender, Thomas R.
    1977   Holocene Woodlands in the Southwestern Deserts. *Science* 198:189–192.

Van Devender, Thomas R., C. Edward Freeman, and Richard D. Worthington
    1978   Full-Glacial and Recent Vegetation of Livingston Hills, Presidio County, Texas. *Southwestern Naturalist* 23(2):289–302.

Waldron, T.
    1993   The Distribution of Osteoarthritis of the Hands in a Skeletal Population. *International Journal of Osteoarchaeology* 3(3):213–218.

Waldron, T., and J. Rogers
    1991   Inter-observer Variation in Coding Osteoarthritis in Human Skeletal Remains. *International Journal of Osteoarchaeology* 1:49–56.

Wallace, Ernest, and E. Adamson Hoebel
    1986   *The Comanches: Lords of the South Plains.* University of Oklahoma Press, Norman and London.

Wells, Phillip V.
 1966 Late Pleistocene Vegetation and Degree of Pluvial Climatic Change in the Chihuahuan Desert. *Science* 153:970–974.

 1977 Post-Glacial Origin of the Present Chihuahuan Desert Less Than 11,500 Years Ago. In *Transactions of the Symposium on the Biological Resources of the Chihuahuan Desert Region, United States and Mexico*, edited by R. H. Wauer and D. H. Riskind, pp. 67–83. National Park Service Transactions and Proceedings Series 3.

APPENDIX I
CERAMICS FROM THE
MILLINGTON SITE (41PS14)

David V. Hill

A sample of 340 ceramic-related objects recovered during the surface collection and testing of the Millington site are analyzed below. Analysis of the ceramic assemblage is oriented toward typological identification, temporal placement, and potential sources of the ceramics.

Methodology

Ceramics derived from the same provenience were checked for cross-mends to keep from over-sampling a single potential vessel during the analysis. All of the Native-made earthenwares were examined under a binocular microscope to classify the ceramic temper to better place the objects in space and time. The colors of the paste of the native-made earthenwares and historic ceramics were classified using the Munsell Soil Color chart. A non-typological attribute-based approach was taken when classifying Native-made ceramics thought to have been produced in the La Junta and Big Bend area. Justification for the use of a non-typological approach for this class of ceramics will be discussed below.

Results of the Analysis

Ceramics from the prehistoric and historic periods were recovered during the surface collection and testing at the Millington site. For the purposes of this analysis these specimens were divided into Native-Made Earthenware and Historic Ceramics subdivided into pottery of Mexican, Euro-American, and Miscellaneous types (Table 1). Ceramic classifications were based on the references

Table 1. Ceramic Types Recovered from the Millington Site (41PS14)

Native-Made Earthenwares

Ceramic Type	Surface	Subsurface	Total
Plain Brownware	21	69	90
Polished Plain Brownware	2	9	11
Polished Incised Brownware		1	1
Polished El Paso Brownware	1	3	4
El Paso Brownware	1	8	9
El Paso Polychrome	6	20	26
Red-on-Brown	13	5*	18
Black-on-White (Historic?)	1		1
Unidentified Polychrome		1	1
Red-on-White	7		7
White Slipped Earthenware	5	2	7
Smudged Brownware	1		1
Red Slipped Earthenware	2	1	3
Polished Red Slipped Earthenware	3	3	6
Black-on-Red	1		1
Black-on-Yellow	1		1
Escondida Polychrome	1		1
Total Native-Made Earthenwares	**66**	**122**	**188**
*Lots 85-1 and 85-4 refit			

Historic Ceramics

Mexican Ceramics

Ceramic Type	Surface	Subsurface	Total
Majolica	66	3	69
Majolica?	1		1
Guanajuato Green Glaze	22	2	24
Presidios Green	4		4
Galera Polychrome	3		3
Sgraffiato Galera Tradition	1		1
Galera Ware	3		3
Galera Pb Glaze		1	1
Black Pb Glaze		1	1
Total Mexican Ceramics	**100**	**7**	**107**

Euro-American Ceramics

Ceramic Type	Surface	Subsurface	Total
Annular or Mocha Ware	5		5
Feathered Edge Ware	1		1

Table 1. Ceramic Types Recovered from the Millington Site (41PS14)

Flow-blue	1		1
Soft Paste Porcelain	2	1	3
Hotel Whiteware	1		1
Stoneware	3		3
Salt-Glazed Stoneware	2		2
Sponge-Decorated	1		1
Decalcomania Porcelain	1		1
Transfer-Printed	11		11
Total Euro-American Ceramics	**28**	**1**	**29**

Miscellaneous Ceramics			
Ceramic Type	**Surface**	**Subsurface**	**Total**
Chinese Porcelain	1		1
Tile	2		2
Unidentified Late 19th / Early 20th Century Euro-American Ceramics	9		9
Porcelain Doll Parts	3		3
Unidentified Circular Porcelain object	1		1
Total Miscellaneous Ceramics	**16**		**16**

cited in the discussion in addition to the prior experience of the author. The surface collection yielded a wide range of prehistoric and historic pottery. Historic ceramics from excavated contexts were confined to the upper two levels of Test Units 4 and 8 and the upper three levels of Test Unit 5. The historic ceramics recovered from subsurface contexts—produced primarily in Mexico with one Euro-American type—are small (less than 2 cm in maximum diameter), and likely represent limited stratigraphic mixing with the surface.

Native-Made Earthenwares

The 2006 Millington site collection contains a total of 188 native-made earthenware sherds, 66 from surface contexts and 122 from the subsurface. This class of ceramics consists of low-fired prehistoric and historic ceramics produced by indigenous peoples of the American Southwest and northern Mexico. The following discussion is presented by ceramic type.

Plain Brownware

Plain Brownwares were the most common ceramics recovered during the project (n=90; 21 from the surface and 69 from the subsurface), accounting for 26 percent of the total ceramic assemblage. The paste of the Plain Brownware sherds ranged in color from light reddish-brown, reddish-brown, brown or reddish-yellow. All had gray cores, regardless of their derivation from surface or subsurface contexts. Interestingly, one brownware sherd from the uppermost level of Unit 8 had an incised line which had later been polished, a reversal of what is typically seen when these applications are combined.

The most common tempering agent observed in the Plain Brownware ceramics is rounded sand composed of various sediments: quartz, white and/or gray feldspars, occasional rounded fragments of mafic or felsic volcanic rock, and most typically a white to gray volcanic tuff. Previous petrographic analysis of brownware ceramics collected by J. Charles Kelley from the Millington Site and secured from the Museum of the Big Bend by William Cloud observed primarily rounded grains of quartz and alkali feldspar in the paste with trace amounts of volcanic tuff and limestone in what are assumed to be locally produced brownware pottery (Robinson 2004). Compositional variability in the minerals and rock fragments observed in the sample of sherds examined by Robinson was attributed to differences in the sources of the raw materials used to make the ceramics. Whether the differences in the tempering agents reported for the different types in the small sample analyzed by Robinson represent differences in the sources of pottery manufacture or variation in a more limited set of ceramic resources remains to be determined through future work.

It has long been recognized that early village occupations at La Junta were using ceramics from the American Southwest and northern Chihuahua (Sayles 1935; Kelley et al. 1940), but undecorated brownwares at these sites were thought to have been produced locally. J. Charles Kelley (1939; Kelley et al. 1940) proposed the names Chinati Plain and Capote Plain and borrowed E. B. Sayles (1936) term Conchos Plain for other distinctive brownwares. However, descriptions of these undecorated ceramics remained unpublished until recently (Kelley 2004). Kelley hesitated publishing his descriptions as he felt they were too broad to be applied to specific cases and that more work needed to be done to clarify them (Ellen Kelley, personal communication 2007).

The non-typological approach taken in this analysis suggests that the three plainware ceramic types described by Kelley from the La Junta area represent continuity in the use of clay and temper resources from the prehistoric and into the historic period. Future composition studies of Plain Brownwares from dated contexts in the La Junta and Big Bend area of west Texas, when combined with the collection and analysis of potential ceramic raw materials, will contribute to our understanding of change in the technology of locally produced undecorated ceramics through time.

Few plainware ceramics could be attributed to specific vessel forms, a problem that has been observed previously in historic native ceramic assemblages from the El Paso, Texas area (Hill 2002). One form of vessel recovered from the Millington site that could be identified was the comal—a ceramic griddle for the preparation of tortillas. Three comal sherds were recovered from the surface of the Millington site. The comal sherds are characterized by a low vertical or slightly incurved rim attached to a flat base (Hill 2002; Leach et al. 1995). Comals appear in the American Southwest in the eighteenth century and seem to represent a change in local foodways, possibly as the result of migration of indigenous people from central Mexico (Warren 1979:241).

Red-on-Brown

Red-on-Brown ceramics constituted 5.3 percent of the overall ceramic assemblage (n=18; 13 from the surface and five from the subsurface). Red-on-Brown ceramics were made using primarily light reddish firing clay similar to that of the Plain Brownwares. Like the Brownwares, the Red-on-Brown sherds were tempered using sand characterized by sediments derived from a combination of plutonic and volcanic sources. The single black-on-white sherd recovered during the project with a paste that is identical in color and the presence of plutonic and volcanic sand temper likely represents a misfired Red-on-Brown sherd.

Previous classifications of red-painted plainware from the La Junta area have either attempted to place ceramics into Capote or Conchos Red-on-Brown (Kelley 2004), or as the approach taken here identifying the Red-on-Brown decorated ceramics present in the site assemblage (Cloud et al. 1994). Capote and Conchos Red-on-Brown are believed to differ in the quality of the line-work and that fewer jar forms tended to be decorated in Capote Red-on-Brown than on Conchos Red-on-Brown (Kelley 2004). Given the highly fragmented nature of most archaeological ceramic assemblages, where identification of vessel forms cannot be easily recognized, the latter typological classification may be difficult to demonstrate.

Seven sherds recovered from surface contexts were coated with a white slip on one or both surfaces and then decorated with a red-firing or in one case black firing mineral-based pigment identical to the paint observed on the Red-on-Brown sherds. Seven additional sherds were coated with a white slip surface (n=5; subsurface n=2). The slip is light gray or white in color forming a thin distinct layer covering the ceramic body. Particles of sand temper frequently protrude through the slip or may reflect the impure nature of the white slip clay.

Brownware ceramics with a white slip have not been reported previously from the La Junta area; however, brownwares with a white slip and red decoration have been reported from sites dating to the eighteenth and nineteenth centuries in the lower valley of El Paso, but are uncommon (Brown et al. 1999; Hill 2002). Given the similarity of the paste of the red-on-white sherds recovered from the Millington site to that of the plain and Red-on-Brown wares, slipped ceramics likely represent a locally produced type. The occurrence of red-on-white ceramics in surface contexts may indicate a historic date for this type. However, the presence of white slipped sherds in subsurface contexts suggests that the use of white slips may have a prehistoric antecedent.

El Paso Polychrome

El Paso Polychrome ceramics make up the major prehistoric ceramic type traded into the Millington site, accounting for 7.6 percent of the recovered ceramics (n=26; six sherds from the surface; 20 sherds from the subsurface). Examination of the ceramic collection excavated by Kelley during his earlier investigations at the Millington site and now curated at Sul Ross State University revealed that El Paso Polychrome formed the bulk of the trade ceramics recovered from this site (Kelley 1985; 1986). El Paso Polychrome sherds are characterized by a reddish brown to black colored paste and are tempered with abundant fragments of quartz along with white and pink alkali feldspar with a trace amount of hornblende and brown biotite—all consistent with the use of granite as a tempering agent (Hill 1991). The lack of sufficient portions of temporally sensitive rim forms precludes assigning these ceramics to a time-span shorter than the total range of production of El Paso Polychrome between A.D. 1100 and 1400 (Miller 1995).

Only the upper one third of the bodies of El Paso Polychrome jars were decorated using red and black colored pigments (Miller 1995). As a consequence, brownware sherds containing minerals derived from granite including quartz, white, gray or pink feldspar and brown biotite mica also observed in the El Paso Polychrome sherds were classified as El Paso Brownware. The granite tempered brownware sherds represented either the undecorated portions of El Paso Polychrome vessels or possibly earlier El Paso Brown ceramics.

Two sherds, both from the surface of the site, have black and red pigments on brown pastes that appear similar in color and presence of plutonic and volcanic sands similar to the majority of the brownware ceramics recovered from the Millington site. It is possible that these two sherds represent local copies of El Paso Polychrome. Without petrographic analysis the compositional similarity of the two presumably local sherds cannot be compared with previous compositional studies of El Paso Polychrome.

Redware

Red-slipped ceramics also constituted a class of ceramics that were brought to the Millington site. Ceramics classified as red-slipped were recovered from both surface (n=5) and subsurface (n=4) contexts. The redwares are highly variable in terms of the degree of surface finish and temper. Of the nine red-slipped sherds, three of them were simply coated with a red clay slip or paint. On the other six sherds, the vessels were then highly burnished with a polishing stone that resulted in a more smooth polished red surface.

One redware sherd from the surface of the site contained very fine angular white feldspar grains. The sherd of Escondida Polychrome, a Medio Period ceramic type from Casas Grandes, also recovered from a surface context contained a similar feldspar-rich tempering agent to the previously mentioned red-slipped sherd. The other redwares were tempered using sands containing quartz and gray feldspar and superficially resembled the temper in the presumably locally produced brownwares.

Redwares containing variable amounts of quartz and feldspar have been reported from the Polvo site (41PS21) located about

21 km (13 miles) south of Millington (Cloud et al. 1994). Red slipped ceramics are a component of Viejo Period ceramic assemblages from the Casas Grandes cultural area (Di Peso et al. 1974). It is possible that some of these sherds could also represent undecorated portions of a Medio Period Casas Grandes type, Playas Red Incised (Di Peso et al. 1974). Playas Red Incised was also produced in the Sacramento Mountains located in southeastern New Mexico (Warren 1992) that may also have served as a source for some of the red-slipped ceramics.

Other Native-Made Earthenwares

Other types of prehistoric pottery were recovered from the Millington site. As mentioned earlier, a sherd of Escondida Polychrome was recovered from the surface (0-246). At least two other sherds, one with a dark yellow slip and dark brown paint (0-80) and another with a blueish gray slip and two very thin red parallel lines (0-81) were also recovered from the surface of the site. These latter two ceramics were likely related to the Medio Period occupation of Casas Grandes. Specimen 0-229, a Red-on-Brown sherd with a highly polished surface and tempered using volcanic tuff, could represent an earlier Viejo Period ceramic product. The three latter sherds were tempered using light-gray colored volcanic tuff a material often used in decorated ceramics recovered from Casas Grandes (Shepard in Di Peso et al. 1974).

Mexican Glazed Ceramics

Majolica

The most common type of glazed Mexican pottery is majolica, a white tin-opacified lead-based glaze. First produced during the late seventh or early eighth century in Basra, the technology of a low-fired high gloss white ceramic traveled with the spread of Islam, eventually being produced in Spain some-time during the twelfth century (Hill 2006). The technology of majolica was brought to Mexico during the early sixteenth century and continues to be produced today at several locations (Lister and Lister 1976). Sixty-nine sherds of majolica were recovered from both surface (n=66) and subsurface (n=3) contexts (Table 2).

The majolica ceramics from the Millington site were small and lack many of the decorative features used for chronological control. However, some temporal control could be derived from the colors of the glaze. Green-colored glazes became popular after 1780, at the expense of blue-colored types (Barnes and May 1972). The presence of predominately green-colored majolica glazes including the use of broad wavy lines, a feature of earlier blue-glazed Huejotzingo Blue-on-White, characterized the majority of the decorated majolica types recovered from the Millington site (Fox 2002).

Green-black, green-yellow, green, green-yellow-pink, green-black-yellow and green-rust-brown represent nineteenth century majolica types (Fournier 1997). The turquoise and turquoise and yellow sherds also likely represent nineteenth century majolica as do the mold-made pieces (Fox 2002).

Black-colored lead glazed ceramics were recovered from the surface and subsurface of the Millington site. Similar black-glazed ceramics were recently recovered from LA 149323, a copper smelter located in Santa Fe, New Mexico that is associated with ceramics dating to the early eighteenth century (Hill n.d.). Black-glazed ceramics were produced well into the mid-nineteenth century (Barnes 1980).

Three majolica sherds had reddish colored pastes. One sherd (0-261) was decorated with a cobalt-blue glaze with an overlying black line. The other sherd with a reddish paste had a single green line (0-49). The third sherd had a blue-on-white design that resembles Puebla Blue-on-White (0-82). Majolica ceramics with reddish-brown colored pastes were probably produced in the state of Guanajuato (Fornier 1997; McKinzie 1989). Majolica ceramics are currently produced in Guanajuato (Whitaker and Whitaker 1978).

Green-glazed ceramics

Two types of green glazed pottery were recovered from the surface and subsurface of the Millington site. The more common type, Guanajuato Green-Glaze is characterized by a reddish brown or dark-brown paste that frequently has a sandy texture (Fournier 1997). Guanajuato Green-Glaze was produced between 1750 and 1850 (Barnes 1980). However, green glazed ceramics continue to be produced in Guanajuato today (Fournier 1997).

The Galera Polychrome and the four undecorated portions of Galera ware characterized by a reddish brown paste coated with a clear lead glaze were likely from Guanajuato. Eight sherds of Galera ware were recovered. Galera Ware first appears in Spanish sites in central Texas around 1750 and continues to be produced today (Tomka and Fox 1998). The Sgraffiato sherd, characterized by a white clay slip with an incised line that exposed the underlying reddish brown paste is also likely to have been produced in Guanajuato, indicating that this sherd was likely to have been an example of the Galera ceramic tradition.

Presidios Green-Glaze is distinguished by a light gray to light pink colored ceramic paste and green-colored glaze (Fournier 1997). Presidios Green-Glaze is believed to have been produced from the sixteenth into the nineteenth century and was defined based on ceramics recovered from Presidio Carrizal, Chihuahua (Brown and Fournier 1998).

Table 2. Decorative Treatments on Majolica from the Millington Site	
Color of the Glaze	**Number of Examples**
Green	23 (1)
Dark Green	1
Green-Rust Brown	12
Green-Black	9
Green-Rust-Black	1
Green-Yellow	2
Dark Green-Yellow	1
Green-Black-Yellow	1
Green-Light Brown	1
Yellowish Green	1
Blue	1 Puebla Blue-on-White
Blue-Black	1 copy of San Elizario Polychrome
Turquoise	3
Turquoise-Yellow	2 (one constructed in a mold)
Yellow-Brown	1
Yellow-Light Green-Dark Brown	1
Yellow-Green-Pink	1
Light Yellow-Green Band	1
Black	1
White Base Glaze	3
Light Yellow-Mold Made	2
(1) Designates number of sherds with Guanajuato pastes	

Euro-American Ceramics

A small but diverse assemblage of Euro-American ceramics was collected from the surface of the Millington site. These ceramics were produced during the late nineteenth or early twentieth centuries, likely reflecting an increase in the availability of Euro-American ceramics with the arrival of the railroad to west Texas.

Transfer-Printed

Eleven Transfer-Printed sherds were recovered from the surface of the Millington site. Nine of the sherds had designs executed in cobalt-blue while the other two sherds have maroon designs. Transfer-Print ceramics were first produced in 1825 (Blake and Freeman 1998). Decalcomania allows the transfer of more complex multicolored designs to ceramics and first appears in 1860 (Berge 1980). A single decalcomania sherd from a plate decorated using a rose pattern was collected (0-192). This sherd had a bottom stamp from the Homer Laughlin China Company. The Homer-Laughlin ChinaCompany has been in operation in East Liverpool, Ohio since 1877 (Kovel and Kovel 1986).

Annularware or Mocha Ware

Five sherds of Annularware were recovered from the surface of the Millington site. Four of the sherds are characterized by parallel blue and black lines (0-33, 0-54, 0-58, 0-70). The fifth sherd has only parallel blue lines (0-142). Annularwares were produced from ca. 1850 into the first decades of the twentieth century (Habicht-Mauche 1988; Price 1979).

Flow-Blue

A single sherd of Flow-Blue was recovered from the Millington site (0-74). Flow-Blue was produced between 1830 and the first decades of the twentieth century (Price 1979).

Feathered Edge Ware

A single sherd of edge-decorated, or Feathered Edge Ware, was collected (0-170). This sherd had a molded floral design below the form of the vessel. Edge-decorated ceramics were produced between 1840 and approximately 1930 (Price 1979).

Sponge-Decorated

A single sherd of Sponge-decorated pottery was also recovered (0-272). Sponge-decorated ceramics were produced beginning in the 1820s or 1830s and continued to be produced into the early twentieth century (Price 1979).

Stoneware and Salt-Glazed Stoneware

Five sherds with stoneware bodies, two of which also exhibited the use of salt-glazing, were recovered (0-96, 0-152). The other Stoneware ceramics recovered were Specimens 0-14, 0-143, and 0-198. The five sherds came from storage crocks. These sherds likely represent the later nineteenth or twentieth century occupation of the site, as such objects are still available on the market.

Soft-Paste Porcelain

Three sherds with grainy white pastes and white glazes are classified as soft-paste porcelain. These sherds were likely produced

during the later nineteenth or early twentieth century (Price 1979). Two of the sherds were recovered from the surface (0-31, 0-273) and one from Level 1, of the subsurface.

Other Historic Ceramics

Another ceramic recovered from the Millington site was produced by the Homer-Laughlin Company (0-184). The base of a tan-orange plate has a top symbol looking like an L going through an X. The design is likely an L piercing an H with a waist produced by the Homer Laughlin Company. If the next word is Nautilus (much of the word is missing) it dates from ca. 1935 to ca. 1950 (Kovel and Kovel 1986:193).

A sherd of white "Hotel Ware" (0-221) and eight unidentified decorative types of twentieth century glazed ceramics, including two sherds from a child's toy cup decorated in copper luster (0-199), are also present in the ceramic assemblage. Three fragments of porcelain dolls, one with the stamp "Japan" on its back (0-84) also represents the presence of children resident at the Millington site.

Although not specifically a Euro-American ceramic, one sherd of Chinese porcelain or Jingdezhen ware was collected from the Millington site (0-200). This tiny sherd is from a small cup or bowl. Given the long span for the production of porcelain and its importation into the New World, this sherd could be attributed to either the Spanish Colonial or more recent occupations at the Millington site.

Discussion of the Millington Ceramic Assemblage

Three distinct periods of occupation of the Millington site are reflected in the ceramic assemblage. The excavated material represents a potential occupation of this portion of the site between the tenth to fourteenth centuries, based on the presence of El Paso Polychrome and ceramics that possibly originated at Casas Grandes. While later occupations dating to the latter portion of the Late Prehistoric and Protohistoric Period (fifteenth and sixteenth centuries) of the Millington site have been posited based on prior excavations, no temporally diagnostic ceramics were recovered that are associated with this more recent period during the current excavations. However, it is possible that some of the Red-on-Brown and undecorated ceramics recovered during the excavations could represent occupations dating to the Late Prehistoric and Protohistoric periods.

A second occupation dating to the later eighteenth century is evidenced by the presence of majolica incorporating green-colored decorative elements from Puebla along with majolica and green-glazed ceramics made in Guanajuato. Based on the presence of decorated native ceramics in the El Paso region, it is possible that at least some of these ceramics are associated with this occupation or possibly in part with the post-fourteenth century component. Without direct dating of the ceramics or features associated with decorated indigenous pottery, the temporal association of the Red-on-Brown and Red-on-White ceramics remains unknown.

The third occupation of the site is evidenced by the presence of late nineteenth and twentieth century Euro-American ceramics. This third ceramically-defined period likely represents a continuum with the late eighteenth and early nineteenth century occupations of the site.

Future excavations at the Millington site will provide greater insight into the Native-made ceramics of west Texas. The current study of the pastes of plain brownwares, redwares, and Red-on-Brown pottery strongly indicates continuity in the sources of the materials used to produce these ceramics. Future analysis of Native-made ceramics from the Millington site should include extensive characterization studies including Instrumental Neutron Activation Analysis and petrographic analysis using a larger sample of ceramics. In conjunction with the composition studies, extensive sampling of local clays and sediment samples should be undertaken. As the pastes of the Native-made ceramics from the Millington site strongly resemble one another the potential for on-site or nearby production of ceramics is high. The clay and temper samples should be analyzed chemically in conjunction with the ceramics. Clay samples also need to be examined for their suitability for the production of pottery including the examination of such properties as shrinkage and firing characteristics.

Prehistoric ceramics identified by this study as derived from other areas of the American Southwest and northern Mexico need to be characterized compositionally. Compositional analysis of imported ceramics will allow for comparison with previous studies—specifically of Casas Grandes decorated pottery types and El Paso Polychrome. Other unidentified decorated ceramics including the redware and unclassified polychrome sherds should also be analyzed.

The phase system for the Big Bend/La Junta region is currently based on few independently dated contexts. Also, the ceramic types that are present in the Big Bend/La Junta region lack appropriate temporal frameworks for seriation purposes. Future excavations at the Millington site and other prehistoric and early historic sites in the Big Bend region need to concentrate on directly dating ceramics through Optically Stimulated Luminescence (OSL) derived from stratified contexts. When possible, OSL dates should be derived from the same contexts as radiocarbon dates for cross-checking dates.

The historic occupation of the Millington site spans the timing of the replacement of indigenous earthenware ceramics with lead-glazed pottery produced in Mexico. The study of historic Mexican and Euro-American ceramics from the Millington site has provided an opportunity to study the phenomena of indigenous, and possibly Central Mexican, migrant acculturation referred to as *Mestizaje* (Brown et al. 1999). Future analysis of historic Mexican ceramics should focus on creating a more complete typology of lead-glazed pottery, including formal/functional and sourcing studies similar in nature to those outlined for the prehistoric pottery and the use of stable lead isotope analysis as an aid in sourcing the historic lead-glazed ceramics. A study of the augmentation and replacement of household ceramic assemblages of indigenous and Mexican-made pottery by Euro-American ceramics should also be conducted during future excavations.

In summary, the current excavations conducted at the Millington site produced a ceramic assemblage spanning the Late Prehistoric and Historic periods of human occupation of the Big Bend/La Junta region of West Texas. The assemblage was characterized by an abundance of Brownware, Red Slipped, Red-on-Brown and Red-on-White ceramics that most likely represent locally produced ceramics. The uniformity of the types of mineral inclusions observed in what are thought to be locally produced ceramics represent considerable continuity in the use of the same ceramic resources. Red Slipped ceramics along with pottery from the El Paso, Texas and Casas Grandes, Chihuahua areas were also traded into the Big Bend region.

Indigenous ceramics were most likely replaced gradually some time during the late eighteenth century by lead-glazed pottery produced at several locations in Mexico. With the arrival of the railroad to West Texas in the late nineteenth century, Euro-American ceramics began to replace the ceramics produced in Mexico. Future analysis of ce-

ramics from the Millington site and other prehistoric sites located in the Big Bend/La Junta region of West Texas should focus on chronology-building using a combination of OSL and radiocarbon dating of short-lived samples to better refine the local prehistoric chronology. The chronological studies should be supplemented with sourcing studies of the indigenous and imported ceramics. Continued efforts should also be made to refine the sourcing and chronological placement of Mexican and Euro-American ceramics from West Texas to understand how the cultures of these two areas influenced the population of West Texas.

References Cited

Barnes, Mark R.
 1980   Mexican Lead-Glazed Earthenwares. In *Spanish Colonial Frontier Research*, edited by Henry F. Dobyns, pp. 91–110. Spanish Borderlands Research No.1, Center for Anthropological Studies, Albuquerque, New Mexico.

Barnes, Mark R., and R. V. May
 1972   *Mexican Majolica in Northern New Spain*. Occasional Paper No. 2. Pacific Coast Archaeological Society, Costa Mesa, California.

Berge, Dale L.
 1980   *Simpson Springs Station: Historical Archaeology in Western Utah, 1974–1975*. Cultural Resources Series No. 6. Bureau of Land Management, Utah.

Blake, Marie E., and Martha Doty Freeman
 1998   *Nineteenth-Century Transfer-Printed Ceramics from the Texas Coast: The Quintana Collection*. Prewitt and Associates, Inc., Austin, Texas.

Brown, Roy, B., and Patricia Fournier
1998   *Proyecto Archeo-Historico de la Frontera Norte: La Expansion del Dominio Español en Nuevo Mexico and Nueva Vizcaya, Analisis de Materiales Arqueologicos.* Manuscript on file, Escuela National de Anthropologia e Historia, Mexico, D.F.

Brown, David O., John A. Peterson, and David V. Hill
1999   Discourse in Clay: Ceramics and Culture in Historic Socorro, Texas. *Bulletin of the Texas Archaeological Society* 70.

Cloud, William A., Robert J. Mallouf, Patricia A. Mercado-Allinger, Cathryn A. Hoyt, Nancy A. Kenmotsu, Joseph M. Sanchez, and Enrique R. Madrid
1994   *Archeological Testing at the Polvo Site, Presidio County, Texas.* Office of the State Archeologist Report 39. Texas Historical Commission and United States Department of Agriculture, Soil Conservation Service, Austin.

Di Peso, Charles C., John B. Rinaldo, and Gloria J. Fenner
1974   Ceramics and Shell. In *Casas Grandes: A Fallen Trading Center of the Gran Chichimeca*, Vol. 6. The Amerind Foundation, Inc., Dragoon and Northland Press, Flagstaff, Arizona.

Fournier, Patricia
1997   Mexican Ceramic Analysis. In *A Presidio Community on the Rio Grande: Phase III Testing and Historical Research at San Elizario, Texas*, edited by Bradley J. Vierra, June-el Piper and Richard C. Chapman, Vol. I, Chapter 8. Office of Contract Archaeology, University of New Mexico, Albuquerque.

Fox, Anne A.
2002   Ceramics. In *Nuestra Señora del Refugio (41RF1), Refugio County, Texas* by Cynthia L. Tennis, pp. 203–220. Archaeological Survey Report 315. Center for Archaeological Research, The University of Texas at San Antonio and Archaeological Studies Program Report 39, Texas Department of Transportation, Austin.

Habicht-Mauche, Judith A.
1988   Historic Artifact Analysis, Hubbell Trading Post, National Historic Site. Manuscript on file, Southwest Archaeological Consultants, Santa Fe, New Mexico.

Hill, David V.
1991   Settlement Patterns and Ceramic Production in the Paso del Norte. In *Actas del Secundo Congreso Historia Regional Comparada*, pp. 29–44. Universidad Autonoma de Ciudad Juarez, Mexico.

2002   Ceramics of San Elizario. In *The 1995 San Elizario Plaza Archaeological Project*, edited by John A. Peterson, Timothy B. Graves, and David V. Hill, pp. 165–182. The University of Texas at El Paso and Texas Department of Transportation, Austin.

2006   *The Materials and Technology of Glazed Ceramics from the Deh Luran Plain, Southwestern Iran: A Study in Innovation.* British Archaeological Reports, International Series 1511, Oxford, England.

n.d.   The Ceramics from LA 149323. Manuscript on file, Lone Mountain Archaeological Consultants Inc., Albuquerque, New Mexico.

Kelley, J. Charles
  1939 Archaeological Notes on the Excavation of a Pithouse near Presidio, Texas. *El Palacio* 44(10):221–234.

  1985 Review of the Architectural Sequence at La Junta de los Rios. In Proceedings of the Third Jornada-Mogollon Conference, edited by Michael S. Foster and Thomas C. O'Laughlin. pp. 149–159. *The Artifact* 23(1–2).

  1986 *Jumano and Patarabueye, Relations at La Junta de los Rios*. Anthropological Papers No. 77. Museum of Anthropology, University of Michigan, Ann Arbor.

  2004 Preliminary Ceramic Type Descriptions from the La Junta Archeological District. In *The Arroyo de la Presa Site: A Stratified Late Prehistoric Campsite Along the Rio Grande, Presidio County, Trans-Pecos Texas*, by William A. Cloud, Appendix IV. Reports in Contract Archaeology 9, Center for Big Bend Studies, Sul Ross State University, Alpine and Archeological Studies Program Report 56, Texas Department of Transportation, Austin.

Kelley, J. Charles, T. N. Campbell, and Donald J. Lehmer
  1940 The Association of Archaeological Materials and Geological Deposits in the Big Bend Region of Texas. *Sul Ross State Teachers College Bulletin* 21(3).

Kovel, Ralph, and Terry Kovel
  1986 *Kovel's New Dictionary of Marks: Pottery and Porcelain: 1850 to the Present*. Crown Publishers, Inc. New York.

Leach, Jeff D., Melinda Wallace-Merton, Robert D. Harrison, John A. Peterson, and Mike Flowers
  1995 Spanish Colonial Through Historic American Period Ceramics. In *Living on the River's Edge*, by Jeff D. Leach, Nicholas P. Houser, Robert D. Harrison, John A. Peterson, and Raymond P. Mauldin, pp. 192–228. Archaeological Research, Inc. El Paso, Texas.

Lister, Florence C., and Robert H. Lister
  1976 Distribution of Mexican Majolica along the Northern Borderlands. In *Collected Papers in Honor of Marjorie F. Lambert*, pp. 113–140. Papers of the Archaeological Society of New Mexico No. 3, Albuquerque.

McKinzie, Clinton M. M.
  1989 Independent Study Report on Guanajuato Majolica in the San Antonio Missions Area. Manuscript on file, Center for Archaeological Research, The University of Texas at San Antonio.

Miller, Myles R.
  1995 Ceramics of the Jornada Mogollon and Trans-Pecos Regions of West Texas. *Bulletin of the Texas Archeological Society* 66:210–219.

Price, Cynthia R.
  1979 *19th Century Ceramics in the Eastern Ozark Border Region*. Center for Archaeological Research, Monograph Series No. 1. Southwestern Missouri State University, Springfield.

Robinson, David G.
  2004 Appendix VI: Petrographic Analysis of Prehistoric Ceramics from Two Sties in the La Junta Archeological District, Presidio County, Trans-Pecos Texas. In *The Arroyo*

de la Presa Site: A Stratified Late Prehistoric Campsite Along the Rio Grande, Presidio County, Trans-Pecos Texas, by William A. Cloud, pp. 227–235. Reports in Contract Archeology 9, Center for Big Bend Studies, Sul Ross State University and Archeological Studies Program Report 56, Texas Department of Transportation, Environmental Affairs Division.

Sayles, E. B.
1935   *An Archaeological Survey of Texas.* Medallion Papers 17. Gila Pueblo, Globe, Arizona.

1936   *Some Southwestern Pottery Types.* Medallion Papers 19. Gila Pueblo, Globe, Arizona.

Tomka, Steve A., and Anne A. Fox
1998   *Mission San Jose Indian Quarters Foundation Project, Bexar County, Texas.* Archaeological Survey Report 278. Center for Archaeological Research, The University of Texas at San Antonio.

Warren, A. H.
1979   Historic Pottery of the Cochiti Reservoir Area. In *Archaeological Investigations in Cochiti Reservoir, New Mexico, Volume 4: Adaptive Change in the Northern Rio Grande Valley*, edited by Jan V. Biella and Richard C. Chapman, pp. 236–246. Office of Contract Archaeology, University of New Mexico, Albuquerque.

1992   Temper Analysis of the Pottery of the Rio Bonito Valley. In *Investigations into the Prehistory and History of the Upper Rio Bonito, Lincoln County, Southeastern New Mexico*, by Robin E. Farwell, Yvonne R. Oakes, and Regge N. Wiseman. Laboratory of Anthropology Notes 297, Office of Archaeological Studies, Museum of New Mexico, Santa Fe.

Whitaker, Irwin, and Emily Whitaker
1978   *A Potter's Mexico.* University of New Mexico Press, Albuquerque.

APPENDIX II
VERTEBRATE FAUNAL REMAINS
FROM THE
MILLINGTON SITE (41PS14)

William A. Cloud, Steve Kennedy, and Sarah Willet

The 2006 Millington site investigation resulted in the recovery of 2,361 faunal specimens from subsurface contexts. The vast majority of these specimens are small scraps of bone salvaged from the screen (1/8" hardware cloth), although a small percentage are larger and more intact, which allowed some degree of identification. These remains were analyzed by Steve Kennedy and Sarah Willet.

Findings

The test units (Test Units 1–8) yielded the majority of the faunal specimens (n=2,096), the remainder (n=265) were recovered from screening Backhoe Trench #1 backdirt. Test unit recoveries were as follows:

Test Unit 1 . . .207
Test Unit 2 . . . 83
Test Unit 3 . . .173
Test Unit 4 8

Test Unit 5 . . .205
Test Unit 6 . . .735
Test Unit 7 . . .420
Test Unit 8 . . .265

The test unit excavated the deepest (Test Unit 6—Level 11) yielded the most specimens. The very low number of specimens from Test Unit 4 is somewhat puzzling, as that unit was dominated by midden deposits where a greater number of bone scraps would be expected to occur. This is perhaps analogous to what was seen with Burial 3, which also was within a midden deposit. A low number of elements and poor preservation of those that were present occurred in that interment and this can probably be explained by soil chemistry in the midden. Identifications from the analysis are proved below:

Mammals   Number of Bones

Large mammal		144
Large to medium mammal		40
Medium mammal		436
Medium to small mammal		23
Small mammal		213
Unidentified mammal		77
Artiodactyla	Even-toed ungulates	128
Cervidae	Deer family	1
Mustelid	Weasel family	1
Leporidae	Rabbit family	4
Cricetidae	Rodent family	3
Odocoileus sp.	Deer	2
Sciuridae sp.	Squirrel	1
Sylvilagus sp.	Cottontail rabbit	26
Lepus californicus	Black-tailed jackrabbit	13
Perognathus sp.	Pocket mouse	6
Peromyscus sp.	Deer mouse	21
Sigmodon sp.	Cotton rat	5
Neotoma sp.	Wood rat	20

Birds
Unidentified bird . . . 6

Reptiles
Unidentified reptile . . . 6

Amphibians
Unidentified amphibian . . . 17

Fish
Unidentified fish . . . 4

Other Unidentified . . . 1,164

Total   2,361

Discussion

Analysis of the faunal remains recovered from the 2006 Millington site investigation provide a listing of animals that either lived at the site and entered the site strata naturally or were brought to the site as foodstuffs. There were no exotic species identified—all of the animals represented above are extant in the general area of the Millington site. Due to the site's proximity to both the Rio Grande and desert environs, these animals would have been common residents within a relatively short distance from the site, perhaps 2 km or less. Interestingly, burned or charred bones were uncommon in the collection, and only a single bone fragment exhibited evidence of modification from use as a tool.

Only 28 bones in the collection exhibited some degree of burning. Twenty-three of these were recovered from Test Unit 7—Levels 2, 4, 5, and 7—in possible association with Feature 12, a rock wall remnant assumed to be a structure of some sort. All but two of these were large mammal fragments. Two other burned bones were associated or possibly associated with features. One of these is an extremely burned medium-sized mammal bone fragment from Feature 6 (ring midden/earth oven). The other is an incomplete left calcaneum from a Cervidae in possible association with Feature 5 (unknown pit structure). The latter was recovered from a small test unit placed in the floor of Backhoe Trench #1 just south of Test Unit 6. The other three burned bones were a *Odocoileus* sp. (deer) ulna fragment recovered from the floor of Backhoe Trench #1, a large mammal bone fragment recovered from Level 3 of Test Unit 8, and a mammal bone fragment recovered from Level 4 of Test Unit 8. Bones that are burned supply more reliable evidence that a specific animal was targeted for food, although even this is not completely demonstrable in many cases, as the bones could have been targeted for other purposes and later tossed into a fire for disposal. Nevertheless, the above data suggest large mammals were cooked on the bone more frequently than other animals at the site through time.

The bone tool is an Artiodactyla long bone diaphysis fragment that is highly polished and could have potentially been used for a number of tasks. It was recovered from near the floor area of Feature 5 (Test Unit 6, Level 11), a pit structure of unknown form that dates to the early portion of the La Junta phase.

Many of the rodent bones recovered from the investigation probably entered the site deposits by natural means. Rodent bones identified in Levels 8–11 in Test Unit 6, within the probable Feature 5 roof residue, were likely attracted to cavities created by the fallen structure. The following numbers of unburned rodent bones were identified from these levels: 18 *Peromyscus* sp. (deer mouse), four *Perognathus* sp. (pocket mouse), 17 *Neotoma* sp. (wood rat), and three *Sigmodon* sp. (cotton rat).

APPENDIX III
GEOPHYSICAL INVESTIGATION

Jaime Hincapié

This report is pursuant to a conductivity/ground penetrating radar (GPR) survey investigation made at three locations at the Millington Site, at the southeastern edge of Presidio, Texas. The purpose of the investigation was to locate buried archaeological objects, if any.

Geophysical Techniques Used

In this survey, conductivity and ground penetrating radar (GPR) were used. The combined data obtained from conductivity and GPR fit the needs of this particular site, since conductivity narrows down anomaly areas, and the GPR provides a better detailed subsurface image of those anomalies. Conductivity changes (conductivity anomalies) are usually associated with changes in material composition. Since conductivity readings average over great depths, the anomaly areas are later surveyed with the GPR to obtain images that resemble a cross section of the subsurface. Because the conductivity method can be carried out rapidly and the data can be downloaded quickly, the preliminary anomaly maps obtained at the site allow a more efficient GPR survey.

The GPR method uses the ability of electromagnetic waves to bounce off surfaces, just like mechanical waves (such as sound waves) do. Differences in electromagnetic properties of materials (dielectric constant, magnetic and electric susceptibility) only allow electromagnetic wave penetration to limited depths. For instance, materials with greater conductivity capabilities will reduce, and even stop, electromagnetic wave propagation, while non-conductive substances allow transmission of the GPR signal. Combining conductivity and GPR data offers a good way to image the subsurface in a fast and reliable manner, since signal changes can be easily associated with changes in the materials in the subsurface.

Equipment

The conductivity was carried out using a Geonics EM-31 conductivity meter, and the GPR survey was done with a Sensors and Software EKKO Pulse ground penetrating radar system. A brief description of the instruments' operation follows.

EM-31 Conductivity Meter

The EM-31 is an instrument designed to detect changes in subsurface material electrical conductivity. It is a pair of coils (transmitter and receiver antennas) inside a frame that keeps them in horizontal position. It operates by sending a polarized electromagnetic pulse into the ground through the transmitter antenna. The electromagnetic field created by the transmitted pulse creates electrical currents in the surveyed materials. The strength and behavior of those currents depends on the electrical properties of the studied materials, and the objects buried in them, if any. Those currents (known as "Eddie" currents) create a set of secondary electromagnetic fields which are detected by the receiver antenna in the instrument on the surface.

Because of the way the instrument is built, the pulse sent into the studied material can be polarized vertically and horizontally. The vertical pulse produces readings that average conductivity values to 6 m below the surface, while the horizontal pulse averages conductivity values to 3 m deep. For this particular study, the horizontal component was used. The measurements obtained for the conductivity are plotted in a contour map. The units in which the measurements are taken are milliSiemens per meter (mSm), and represent the conductivity of the material—the higher the measurement, the more conductive the material is.

Ground Penetrating Radar

The GPR employs the imaging of weak reflections. It uses a transmitter that sends a high frequency electromagnetic pulse into the ground, and a receiver that captures the energy that bounces (echoes) off the discontinuities inside it. The electromagnetic pulse frequency ranges from several megahertz to a few gigahertz, and the lower the frequency, the deeper the penetration. However, this has a tradeoff—the lower the frequency, the lower the resolution (the size of the smallest object detectable with the technique increases as resolution decreases). In soils, GPR penetration is also constrained by humidity content and clay content. Humidity and clay minerals act as barriers that inhibit signal penetration. The 250MHz central frequency antenna was used in this survey, allowing a clear signal penetration down to 4 m in dry non-clayey materials. The measuring units used for the GPR are initially time units (nanoseconds; $1ns = 1x10^{-9}$ sec), that are converted to depth depending on the electromagnetic velocity of the material. For instance, when operating on dry sand, the average electromagnetic wave velocity is 0.15 meters per nanosecond (m/ns, with a dielectric constant ranging from 3–5), while operating in saturated sand, the electromagnetic velocity is 0.06 m/ns (dielectric constant 20–30).

Detailed descriptions of these methods and rigorous mathematical and physical support material can be found in multiple references, such as Telford et. al. (1976) and Sharma (1982).

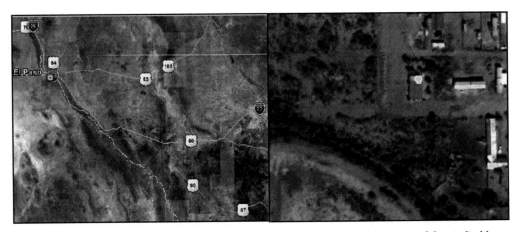

Figure 1. Location of the Millington Site in West Texas (left), and an aerial picture of the studied locations (right).

Field Procedure

The three studies are labeled Areas A, B, and C, and they are located at the southeast edge of Presidio, Texas (Figure 1). These areas were selected by the archaeology team that requested this survey. Each location was a 10 x 10 m square, and the sides were oriented to magnetic cardinal directions. Each area was gridded into 1 x 1 m squares, and conductivity readings were taken at each grid node.

Once the conductivity readings were obtained, a preliminary conductivity map was created at each area. The purpose of the conductivity anomaly maps was to identify and locate areas where strong conductivity changes appeared. These strong conductivity anomalies are suggestive of material changes, which could be representative of buried features or materials. The GPR survey was carried out along lines that intersected suspicious areas where conductivity anomalies were found. On Areas A and B, the GPR lines started at a baseline that cut through the northwestern corner (see dashed line in Figures 3 and 5). Some geophysical processing was applied to the signals in order to enhance the appearance of the observed features detected by the exploration techniques.

Conductivity Results

Area A exhibited a series of conductivity anomalies with a northeast-southwest trend (medium shades in Figure 2). These anomalies could be the result of changes in soil composition, or the presence of buried objects that yield a strong conductivity contrast compared to the surrounding soils. The more or less linear layout of the anomaly (especially noticeable in the southwest corner where the big anomaly seems to split) suggests that, if it was produced by buried man made structures, a better view of their edge(s) would be provided by GPR lines going across it. Figure 3 shows the directions of the GPR lines carried out at Area A. A more in-depth explanation of the findings with the GPR is provided later in this report. The very high magnitude anomaly on the northeast corner (lighter shades) was likely caused by the nearby fence.

Area B yielded anomalies with a similar trend as Area A (northeast-southwest). These anomalies, however, are lower in magnitude (Figure 4). The shape of the anomaly seems to start a little below the center of the area, and grows in magnitude towards the northeast, with a slight bend towards the north. This anomaly was also inspected with

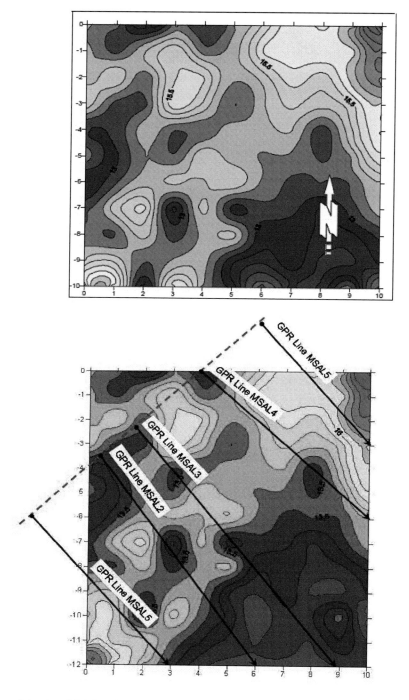

Figures 2 (top) and 3 (above). Conductivity anomaly map for Area A. In this figure, and all conductivity maps, areas with same shades have the same average conductivity. Light shades are the high conductivity end, while dark shades represent the lower end of conductivity. The dashed line on Figure 3 is the base line where GPR lines started.

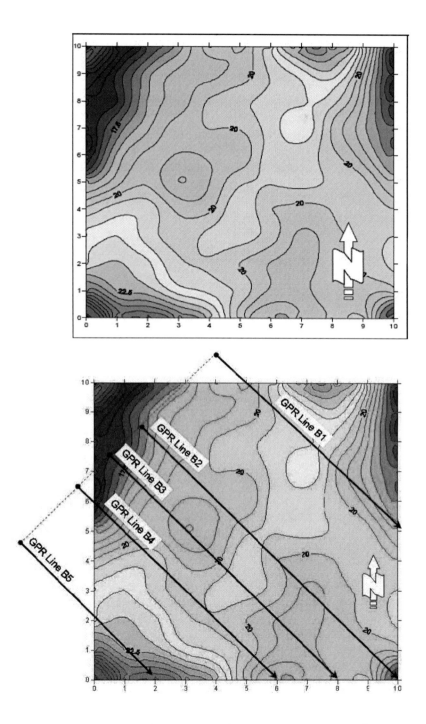

Figure 4. (top) Area B conductivity survey. Distances along both axes are in meters.

Figure 5. (above) Area B GPR lines.

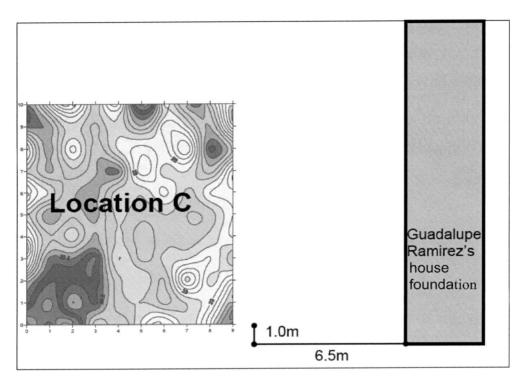

Figure 6. Area C relative to Mr. Ramirez's house and sidewalk.

the GPR in a perpendicular direction, so the objects that were causing it, if any, could be localized. Figure 5 shows the GPR lines used on Area B.

Area C is located southwest of the property across the street from BHT #1. The southeast corner of Area C is 6.5 m west, and 1.0 m north of the sidewalk that borders Mr. Guadalupe Ramirez's property (Figure 6). Area C presents several conductivity anomalies that don't seem to follow a linear pattern. A very strong conductivity low is observed in the southwest corner (darker shades on Figure 7), while conductivity highs are more widespread in the area, represented as small patches of about 1 m² in average size. Along X=0, several conductivity highs can be seen at Y=3.5, Y=6.0, and Y=7.8. These strong conductivity values may reflect the presence of a metal pipe and/or metallic tools used by the archaeology crew working at the site. The high conductivity at X=1.7, Y=10 was probably a reflection of the metal sieve installed at about 2 m off the northern end of the study area. Anomalies observed at the south and north ends of the eastern edge of Area C were probably caused by construction debris, piping, or cables associated with the house across the street (Mr. Guadalupe Ramirez's). Due to the sparse location of these anomalies, running GPR along selected lines would cause good coverage of some points, and missing others. Taking advantage of the fact that Area C was on the street, we covered it by running GPR lines from west to east, and at 1.0 m spacing from each other (Figure 8).

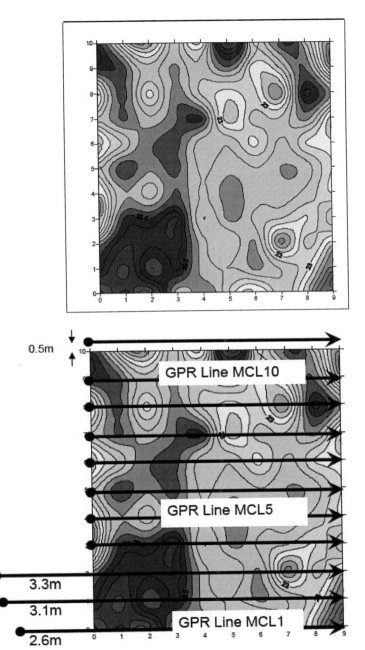

0.5m

GPR Line MCL10

GPR Line MCL5

3.3m

3.1m

GPR Line MCL1

2.6m

Figre 7. (top) Area C conductivity survey. Distances along both axes are in meters.

Figure 8. (above) Area C GPR lines.

GPR Results

The signal enhancement process includes "*dewowing*," and AGC with 1.0 sec window, and 500 as maximum gain.

Five GPR lines were run over Area A, in a direction intended both to intersect the conductivity anomalies, and to get a cross-section of the buried object(s), if any (see Figure 3). The same procedure was applied at Area B (see Figure 5). Area C was treated differently: since it was located on a flat unobstructed surface, the survey was carried out at a faster pace. GPR lines here were run along west-east lines, at 1.0 m spacing, starting at the southwestern end of the area (see Figure 8). Area C had complete GPR coverage.

The anomalies found within Areas A and B were marked and labeled in the field by members of the archaeology and geophysical teams. Anomalies in Area C were not flagged. The complete set of GPR findings can be summarized in Table 1. Note: starting point indicates the point where the GPR line intersects the baseline.

Area A

GPR Line name (Same label as in Figure 3)	Area Name	Dist. from Starting Point (m)	Approx. depth to object (m)
MSLA1	MA1a	2.0	1.0
	MA1b	6.0	1.0
MSLA2	MA2a	2.0	1.7
	MA2b	5.5–7.0	1.5–1.7
	MA2c	7.7	1.9
MSLA3	MA3a	2.5	1.3
	MA3b	6.0	1.2
	MA3c	8.0	0.9

Area B

GPR Line name (Same label as in Figure 5)	Area Name	Dist. from Starting Point (m)	Approx. depth to object (m)
GPR Line B1	MB1a	1.3*	1.0
	MB1b	5.5*	1.5
GPR Line B2	MB2a	2.0	1.3
	MB2b	7.8	1.0
GPR Line B3	MB3a	3.0*	0.7
	MB3b	8.5*	1.0

* An anomaly can be followed between these two locations.

Area C

GPR Line name (Same label as in Figure 8)	Dist. from Starting Point (m)	Approx. depth to object (m)
GPR Line MCL1	0.0–2.5	0.5
	2.5–5.5	1.0
	5.5–7.5	1.4
GPR Line MCL2	0–10 [1]	1.0
GPR Line MCL3	0–10 [2]	1.0
GPR Line MCL4	2.0–3.5	1.1
	5.70–9.0	1.4
	9.0–10.0	1.1
GPR Line MCL5	0.5–3.0	1.1
GPR Line MCL5	2.5–4.6	1.0
	5.5–7.5	1.0
	8.8–10.0	1.0
GPR Line MCL6	1.75–4.0	1.25
	7.25–9.0	1.0
GPR Line MCL7	3.0–4.5	0.7
	8.5–10.0	1.0
GPR Line MCL8	1.0–3.0	1.0
GPR Line MCL9	0.0–2.5	0.8
	4.5–9.0	1.1
GPR Line MCL10	1.0–3.5	1.2
	4.2–7.0	1.25

	8.2–9.5	1.25
GPR Line MCL11	4.0–8.0	1.25

(1)
Continuous disturbance at depth ~1.0 m. The cause of this disturbance is not clear on the signal.

(2)
Same disturbance as in GPR Line MCL2, at about 1.0 m, however, at distance 0.0–2.5 m. At 9.0–10.0 m another perturbation appears as a diagonal that starts at a depth of about 1.0 m and stops at about 0.7 m. This anomaly could be due to construction and/or construction debris.

The disturbances in Area C could be due to many reasons, especially to reflections of the GPR signal from leftovers of construction material under the pavement (such as from Mr. Ramirez's property construction).

References

Burguer, H. R.
2002 *Exploration Geophysics of the Shallow Subsurface.* Prentice Hall P.T.R., Englewood Cliffs, New Jersey.

Dobrin, Milton B.
1976 *Introduction to Geophysical Prospecting.* McGraw-Hill Inc., New York.

Geonics Inc.
EM-31 Conductivity Meter Reference Manual.

Golden Software Inc.
Surfer 8 Data Processing Package Reference Manual.

Sensors and Software Inc.
EKKO PULSE 1000 GPR Reference Manual.

Sharma, P. V.
1982 *Environmental and Engineering Geophysics.* Cambridge University Press, London.

Telford W. M., L. P. Geldart, R. E. Sheriff, and D. A. Keys
1976 *Applied Geophysics.* Cambridge University Press, Cambridge, England.

APPENDIX IV

GEOPHYSICAL SURVEY AT TWO LA JUNTA SITES

Chester P. Walker

This report outlines findings from geophysical survey at the Polvo (41PS21) and Millington (41PS14) sites in Presidio County, Texas. A fluxgate gradiometer, conductivity meter and ground penetrating radar (GPR) were used on an area totaling 200 m². Geophysical survey was conducted by Chester P. Walker who was aided by William A. Cloud, Barbara Baskin, David Duke, Bill Moorehouse, and Gilberto Velasco.

Equipment Used

Instrument	Sample Density	Area Surveyed
Geonics EM38B - both Quadrature and In Phase recorded	1 m Traverse Interval 4 Readings per Meter	200 m²
GSSI SIR 2000 GPR with 400 Mhz Antenna	0.5 m Traverse Interval 32 Readings per Meter	200 m²
Bartington 601-2 Fluxgate Gradiometer	0.5 m Traverse Interval 8 Readings per Meter	200 m²

Survey Objectives

Record and locate Spanish Colonial architecture associated with two mission sites.

Site Locations

Site	Easting	Northing
The Polvo site (41PS21)	578430	3256310
The Millington site (41PS14)	562712	3268753

Site Location

Both sites are located in Presidio County, Texas. UTM coordinates above are in zone 13 north and referenced to the WGS84 datum.

Summary of Results

The geophysical survey at both sites recorded patterning of possible cultural origin that fit the approximate shape and size of the archaeological features targeted. At both sites the GPR data shows the patterning of the possible structures with the most clarity. Results from the Millington site are much more compelling than the results from the Polvo site. Ground truthing in these areas is suggested to confirm these findings.

Areas of Investigation

Detailed survey using a fluxgate gradiometer, electromagnetic conductivity meter, and a GPR totaling 200 m² was conducted at two sites in Presidio County. Survey grids were laid out using tapes.

Ground Conditions & General Considerations

Ground cover at both sites was exposed soil. Both sites are located in areas with a significant amount of mesquite and creosotebush. Each showed clear signs of modern cultural activity.

Data Processing

Magnetometer and EM data was processed using ArchaeoSurveyor 2.1.4.5 by DW Con-

sulting. GPR data was processed using GPR Slice 5.0 by the Geophysical Archaeometry Laboratory.

Data Processing - Polvo Site 41PS21 Magnetometer

1 Base Layer
2 Clip from -50 to 50
3 De Stagger: Grids: All Mode: Both By: -4 intervals, 10.00 cm

---

Data Processing - Polvo Site 41PS21 Conductivity

1 Base Layer
2 Despike Threshold: 1 Window size: 6 x 3

Data Processing - Polvo Site 41PS21 Magnetic Susceptibility

1 Base Layer
2 Despike Threshold: 1 Window size: 6 x 3
3 Low pass Gaussian filter: Window: 3 x 3

Data Processing - Millington Site 41PS14 Magnetometer

1 Base Layer
2 Clip from -50 to 50
3 De Stagger: Grids: All Mode: Both By: -3 intervals, 10.00 cm

---

Data Processing - Millington Site 41PS14 Conductivity

1 Base Layer
2 Clip at 1 SD
3 Clip at 2 SD

Data Processing - Millington Site 41PS14 Magnetic Susceptibility
1 Base Layer
2 Clip at 1 SD
3 Clip at 2 SD
4 Low pass Gaussian filter: Window: 3 x 3

GPR data was assembled into a three dimensional data cube and "sliced" into a series of amplitude slice maps. Amplitude slice-maps are a three-dimensional tool for viewing differences in reflected amplitudes across a given surface at various depths and are generated through a comparison of reflected amplitudes between raw vertical profiles.

Velocity analysis was preformed on the data at both sites to determine the relative depths of each time slice. When travel times of energy pulses are measured, and their velocity through the ground is known, distance (or depth in the ground) can be accurately measured. The geometry of hyperbolic reflections can be used to calculate the relative dielectric permittivity (RDP) of the ground and in turn this can be used to calculate the velocity of the signal then employed to calculate the various depths of objects or individual amplitude slice maps.

Survey Results

Initial results from both sites show promising trends in the data—especially the GPR data—that correspond to the rough size and shape of the archaeological features targeted by this investigation. Data from the Millington site is more legible than the

data from the Polvo site, however, ground truthing excavations is needed at both sites to confirm these findings. While neither site produced data with cultural patterns that can be unequivocally interpreted as remnants of the buildings targeted, both sites produced data trends that can be interpreted as possible structures.

Polvo (41PS21)

The Magnetometer (Figure 1) data from the Polvo site shows two strong dipolar anomalies in the upper southwest and lower northeast corners of the collection grid. A northwest running series of monopolar positive anomalies, centered on the southern dipolar anomaly are also present. To the northwest of the two dipoles is a series of monopolar negative magnetic anomalies.

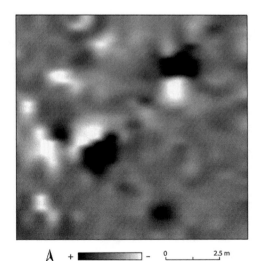

Figure 1. Processed Magnetometer data from the Polvo site.

Velocity Analysis Results

Site	RDP	Velocity (m/ns)	Depth of Hyperbola
The Polvo site (41PS21)	7.75	0.109	3.25 m
The Millington site (41PS14)	20.58	0.066	0.45 m

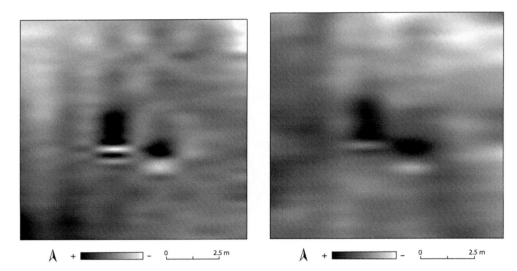

Figure 2. (left) Processed Conductivity data from the Polvo site.
Figure 3. (right) Processed Magnetic Susceptibility data from the Polvo site.

The conductivity (Figure 2) and magnetic susceptibility (Figure 3) both show two strong positive anomalies roughly in the center of the collection grid. Neither of these two data sets produced any data trends that can readily be interpreted as being cultural in origin.

The GPR surveys (Figure 4) at the Polvo site did locate patterns that are possibly cultural in origin. These patterns, however, are only legible in the upper 20 cm below the ground surface. Magnetometer data help to confirm the trends observable in the GPR data with two strong dipolar returns and several small positive monopolar returns that conform to this patterning. Neither the conductivity nor magnetic susceptibility data show any patterning that correlates well with the ones observed in the GPR data.

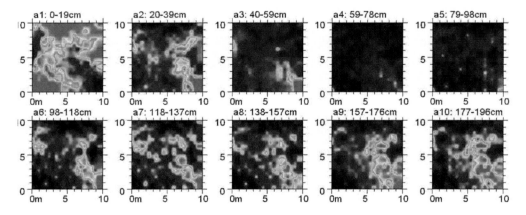

Figure 4. Processed GPR Amplitude Slice Maps from the Polvo site.

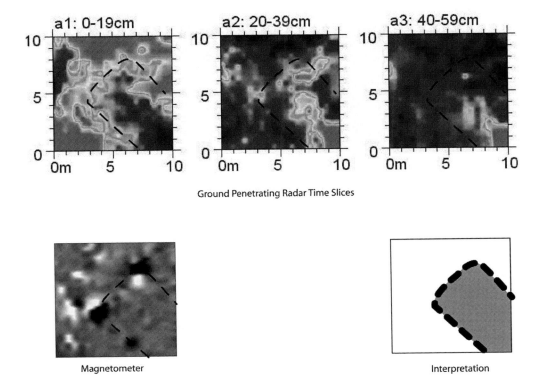

Ground Penetrating Radar Time Slices

Magnetometer

Interpretation

Figure 5. Interpretations of geophysical data from the Polvo site.

Interpretations of the geophysical data from the Polvo site (Figure 5) suggest the location of a possible rectangular structure orientated on a northeast axis. The portions of this structure caught by the collection area measures approximately 5.5 m wide by 6 m long. This possible structure appears to extend outside the collection area to the southeast.

Millington Site (41PS14)

The magnetometer data (Figure 6) from the Millington site displayed several complex dipolar anomalies. These were concentrated on the northeastern and southeastern corners of the grid as well as slightly to the west of the center of the grid. A trend of monopolar positive anomalies is present throughout the data with the notable exception of the area in

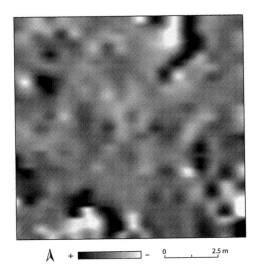

Figure 6. Processed Magnetometer data from the Millington site.

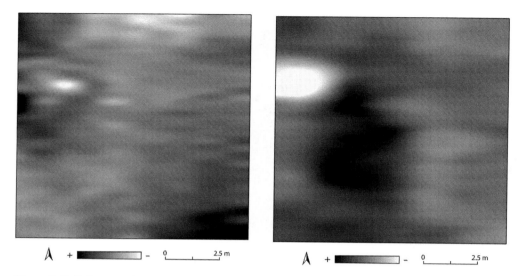

Figure 7. (left) Processed Conductivity data from the Millington site.
Figure 8. (right) Processed Magnetic Susceptibility data from the Millington site.

the center of the collection grid. The center of the collection grid is notably more quiet (displaying lower amplitude magnetic anomalies) than the rest of the area.

The conductivity data (Figure 7) displays a large, diffuse monopolar positive anomaly in the southeast corner of the collection area. The northwestern edge of the collection grid also show monopolar positive anomalies. A diffuse low conductive trend is noted along the northern edge of the collection grid that corresponds to a washed out area on the surface of the ground that was noted during data collection.

Magnetic susceptibility (Figure 8) data is dominated by a strong positive monopolar anomaly just off center of the collection grid. This anomaly is adjacent to a strong monopolar negative anomaly.

The GPR data from the Millington site (Figure 9) shows an interesting square trend on a northwest axis. This trend is the most legible in the first time slice from 0–12 cmbs. This time slice shows a high amplitude background response (shown in a medium shade) and three large low amplitude anomalies

(shown in darker shades). These low amplitude returns form a rough square pattern. This square trend is also legible in the second and third time slices measuring 12–24 and 24–36 cmbs, respectively. In these two time slices the high amplitude initial response is no longer present and the background a low amplitude return (dark). The outline of the square trend consists of low to medium amplitude returns (medium to light).

Interpretations from the data collected at the Millington site (Figure 10) include a possible square structure measuring approximately 7 x 7 m orientated on a northwest axis. This possible structure is defined in the magnetometer data by a series of strong dipolar anomalies and several smaller monopolar positive magnetic anomalies. Interestingly there is a quite area in the magnetometer data that corresponds to the center of the possible structure. A strong positive magnetic susceptibility anomaly is also located in the interior of the possible structure. GPR data shows the square pattern with the most clarity and gives a relative depth, suggesting the deposits are present in the upper 12 cmbs and start to

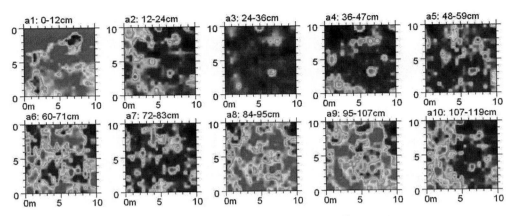

Figure 9. (above) Processed GPR Amplitude Slice Maps from the Millington site.
Figure 10. (below) Interpretations of the geophysical data from the Millington site.

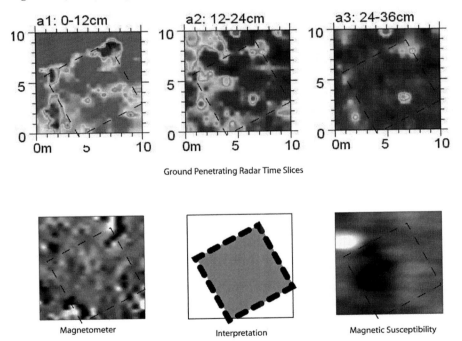

Ground Penetrating Radar Time Slices

Magnetometer   Interpretation   Magnetic Susceptibility

pinch out below 36 cmbs and appears to not extend below 47 cmbs.

It is important to caution that the archaeological interpretations of the geophysical data from both sites was difficult to make based on the limited coverage areas. Larger scale archaeogeophysical surveys would produce more immediately interpretable data which could directly address the research goal stated earlier in this report.

Recommendations

Recommendations for both sites include expanding the geophysical survey to include wide coverage with the magnetometer and EM. The resulting three data sets can then be used to help strategically locate areas of archaeological interest for closer investigation using GPR and a resistance survey as well as excavation.